Twilight

of a

Golden Age

JUDAIC STUDIES SERIES

Leon J. Weinberger
General Editor

Twilight of a Golden Age
Selected Poems of
Abraham Ibn Ezra

Leon J. Weinberger

The University of Alabama Press

Tuscaloosa

Copyright © 1997
The University of Alabama Press
Tuscaloosa, Alabama 35487-0380
All rights reserved
Manufactured in the United States of America

∞

The paper on which this book is printed meets the minimum requirements of
American National Standard for Information Sciences-Permanence of Paper for
Printed Library Materials, ANSI Z39.48-1984.

ISBN: 978-0-8173-5679-8 (paper)
ISBN: 978-0-8173-8573-6 (electronic)

A previous edition of this book has been catalogued by the Library of Congress.

Library of Congress Cataloging-in-Publication Data

Ibn Ezra, Abraham ben Meïr, 1092–1167.
    [Poems. English & Hebrew. Selections]
    Twilight of a golden age : selected poems of Abraham Ibn Ezra / edited
and translated with introduction and notes by Leon J. Weinberger.
        p. cm. —(Judaic studies series)
    Contains the Hebrew text of selected poems with English translation.
    Includes bibliographical references and index.
    IBSN 0-8173-0878-4 (alk. paper)
        1. Ibn Ezra, Abraham ben Meïr, 1092-1167—Translations into English.
    I. Weinberger, Leon J. II. Title. III. Series: Judiac studies series
    (Unnumbered)
    PJ5050.I18A25 1997
    892.4'12—dc21   97-1624

For
Lynn and Gary
Ellen and David
Lisa and Tom

CONTENTS

SACRED POETRY   129

God: 129

The Soul: 167

PREFACE

My purpose is to offer the reader a representative selection of Abraham Ibn Ezra's secular and sacred poetry in the original Hebrew with English translation. The Hebrew texts are based on I. Levin, ed., *Sirey Ha-Qodeš Šel Avraham Ibn Ezra*, 2 vols. (Jerusalem: 1975–80) and H. Schirmann, ed., *Ha-Širah Ha-'Ivrit Bi-Sfarad U-V-Provans*, 2 vols. (Jerusalem: 1959). For the most part I have relied on Levin's later edition which incorporated some recently discovered Ibn Ezra poetry in the Cairo Geniza. When I choose Schirmann's reading over Levin's, I give my reason. The scansion of the poems follows the classic quantitative principle in which two elements forming a Hebrew syllable, the *tenu'a* (movement = {-}) and *yated* (peg = {ʊ}), designated by the mobile *šewa'* and its *hataf* derivatives, are used in combination. When the poem does not include the *ṣewa'* and *hataf* derivatives in its scansion I have noted the number pattern of vowels in each stich. I have also added "verse" to the scansion when a Scriptural refrain follows the strophes.

I should like to thank Malcolm MacDonald and Nicole Mitchell for their encouragement and support. Debra J. Rosen has my gratitude for her thorough and competent editing of the text. My colleague Professor Thomas Rabbitt read the manuscript, and I am indebted to him for his helpful suggestions.

My wife Marcy has been a blessing to me and I am grateful to have her at my side.

As always, my chief thanks are due the One who graciously grants intelligence and preserves us in life.

Leon J. Weinberger
The University of Alabama
Tuscaloosa, Alabama
8 Tammuz, 5756
June 25, 1996

A NOTE ON TRANSLITERATION

In giving each Hebrew word a phonetic transcription into English I have distinguished between *'alef*, א (= ') and *'ayin*, ע (= '), and have designated the following values for the other Hebrew letters giving the name, symbol, equivalent and character: *bet b b*ar ב; *vet v v*ent ב; *gimmel g g*ood ג; *dalet d d*oor ד; *he' h h*ot ה; *waw w (vowels u, o).* win ו; *zayin z* zoo ז; *ḥet ḥ* Bac*h* ח; *ṭet ṭ t*ea ט; *yod y (vowel i)* yo u י; *kaf k k*in כ; *khaf kh* Bac*h* כ; *kaf sofit kh* Bac*h* ך; *lamed l l*a n d ל; *m e m m m*int מ; *mem sofit m m*int ם; *nun n n*oun נ; *nun sofit n n*oun ן; *samekh s* soft ס; *peh p* park פ; *feh f f*air פ; *peh/feh sofit p, f,* pa r k, fair ף; *ṣadiy ṣ* cats צ; *ṣadiy sofit ṣ* cats ץ; *qof q k*in ק; *reš r r*un ר; *šin š sh*oe שׁ; *sin s s*oft שׂ; *taw t t*ea ת.

I have not distinguished between *samekh* and *sin* because they are often interchangeable in Hebrew literature. The letter *e* is used to indicate the *segol*, as in *homer* and *qedem*; the *ṣereh*, as in *nerot* and *yošev*; and the *šewa' na'*, as in *qerovah* and *telunah*. The letter *a* indicates *pataḥ*, as in *baqqašah*; *qameṣ*, as in *magen*; and *hataf patah*, as in *mahazor*. The letter *o* designates a *holam* as in *rofe'* and a *qameṣ hatuf* as in *hokhmah*. The doubling of letters, as in *'ammim, huqqim* indicates a *dageš hazaq.*

ABBREVIATIONS

Tractates in the Talmud

AZ = 'Avodah Zarah

BB = Bava' Batra'

Ber = Berakhot

Bes = Besah

Bikk = Bikkurim

BM = Bava' Meṣi'a'

BQ = Bava' Qamma'

'Eruv = 'Eruvin

Git = Gittin

Hag = Hagigah

Hor = Horayot

Hul = Hullin

Ket = Ketubot

Makk = Makkot

Meg = Megillah

Men= Menahot

MQ = Mo'ed Qatan

Pes = Pesahim

Qid = Qiddušin

RH = Roš ha-Šanah

Šab = Šabbat

San = Sanhedrin

Šeq = Šeqalim

Sot = Sotah

Sukk = Šukkah

Ta'an = *Ta'anit*

Tam= *Tamid*

Yev = *Yevamot*

----

b = *Babylonian Talmud*, M. Romm ed. (Vilna 1881); English trans. ed. I. Epstein (London, 1948–52)

EJ= *Encyclopaedia Judaica* (10 vols.; Berlin, 1928–34)

EJ= *Encyclopaedia Judaica* (16 vols.; Jerusalem, 1972)

HUCA= *Hebrew Union College Annual*

j= *Jerusalem Talmud* (New York, 1959)

JQR= *Jewish Quarterly Review*

m= *Mišnah*, var. eds.; English trans. H. Danby (Oxford, 1933)

MGWJ= *Monatsschrift für Geschichte und Wissenschaft des Judentums*

REJ= *Revue des études juives*

t = *Tosefta*, ed. M. S. Zuckermandel (Pasewalk, 1881)

Twilight
of a
Golden Age

INTRODUCTION

BIOGRAPHY: CRISIS AND DECISION

Abraham ben Meir Ibn Ezra (1092–1167) was born in the northeastern Spanish province of Navarre in the city of Tudela, the home of his older contemporary and sometime traveling companion, the poet–philosopher Judah Halevi, whose daughter, Ibn Ezra's son Isaac is said to have married.[1] During Ibn Ezra's travels in Spain in the first third of the twelfth century, the two frequently met in the social and literary circles of the Lucena–Seville–Cordoba courtly culture triangle; Halevi is often mentioned in Ibn Ezra's Bible commentaries.[2]

Abraham Ibn Ezra's personal life was marred by tragedy. The same Isaac, a gifted poet in his own right, may have converted to Islam. This is suggested by Judah Al-Harizi (1170–1235):

> Isaac, his son, also drew from poesy's fount...
> But when he arrived in the lands of the East,
> The glory of God did not shine upon him;
> He shed the mantle of precious faith,
> Removed his garments and dressed in different clothes.[3]

The reference to Isaac's travels in the "lands of the East" may be related to his association with the philosopher–physician Nethanel b. Ali during his stay in Baghdad. Nethanel, who did convert to Islam, was aided by Isaac in copying the former's Arabic commentary on Ecclesiastes.[4]

---

1. The view that Isaac Ibn Ezra married the daughter of Judah Halevi was first advanced by S. D. Goitein and was recently confirmed by E. Fleischer. See Fleischer, "Yehuda Halevi--Remarks Concerning his Life and Poetical Ouevre" [Hebrew], pp. 264–70.

2. See Goitein, *A Mediterranean Society*, 1: 303; Levin, *Avraham Ibn Ezra, Hayyaw We-Širato*, p. 15.

3. Al-Harizi, *Tahkemoni*, p. 45.

4. See Schmelzer, *Isaac...Ibn Ezra, Širim*, pp. 10–11, and see poem #36 (pp. 44–45) which Isaac wrote in honor of Nethanel upon the completion of the commentary.

However, in a poem attributed to Isaac (*Yerivuni 'aley 'ozvi berit 'el*, They quarrel with me for forsaking God's covenant), he appears to have converted to Islam for appearances sake only and not from conviction:

> I am convinced that the prophet of Allah (Muḥammad) is a madman;
> Although I thanked him in every prayer
> With my lips only, while my heart said,
> "You lie and your testimony is false!" [5]

Isaac died during his father's lifetime. The latter's grief is revealed in his elegy:

> In my declining years I had hoped
> That he would bring me relief and deliverance;
> Alas, I labored in vain
> And sired a son to dismay me!

The passing years did not lessen the father's anguish:

> When I recall, three years past,
> His death among foreigners,
> And his vagabond life,
> And my longing for him... [6]

Abraham Ibn Ezra's early years were a time of troubles for his native Spain. The early Reconquest pitted Christian princes against Arabs who invaded the peninsula in 711. Jews were often forced to choose between the warring camps. Some opted to flee the war-torn country rather than take sides. Abraham Ibn Ezra, one of the thousands made homeless by the wars of the early Reconquest, found refuge in

---

5. Schirmann, *Ha-Širah Ha-'Ivrit*, 1: 628; Schmelzer, *Isaac...Ibn Ezra*, p. 147. In another poem *'Ani ha-'iš 'ašer nilkad be-ḥeṭ'o* (I am the one who was trapped in his sin), Isaac confesses that he violated God's commands and regrets his actions. See Schmelzer, p. 146.

6. Levin, *Yalqut Avraham Ibn Ezra*, pp. 103–04; Schirmann, *Ha-Širah Ha-'Ivrit Be-Sefarad U-Be-Provans*, 1: 580–81; Poem #13, below.

Lucena in Andalusia. There he was warmly welcomed into an intimate literary circle that included Judah Halevi, Solomon Ibn Al-Muāllim and Isaac Ibn Muhājir of Seville, Joseph Ibn Ṣaddiq of Cordoba, and Abraham Ibn Rabīb among others. Several panegyrics by Ibn Ezra from this period in honor of his colleagues and patrons have been preserved as have the *laudes* dedicated to him. Reminiscing about this happy interlude in Lucena, in an otherwise turbulent life, he wrote:

> Early in my youth
> I fashioned my verses,
> And set them as jewels
> Upon Israel's neck. [7]

He departed Spain for a short visit to North Africa in 1140, the year that Judah Halevi set out for the Holy Land via Egypt. In the opening chapter of his commentary on Lamentations, Ibn Ezra gave the reason for leaving his homeland: "The fury of the oppressor expelled me from Spain." Presumably, he had in mind the deteriorating conditions in Andalusia following its conquest by the Berber Almohads in 1140. In 1090 the legalist Muslim Almoravids led by Yusuf Ibn Tashufin disrupted Jewish courtly life in the Spanish southland and many prominent families lost their estates and were forced to flee. Among the refugees following the Almoravid invasion was Moses Ibn Ezra. When the Almohades under 'Abd al-Mu'min attacked southern Morocco, the surviving Jews of Andalusia still reeling from the Almoravid incursion, feared the worst. Their concerns were justified when Spain was invaded by the forces of 'Abd al-Mu'min, who, in 1146 forced the Jews (and Christians) in his realm to publicly renounce their religious faith. [8]

Ibn Ezra, whose final departure from Andalusia was on the eve of the Almohad invasion, laments the latter's destruction of North African and Hispanic Jewish settlements which he names:

> I weep like an ostrich for Lucena (cf. Lam. 4: 3 and Mic. 1: 8).
> Her remnant dwelt innocent and secure...

---

7. Schirmann, *Širim Ḥadašim Min Ha-Geniza*, pp. 267-68; D. Kahane, *Rabbi Avraham Ibn Ezra*, 1: 22.
8. Cf. S. Baron, *A Social and Religious History of the Jews*, 3: 124-25.

Alas, the city of Cordoba is forsaken, her ruin as vast as the sea!
Her sages and learned men perished from hunger and thirst.
Not a single Jew was left in Jaen or Almeria;
Majorca and Málaga struggle to survive...
I cry out like a woman in labor for the congregations of Sijilmasa—
A city where genius and wisdom flourished; their brilliance
    obscured the darkness...
Woe, the congregation of Fez is no more; this day they are
    given to the plunderer;
Where is the protection for the congregation of Tlemsan?
    Its glory is melted away.
A bitter voice I raise over the fate of Ceuta and Meknes;
I rend my garments for Dar'ī already vanquished...[9]

Abraham Ibn Ezra's stay in Africa was brief and in the same year we find him in Italy, where he remained until 1147. While in Africa, Ibn Ezra was graciously received by the Jewish families of Alexandria who competed for the honor of paying tribute to their illustrious guest. R. Abraham's literary remains during his African sojourn include several panegyrics to patrons, including a *muwashshah*, "How will you comfort me, my friends after my playful gazelle has left?" dedicated to Samuel Ibn Jāmiʿ of Gabes, Tunisia. It is likely that the poet made his home with Ibn Jāmiʿ when he left Andalusia. Ibn Ezra's *maqāmah*-style (a narrative in rhymed prose) *Hay ben Meqis*, based on Avicenna's *Hay ben Yaqzān*, was dedicated to his host. Given his numerous encomia honoring friends and patrons in Algiers and in Sijilmasa, Morocco, it is likely that he often visited those countries prior to his final departure from Spain. [10]

Upon his arrival in Rome, Abraham Ibn Ezra was again well received by the Jewish notables who were familiar with his writings. Rome's Jewish population comprised some "two hundred prominent families who were exempt from paying taxes," according to a report by Benjamin of Tudela who visited there between 1165 and 1167.

---

9. Poem #14, below.

10. See Schirmann, *Širim Hadašim Min Ha-Geniza*, pp. 268–69, 275–76; Levin, *Yalqut*, p. 11.

Under the generous reign of Pope Alexander III, Jews were also privileged to serve at court. During Ibn Ezra's stay in Rome the ruling Pope, Innocent II, was equally well-disposed to his Jewish subjects. [11] Why Ibn Ezra chose to return to Europe is not clear. Writing in the third person, he reveals his anxiety upon arriving in the Eternal City:

> He has been separated from home
> Which is in Spain;
> He has come down (*yarad*) to Rome
> And is fearful. [12]

The choice of the word *yarad* suggests that he, scion of an erudite Hispanic-Hebrew tradition, was being demoted to live in a backwater. Particularly irksome were the charges brought by Jewish zealots in Rome against Spanish scholars whom they accused of apostasy.

Concerned that the "fury of the oppressor" which led him to leave his native land would soon put an end to all courtly culture and tradition, Ibn Ezra began to see himself as a survivor with a mission. In the Rome, Lucca-Pisa, and Mantua-Verona triangle where he was a frequent guest, he introduced Hispano-Hebrew learning to Christian Europe. He translated from the Arabic, which the Italians could not read, into Hebrew the pioneering language studies of Judah ben David Hayyuj (tenth century) who rediscovered the tri-consonantal root structure of Hebrew. Ibn Ezra's own contributions to Hebrew philology during this period included the *Sefer Mo'znayim* (Book of Scales), based on the earlier studies of Hayyuj and Jonah ben Janah's (eleventh century) *Sefer Ha-Šorašim* (Book of [Hebrew] Roots); *Yesod Ha-Lašon* (Principles of Language); *Sefat Yeter* (On Verbosity); *Sefer Ha-Sahut* (On Purity [in Usage]); and *Safah Berurah* (Clarity in Language).

---

11. See Benjamin of Tudela, *Sefer Massa'ot Šel R. Binyamin*, pp. 6–7; Levin, *Avraham Ibn Ezra, Hayyaw We-Širato*, p. 24.

12. Ibn Ezra, Introduction to the commentary on Ecclesiastes, in *Commentary on the Torah.*

The time spent in the Lucca–Pisa region also produced the first draft of his influential treatise on astronomy, the *Tabulae Pisanae*. Although Lucca in the 1160s comprised only forty Jewish families according to a report by the voyager Benjamin of Tudela, it boasted of an academy of learning under the leadership of the Kalonymide family. Never missing an opportunity to share his knowledge, he taught his eager Italian audience the new Indian and Arabic mathematics with his *Sefer Ha-Mispar* (Book of Numbers). In addition to the scientific writings, his Italian period produced the widely known short commentary on the Pentateuch, the influential commentaries to Ecclesiastes, Job, and Daniel. and the *Sefer Ha-'Ibbur*. The latter became a seminal study on the intercalation of the Jewish religious calendar, a subject much in dispute by Rabbanites and Karaites in his day. [13]

In 1147 the restive Ibn Ezra left Italy for France where he divided his time between Narbonne and Beziers in Provence, and Rouen in the north. There he soon came to know and admire the grandson of R. Solomon ben Isaac (RaŠI), R. Jacob ben Meir (Rabbenu Tam, ca. 1100–1171), a prominent rabbinic scholar and master of the academy at Champagne. The letters the two men exchanged reveal both the elitism of Ibn Ezra and his generosity. Following is his sneering reaction to R. Jacob's attempt to compose metric poetry in the style of the Hispanics:

> Who let the Frenchman into poesy's mansion?
> [Who permitted] the stranger to trample upon the holy place?
> Were Jacob's verses as sweet as manna,
> I am the sun, and I grow hot and they melt. [14]

The allusion to Ex. 16: 21 was not lost on the younger man who graciously conceded that he had met his master:

> I am a servant employed by Abraham;
> I bend the knee and bow before him! [15]

---

13. Cf. Levin, *Avraham Ibn Ezra*, pp. 24–30; idem, *Yalqut*, p. 33.
14. B. Dinur, *Yisra'el Ba-Golah*, II, 3: 83.
15. Ibid.

Impressed by R. Jacob's allusion to Gen. 23: 17-18, but not to be outdone, Ibn Ezra replied with mock-reproach:

> Is it proper for the gallant shepherd of God's flock
> To abase himself in writing before one despised?
> Heaven forbid that the Lord's angel
> Should bend the knee and bow before a vagrant. [16]

His furious pace of writing continued in France with a treatise on astronomy, *Ta'amey Ha-Luḥot* (Understanding the Calendar), a work begun in Lucca and completed in Narbonne, and two tracts on astrology, *Re'šit Ḥokhmah* (The Beginning of Wisdom) composed in the summer of 1148 at Beziers, and *Mišpat Ha-'Olam* (The Manner of the Universe) written in the fall of 1149. At Beziers, where according to Benjamin of Tudela there flourished "a congregation of learned men" [17] Ibn Ezra was commissioned by community leaders Abraham b. Ḥayyim and Isaac b. Judah to prepare a study of the Divine Name, which he published under the title, *Sefer Ha-Šem*. While in the north of France, he composed his commentaries on the Pentateuch, Psalms, Canticles, Esther, and a longer work on Daniel. The commentary on Daniel was completed in the fall of 1155 at Dreux and was followed by a book on the Minor Prophets in 1158.

In the same year he crossed the Channel into England, ruled by Henry II, and settled in London. There he wrote the widely copied *'Iggeret Ha-Šabbat* (Epistle on the Sabbath). The work was subsequently (in 1739) included in the printed editions of the authoritative *Šulhan 'Arukh* (Prepared Table [of Jewish Law]) by R. Joseph Qaro. The year 1158 was a highly productive one for Ibn Ezra. In addition to completing the Epistle, he composed his major philosophic treatise, the *Yesod Mora'* (Principles of [God] Fearing), a work that was commissioned by his English patron, Joseph b. Jacob of Maudeville (or Morville). Soon thereafter, the latter presented to England's

---

16. Ibid.
17. Benjamin of Tudela, *Sefer Massa'ot*, p. 3.

Jewry Ibn Ezra's Commentary to the Minor Prophets which he copied "from the author's handwritten text." [18]

His decision to make the hazardous Channel crossing on the eve of his sixty-sixth birthday was prompted, in part, by a desire to see "the land at the far end of the earth," a characterization of England (Angleterre) assimilated with the biblical usage "end of the earth" (Deut. 13: 8). Throughout his life, he seemed to be driven by a need to observe and understand all that is worth knowing, even as he felt an obligation to impart his Andalusian-Hebrew scholarship to a distant outpost of civilization. Although he may have thought of England as the last frontier, Ibn Ezra was undoubtedly informed about the prosperity and well-being of the Jews in the realm of Henry II. The English monarch's French holdings at that time included Dreux and its environs, and his protection saved Jewish settlements from the excesses of the mob during the Second Crusade.

Following his sojourn in England, Ibn Ezra returned to the European mainland and visited friends in Italy and France. In 1161 his presence is observed in Narbonne. He leaves no traces in the years following. According to one early copyist of his Commentary to the Pentateuch, Ibn Ezra is said to have written his own epitaph. Paraphrasing Gen. 12: 4: "And Abraham was seventy five years old when he departed from Ḥaran," he wrote, "Abraham was seventy five years old when he departed from God's anger [me-ḥaron 'af 'adonay]." The same copyist noted that "on the second day, of the New Moon of the first month of Adar in 4924 (January 23, 1167) Ibn Ezra died." Where he died is not known. I. Levin believes that he never left England and died there. Others suggest that since he is last heard from in Narbonne, it may have been his wish to return to his native Tudela in nearby Navarre and die there. [19]

Abraham Ibn Ezra was the last of a celebrated quintet of Hispanic-Hebrew Golden Age poets, including Samuel Ibn Nagrela (993-1056), Solomon Ibn Gabirol (ca. 1020 - ca. 1057), Moses Ibn Ezra (ca. 1055 - d. after 1135) and Judah Halevi (ca. 1075-1141). A transitional figure, he anticipated the decline of Hispano-Hebrew courtly culture in Spain even as he participated in the newly emerging centers of

---

18. The quote is from the colophon notation in Ms. British Museum #24896 and Jews' College, Ms. Montefiore #34, 2.
19. See Levin, *Avraham Ibn Ezra*, pp. 37, 42; idem, *Yalqut*, p. 16.

learning in Italy and France which he visited and influenced. The decline of Andalusian values and life-style was already signaled by Judah Halevi. Halevi, the immensely gifted and highly admired darling of Andalusian society, renounced the wit and wisdom of Spain as spurious even as he affirmed the eternal truth of the Torah and the sanctity of the Land of Israel. Departing from Spain on his way to the Holy Land he wrote:

> The grandeur of Islam, the glory of Greece
> Are vanity beside the Urim and Tummim (Ex. 28: 30).
> Zion's annointed, its Levites and princes
> Cannot be replaced, for they are unique. [20]

With Abraham Ibn Ezra's departure from Spain an illustrious chapter of Jewish learning and culture came to an end in the region, even as it was to spread its influence throughout the rest of Europe.

Ibn Ezra was one of the best known and admired Jewish figures in the West. His *Pisan Tables* in astronomy were the authoritative guides for Roger Bacon (ca. 1214-1294), Nicolas of Cusa (1401-1464), and Pico della Mirandola (1463-1494), and he was remembered for his pioneering efforts in introducing the mathematics of the Arabs to the Europeans. In Victorian England, he was the model for Robert Browning's (1812-1889) "Rabbi Ben Ezra" whose philosophy reflected "robust hope and cheerfulness." [21]

His range of interests was impressive, even for a polymath. Author of over one hundred books on medicine, astronomy, mathematics, philosophy, poetry, Bible, Talmud, and linguistics, he was the model itinerant sage, teaching and writing both in his native Spain as well as in north Africa, Italy, Provence, northern France and England. The literary critic and poet, Moses Ibn Ezra, ranked him with Judah Halevi and praised his poetry for its "clarity and its rhetoric." Judah Al-Ḥarizi, Hebrew poet and translator, lavished extravagant praise upon him and characterized his poetic

---

20. The translation of Judah Halevi's "Ode to Zion" (*Ṣiyyon ha-lo' tiš'ali*, see Halevi, *Širey Ha-Qodeš...Ha-Levi*, pp. 913ff) is by Gerson Cohen; see Ibn Daud, *Sefer Ha-Qabbalah*, pp. 296-300.

21. J. M. Millás Vallicrosa, *El Libro de los fundamentos de los Tablas astronomicas de R. Abraham Ibn Ezra*, pp. 77ff; W. C. DeVane, *A Browning Handbook*, pp. 292-95.

writing as "a timely help in trouble, a refreshing bounty of rain in time of drought...they have no equal." [22]

The Provençal poet and critic, Yedayah Ha-Penini (ca. 1270 – ca. 1340) of Beziers described the excitement caused by his arrival in the south of France and the enthusiasm of the French rabbis who thanked him for "enlightening us in our region" with new insights in biblical interpretation, philosophy, and mysticism. Moses Maimonides (1135–1204), influencial rabbinic authority, codifier and philosopher, when counseling his son Abraham to study the Bible urged him to consult only the commentaries of Abraham Ibn Ezra whom he admired for his "fearlessness" and "independence." Maimonides, not generally given to hyperbole, wrote that Ibn Ezra was favored with an insight (be-ruah) similar to that of Abraham the patriarch. Joseph Solomon Delmedigo of Candia (1591-1655), rabbi, philosopher, mathematician, astronomer, and a polymath in his own right, summed up the esteem in which Abraham Ibn Ezra was held, "This is the man who, all the days of his life, wandered around the world from the extremity of the western sea to Lucca and Egypt, Ethiopia and Elam. He had no money, not even a few coins, for he despised these all his days. He had only the garments he wore and the bag which contained his astrolabe, a stout heart and the spirit of God within him." [23]

Like Maimonides, Abraham Ibn Ezra had his detractors. R. Moses b. Nahman (Nahmanides, 1194–1270), rabbinic authority, philosopher, and kabbalist, charged (in his comments on Gen. 9: 18) that at times Ibn Ezra does not interpret Scripture according to its plain meaning "and resorts to lying." Nahmanides condemned Ibn Ezra for his disdain of rabbinic legends (aggadah), for favoring reasonable interpretations of Scripture, and for claiming to have access to unfounded kabbalistic traditions. [24] Despite their differences, Nahmanides noted (in his comment on Prov. 27: 5), "For R. Abraham Ibn Ezra we will have open rebuke and concealed love."

---

22. M. Ibn Ezra, *Kitab al-Muhādara wal-Mudhākara*, fol. 42b (p. 79); Al-Harizi, *Tahkemoni*, #3 (p. 45).

23. See Yedayah Ha-Penini, "'*Iggeret Hitnaṣlut*." In Solomon b. Abraham b. Adret (RaŠBA), *Še'elot U-Tešuvot Ha-RaŠBA*, 1. 418, p. 166; Maimonides, *Koveṣ Tešuvot Ha-Rambam We-'Iggerotaw*, 2. 39.

24. See Nahmanides comments on Gen. 1: 1, 11: 28, 24: 1, and 46: 15. See also the comments on Gen. 18: 20: 24: 1; Ex. 3: 2, 6: 7, 13: 21, 14: 19, 28: 30; and Num. 8: 2.

Commenting on the Ibn Ezra–Naḥmanides relationship, B. Septimus observes that "Naḥmanides' 'love'—his sense of spiritual kinship with Ibn Ezra—is often to be found hiding not far from his 'rebuke.'" Openly hostile to Ibn Ezra were the anonymous critics cited by Joseph b. Eliezer Ṭov Elem in his supercommentary *Ṣofnat Paneah* on Ibn Ezra's commentary on the Pentateuch. The former claimed that they were misled by Ibn Ezra's terse and epigrammatic style of commenting on Scripture and suspected him of being a heretic and apostate (*min we-'apiqoros*). [25]

THE VAGABOND LIFE

The rigors of travel took their toll. In the following lament attributed to Ibn Ezra, [26] he bares his fears:

Wandering has sapped my strength and confused my mind;
My speech is halting, my tongue is chained...

My books were written wherever I found a home
In them I made mysteries
Clear like a molten mirror...

Now I have fallen on hard times and am mired in dirt;
I pray God to raise me from the dungeon;

I have become an example to be avoided by all men;
Honor and glory have left me and abuse remains! [27]

Easing the hardships were people like Samuel Ibn Jāmiʿ with whom he corresponded and to whom he dedicated the *Hay ben Meqiṣ*; Benjamin b. Joab

---

25. See B. Septimus, "'Open Rebuke and Concealed Love,' Nahmanides and the Andalusian Tradition," pp. 17–23; Joseph b. Eliezer Tov Elem, *Sofnat Paneah*, 1: 6–7.
26. Masha Itzhaqi, in a private communication, is of the opinion that it is likely that Ibn Ezra wrote this poem.
27. The Hebrew text is in Levin, *Avraham Ibn Ezra*, p. 206.

Matara of Rome who commissioned his Commentary to Job; Abraham b. Hayyim and Isaac b. Judah, both of Beziers, who subsidized his *Sefer Ha-Šem*; Moses b. Meir of Lucca for whom he composed the Commentary to the Pentateuch at age sixty-four, and who nursed him back to health following a severe illness; Solomon of London for whom the *'Iggeret Ha-Šabbat* was written, and the ever generous Joseph b. Jacob of Maudeville. However, others were not as giving, and in a telling confession the poet laments the inaccessibility of the wealthy Maecenas:

> Early I set out for the patron's home;
> They say: He is off riding;
> I return toward evening,
> They say: He is already sleeping;
> He either mounts a horse or climbs into bed... [28]

Nor were all receptions as enthusiastic as in Alexandria or Beziers. On more than one occasion he complained that he was slighted by his hosts:

> No wine is to be found in the emptied flask,
> The cheese is missing--stolen as it were--
> And the hostess is blind in one eye;
> Limping and bent she hobbles toward the well;
> The natives are kin to Cain,
> Barely superior to beasts. [29]

On another occasion he protests the insensitivity of his host who did not accord him the seat of honor at the dinner table:

> My honor is intact, though I humble myself
> And choose not to sit among those whose reputation is flawed

---

28. Kahane, *Rabbi Avraham Ibn Ezra*, 1: 69-70; Schirmann, *Ha-Širah Ha-'Ivrit*, 1: 575; Poem #1, below.
29. Schirmann, *Ha-Širah Ha-'Ivrit*, 1: 578; Poem #6, below.

But who like to think that they occupy the head table,
Hoping that the dais will cover their disgrace.[30]

Whether these slights were real or imagined is not known. It is likely that the proud poet, a privileged associate in the elite circle of Andalusia's courtly culture, did not feel at home among the "barbarians" in the "land of Edom," his reference to Christian Europe. [31] Like the Muslim Arabs in the High Middle Ages, Ibn Ezra had little regard for the Europeans north of the Pyrenees. His cynical impression in *Ḥay ben Meqiṣ* characterizes the "men of Edom" as:

Ruddy [men], spilling blood [32]
Schemers resorting to flattery,
They plunder at will...
War is their specialty.
After taking bribes
They murder their victims...
They love being wicked and deceitful,
And despise learning and prudence. [33]

Earlier, Moses Ibn Ezra was no less critical of the people he encountered on his travels in Christian Spain. He characterized them as men "famished for the lack of the bread of reason...would-be seers without vision...savages who love corruption and set an ambush for the blood of the righteous and innocent." [34] However, unlike Moses who was never reconciled to the vagabond life, Abraham Ibn Ezra had the generosity to find comic relief in his misfortune:

Were I a merchant of candles, the sun would not set until I died!...

---

30. Schirmann, *Ha-Širah Ha-ʿIvrit*, 1: 577; Poem #5, below.
31. See Schirmann, *Ha-Širah Ha-ʿIvrit*, 1: 595.
32. A play on the words *'Edom* (Edomites); *"anašim 'adumim"* (ruddy men); *šofkhey damim* (spilling blood).
33. Schirmann, *Ha-Širah Ha-ʿIvrit*, 1: 595–96; Poem #17 G, below.
34. See Moses Ibn Ezra, *Širey Ha-Ḥol*, 1: 13: 17–26; 1: 20: 43; 1: 67: 31–32; 1: 112: 14, 29.

Were I to trade in shrouds, men would not die in my lifetime!...
Were I to seek on a rainy day some water from the sea,
    it would dry up!
Were I to sell armaments, all enemies would be reconciled and
    not make war! [35]

This mock-serious tone was also used in describing the pitiful garment that he wore during the day and as a night cover when sleeping:

I have a mantle; it resembles a sieve
For sifting wheat or barley;
In the dark of night I unfurl it like a tent
And heavens' starry radiance filters through;
I behold the moon and the Pleiades,
Even Orion's lustre is reflected;
I grow weary counting its holes...
Were a fly to descend on it compulsively
Like a fool, he would soon regret it... [36]

POETRY IN TRANSITION: REALISM AND REALITY

Ibn Ezra's choice of subject in writing about his tattered cloak is a departure from the earlier courtly and chivalric themes of Samuel Ibn Nagrela and Solomon Ibn Gabirol. He reflects the new realism in Hebrew letters following the decline of Jewish life in Andalusia after the Almohade invasion in the fourth decade of the twelfth century. Ibn Ezra pioneers the change in themes with a mock-heroic treatment of life's daily difficulties. In his diatribe against the pesky housefly, he echoes a complaint heard by humans throughout the world:

Where can I find refuge from my oppressors?
I cry for help from the robber flies
Who give me no respite.
Like arch-enemies they tyrannize me with a vengeance;

---

35. Levin, *Avraham Ibn Ezra*, pp. 199–200; Poem #2, below.
36. Schirmann, *Ha-Širah Ha-'Ivrit*, 1: 576; Poem #3, below.

They run races on my eyes and eyelids,
They croon lusty lyrics at my ears.
I had planned to eat my bread alone,
But there they were, like wolves, feeding on it...
I yearn for winter and windy rains and icy snows
To put an end to them... [37]

Like most Hispanic-Hebrew vagabond poets, Ibn Ezra was beholden to patrons for support. In Andalusian-Hebrew courtly circles the poet served at the patron's pleasure composing encomia to flatter his vanity and heaping abuse upon his enemies. Ibn Ezra's encomia, following established practices of the period, were constructed in the form of the Arabic *qaṣīdah* and *muwashshaḥ*. The *qaṣīdah* featured one unvarying rhyme throughout the poem and one quantitative meter dividing each verse into hemistichs; the *muwashshaḥ*, or "belt" poem, combined fixed and variable rhyme components. Each strophe had a different rhyme and was followed by a "belt" of a varying number of verses with a constant rhyme. The constant rhyme recurred only in the "belt" verses. The *qaṣīdah* encomium generally opened with an introduction providing setting and tone and continued with a list of the honoree's virtues. A favorite setting of the poets was the festive garden drinking party with its flirtatious cup-bearer and its generous host. Now the poet changes the landscape and shows the solitary lover departed to a distant land lamenting the absence of his beloved patron. The encomium closes in the hope that the pair will be reunited. This is followed by a coda of good wishes and dedication of the poem to the patron. The encomium was generally divided into two major parts: the introduction, modeled to some degree after the Arabic *nasīb*, an amatory prelude of the *qaṣīdah*, and the body of the *laudes*. From the introduction alone it was often impossible to tell that a tribute to a friend or patron would follow since the honoree was not mentioned. The transition couplet or triad leading to the *laudes* was intended to surprise the unsuspecting listeners and the skilled poet would make the most of this opportunity. An effective use of this tactic is Ibn Ezra's tribute to his patron R. Menaḥem of Rome and his son Moses (Poem #11, below). In the lengthy introduction featuring a debate between the limbs of the body with each claiming superior status there is no hint that a tribute to a patron is intended. The linking triad, "Find an agreeable way to resolve your dispute / Seek out Rabbi Menaḥem..."

---

37. Schirmann, *Ha-Širah Ha-'Ivrit*, 1: 576-77; Poem #4, below.

comes as an agreeable and unexpected shock and succeeds in flattering the benefactor by its indirection.

Less common was the encomium in the form of a *muwashshaḥ*, although its theme and setting were often similar to the *qaṣīdah*. The *muwashshaḥ* (belt-poem) was a poetic form commonly used in Arabic drinking songs (*khamriyyāt*) from Andalusia. The early "belt poems," built in multi-rhymed, strophic verse-forms written in classical Arabic, ended with the *kharjah* (exit) often in colloquial Arabic or Romance acting as a punch line. The Hispanic–Hebrews were widely attracted to the *muwashshaḥ* and used it in their panegyrics and wine and wedding poems complete with the vernacular closing. The widespread practice elicited a condemnation from Maimonides who complained, "Both [the Hebrew and Arabic *muwashshaḥāt*] are designed to arouse immoral behavior." Samuel Ibn Nagrela, model courtier–rabbi and poet, refrained from using the "belt-poem" in his writings for the synagogue, although he had no such qualms when it came to his secular poetry.

Following Nagrela, Hebrew poets freely adopted the *muwashshaḥ* for liturgical use, omitting the closing *kharjah*. Solomon Ibn Gabirol was probably the first among the Andalusians to engage in this practice, and by the time of Abraham Ibn Ezra it was a commonplace. The *muwashshaḥ* with its variable "belt" verses easily lent itself to choral reponses, which, in large part, accounted for its popularity. The *muwashshaḥ* and the *qaṣīdah* with its metrically balanced hemistichs in monorhyme were the two dominant forms in Hispano–Hebrew poetry.

Following is a selection from Ibn Ezra's *muwashshaḥ* encomium in honor of his patron, Joseph b. Amram, a judge (*dayyan*) in Sijilmasa, Morocco. The latter was martyred in 1146 by the invading Almohades:

> The image that revived me,
> Can it now hasten my death?

> The face of my choicest love
> Is like the cherub's flaming sword
> Standing guard over Eden;

His gaze barring my approach
Keeps me at bay.

Though rejected, I do not detest him;
What can I do? I love him!
[In his absence I am like the moon, pale with grief]
He makes me glow like the sun;
The lustre in his eye excites me.

May his love for me endure
Even now when he hates me;
A slight motion of his lips
Would lift my spirits
Like an enchantress calling

Will the cloud forever settle
On the face of the moon... [38]

Beyond the conventional hyperbole and stock figures adapted from Arabic love poetry (*ghazal*) is the poet's request for support from the Maecenas ("A slight motion of his lips Would lift my spirits"). The unresponsive patron is likened to the cruel beloved who rejects the humble lover. The beloved's indifference causes untold suffering to the yearning suitor which he endures out of helplessness. Adding to the suitor's predicament is the "reproacher" (Heb. *meriv*). In Arabic poetry, he is often the watcher or spy (Arab. *raqīb*) guarding the interests of the beloved. In Ibn Ezra's tribute to his patron, Barukh Ibn Jau, the *meriv* seeks to bring some good sense and cold wisdom to the emotionally overcome lover:

You who reproach me with complaints and quarrels,
I beg you to cease

---

38. See Maimonides, *Peruš Le-Massekhet 'Avot*, 1. 16; Schirmann, *Ha-Širah Ha-'Ivrit*, 1: 579; Poem #8, below.

Now that my beloved has deserted me
And taken with him my heart and my good sense. [39]

The obverse of the encomium (*ševaḥ*) in praise of the benefactor was the reproach (*genay*) heaped on his enemy. In the service of the Maecenas barbed sarcasm and satire--characteristic of the reproach--were often directed at unresponsive hosts encountered in the poet's travels. In his "The Denizens of Morah," Ibn Ezra refers to the townspeople as "kin to Cain,/ Barely superior to beasts." In "My Honor" he ridicules those "who like to think that they occupy the head table,/ Hoping that the dais will cover their disgrace." In both poems he combines sarcasm with complaint and ends with self-praise, "Were I not to live among them (the people of Morah), / They would suffer the fate of Gemorah," and "As for me, I define my place, – / While they use it to conceal their blemishes." [40]

Occasionally, Ibn Ezra would modulate his diatribe against a less talented peer. In ridiculing the efforts of R. Jacob b. Meir to compose in quantitative meter (see above), he is much less sanguine than in the following unrestrained invective against the less prominent Rabbi Isaac b. Malkiṣedeq of Salerno, Italy:

To his confused students, he bragged: I am thoroughly familiar
With the [laws of] "Seasons" and "Seeds," "Women" and "Damages."
His raving and ranting reached the clouds
Though he barely knew the "Ethics of the Fathers" and the
     rules of Sabbath candles.
The obstinate man's abuse of learning even a child could observe;
He would attempt to read [the laws] on "Purities" and stumbled on
     verses of Scripture;

---

39. See A. Hamori, "Love Poetry (*Ghazal*)," in *'Abbasid Belles-Lettres*, pp. 209–13; Poem #10, below.
40. Poems #5 and #6.

Its very opening chapter, known to every child, was
too difficult for him... [41]

IBN EZRA'S ASTROLOGY

Upon entering Ibn Ezra's world one is struck by his frequent references to astrology.
He complains that he is "unlucky" [42] and blames a defective stellar configuration at
his birth for his ill-fortune. He faults "the stars and their planets [who] strayed in
their orbits." They "have played false with me." [43] Like his Hispanic contemporary,
Abraham ben Ḥiyyah, Ibn Ezra was persuaded that the governance of the sublunar
world has been delegated by God to the stars. The poet found support for this view
in Gen. 2: 3, "And God rested from all the work that He had done in creation." [44]

Although he regrets his dependence upon unfeeling patrons and is unhappy
with astral behavior, he accepts his fate. The "wisdom" that he possesses
compensates—to some extent—for his lack of wealth. Yet, even the wisest must take
note of stellar patterns, as he reveals in his Sefer Ha-Mivḥarim:

He whose astral fortune is good, and who chooses for all of his doings and
affairs auspicious hours, auspicious days, and auspicious rising signs, will add
to his good fortune, or, [if] he possess astral misfortune, he will mitigate
somewhat his misfortune. Therefore Ptolemy (Claudius Ptolemaeus) said, "Be
careful in choosing a day on which to embark on a journey..."[45]

Ptolemy's Almagest, which was translated from the Greek into the Arabic in
the ninth century, was known to European scholars. Following Ptolemy's
recommendation Ibn Ezra composed his astronomical treatise "The Beginning of

---

41. Ibn Ezra, Commentary on Isaiah. p. xxiii. "Seeds," "Seasons," "Women," "Damages,"
and "Purities," are five of the six parts of the Mišnah. "The Ethics of the Fathers"
(Pirqe 'Avot) is a tractate in "Damages."

42. Poem #1.

43. Poem #2

44. Ibn Ezra's comment on Eccles. 7: 13.

45. Ms. Jewish Theological Seminary, New York, Mic 2626, f. 131a; Y. Tzvi
Langermann, "Astrological Themes in Ibn Ezra," pp. 51-52.

Wisdom" (*Re'šit Ḥokhmah*) in Lucca, Italy, between 1146 and 1148. In it he deals with the signs (*mazalotaw*) and figures in the sky, its seven "planets" (*kokhevey lekhet*), their celestial influence (*kokham*), and their power (*u–memšaltam*). [46]

In his lengthy, 130–line poem "*Šim'u na' 'el divrey ha–rofe'*," he refers to himself as "the physician" and offers advice on how to avoid the several perils associated with each of the twelve months in the year. Its twenty–six strophes comprise a longer six–line unit and a shorter four–line summation:

> Wise kinsmen, both strong and weak,
> Pay attention to the words of the physician
> Who offers a cure for every malady:
> How one can anticipate from month to month
> [The climate] that affects the body [and regulate the food
>   he puts into] the mouth
> In order to remain healthy and praiseworthy.

> That man will be admired
> And live a long life
> Who observes the rules of [good health],
> Its demands and practices.

> Tišri is the first month of the year,
> In it the winds blow fiercely
> And cool the body's temperature;
> Therefore it is advisable to eat [garden] leeks, [47]
> And peppers, both seed and stalk
> In order to treat infected kidneys...

> Hasten to purify the

---

46. See Abraham Ibn Ezra, *Re'šit Ḥokhmah*, pp. 152–53.

47. See *bPes* 116a where leeks are recommended for blockage of the urinary tract.

Kidneys from their humor [48]
And to sweeten the blood,
Drinking milk is recommended...

Nisan is the season of growth
In the [Holy] Land; it is also a time for roses.
In this month there is an increase of irritation from boils
On the body and diseases of the throat
Caused by an increase of humor settling in the blood
Of young men, but not the aged.

Prefer a steam bath;
Blacken the meat you roast;
Draw blood and relax the bowels,
But not in excess for it is harmful...

Elul is the last of the months
When the leaves fall and plants wither;
Thick clouds gather threatening,
And the clear season changes,
And the young lads are feverish;
Take care not to eat apples [or watermelons].

Whoever falls into deep melancholy
Call [his attention] to his impure [balance];
Let him eat heated foods,
Onions and garlic. [49]

However, the power of the stars is not absolute; it can be modified by the
efforts of the soul which "comes from a place higher than all the stars." That place is

---

48. The humor referred to one of the four chief fluids in the body (blood, phlegm,
choler, and melancholy or black choler), by the relative proportion of which a
person's physical and mental qualities and dispositions were held to be determined.
49. M. Yizḥaqi, "Megamot Didaqṭiyot Be-Širat Ha-Ḥol Šel Avraham Ibn Ezra," pp.
19-27.

the universal soul (nešamah ha-elyonah). The "power of the soul, which is wisdom" can overcome an astral decree. [50] These perceptions are reflected in Ibn Ezra's hymn "In the Dark of my Folly."

> I want to serve You, but my ill-fortune (zemani) prevents me;
> I look for Your light in the dark of my folly. [51]

Astral rule may also be mitigated when it affects the Jewish people. This would appear to be the view of Ibn Ezra in his commentary on Deut. 4: 19, "It is known from experience that each people has a definite star and sign...God has given Israel a great stature, in that God is their adviser. They have no star...Israel belongs to God...God has appointed the various heavenly bodies to govern the other nations, reserving Israel for His special guardianship." However, in other writings, Ibn Ezra places the Jews under the governance of the planet Saturn and the Zodiacal sign Aquarius and assigns the angel Michael to be their minister (sar). The latter view is echoed in his lament over Israel in exile, "The Song of a Bird Frightens Her."

> The evil decreed by the stars (ra'ah gazru šehaqim)
> Has overcome her. [52]

It is likely that Israel enjoyed the privilege of God's "guardianship" only when it lived up to its potential. Commenting on Deut. 4: 7, "For what other great nation has a god so near to it as the Lord, our God is whenever we call to him?" Ibn Ezra notes that Israel is designated a "great nation" because of its wise and God-fearing people.

THE USES OF WISDOM

Wisdom and the fear of God are accessible not only to Israel but to the entire human race. Commenting on Eccles. 3: 21, "Who knows whether the human spirit

---

50. Ibn Ezra, Sefer Ha-Mivharim, 131a; idem, Sefer Ha-Moladot, Ms. Oxford, Bodley, Opp. 707 (Neubauer 2025), fol. 156a; Langermann, "Astrological Themes," pp. 53-54; Ibn Ezra commentary on Ps. 49: 16.
51. Poem #39.
52. Poem #48.

goes upward and the spirit of animals goes downward to the earth?" Ibn Ezra argues that "one cannot find even one in a thousand" among Jews and non-Jews who fulfill their full human potential. Only the "learned (ha-maskilim) whose thoughts have been purified in the scales of wisdom" can qualify. In line with this is Ibn Ezra's interpretation of Ex. 18: 7, "Moses went out to meet his father-in-law; he bowed down and kissed him; each asked after the welfare of his colleague (re'ehu). He (Jethro, the non-Israelite) is called a colleague because of his high level of wisdom (ma'alato be-ḥokhmah)."

This universalism as regards the human spirit and its potential Ibn Ezra shared with the Andalusian-Hebrew intellectual elite of his day. The classic formulation of this cosmopolitanism was expressed by Solomon Ibn Gabirol in his "The Kingly Crown" (Keter Malkhut) 8:

> You are God:
> > Every creature is Your servant and Your devotee
> > Your glory can never be diminished;
> > Although they may worship others,
> > They intend to come to You." [53]

How does one "come to You?" In his philosophical study, "Fountain of Life" (Meqor Ḥayyim), 1.3 Ibn Gabirol suggests that the soul that has cleansed itself from the pollutants of the material world by knowledge and virtuous activity can return to its divine source. There is no indication that this "activity" implies the performance of the six hundred and thirteen commands as proposed by the rabbis (in bMakk 23b-24). [54]

Abraham Ibn Ezra shares with Ibn Gabirol the Neoplatonic view that the soul imprisoned in the body can free itself with the aid of wisdom. However, "wisdom" alone is not sufficient. God's help is required:

> O my soul, return to God and be saved

---

53. Langermann, "Astrological Themes," pp. 59–60; Scheindlin, The Gazelle, pp. 11–12.
54. See C. Sirat, A History of Jewish Philosophy, p. 72.

From Time's snare. How long must you crave foolishness?...
Take hold of Wisdom and turn to the Intellect;
Pray night and morning and know Who [confronts you].
Put on Reason's valued garment; wrap it around you...
Fortify yourself with His love—and you will find peace
Forever in His holy heights, there rejoicing. [55]

Notably absent in this poem is the requirement to respond to God's commands (*miṣwot*). It would appear that the soul's main challenge is avoiding the enticements of personified Time and the World. With the aid of reason it is possible to separate the illusory and transient attraction of the phenomenal world from the reality of the World-To-Come:

Be well-advised in this World so that
In the World-to-Come you may be bound up with the Lord. [56]

However, in his hymn "I live by adhering to God's Torah" (Poem #34) Wisdom is gained by knowledge of the Torah and living by its precepts:

I have found You (God) with my mind's eye and again
With Your Torah's help, O Glorious In Power.
Give me wisdom to do the right.

Taken to extremes, the renunciation of the World's "enticements" often led to a melancholy view of humankind. This is evident in Ibn Ezra's meditation on the Ages of Man:

At age thirty he falls into a woman's hands.
Coming to, he finds himself entrapped,
Harried on all sides by a host of arrows:
  The needs of his wife and children.

Shaken and humbled at forty he must

---

55. Poem #36.
56. Poem #37.

Be content with his lot—whether good or bad.
He hastens on his way; forsakes his friends;
  Dutifully, he stands at his post.

At fifty, remembering the wasted years,
He laments that death's day is approaching.
He holds the world's riches in contempt,
  He fears that his end is at hand. [57]

In its more moderate form "renunciation" implied a realistic assessment of man's limitations and a stoic indifference born from an awareness of human mortality:

O World, why have you enticed me with vapors?
I no longer care if you are gracious or cruel!
O Time, why should I rejoice at good fortune or mourn a tragedy?
I am but a transient here indifferent to your praise or blame,
  Your success or failure, tranquility or terror.
  Whether I be master or slave, death will ultimately
  Separate us! [58]

Compensating for the World's "enticements" are the joys that await the purified soul in the Garden of Delight (*gan ta'anug*), or Eden. [59]

Among the uses of "wisdom" is its effectiveness in enabling earth-bound man to escape from his confinement. This is the theme of Ibn Ezra's *maqamah*-style, *Hay ben Meqiṣ*, an account of his tour of the "heavens." His guide is personified "Wisdom" in the form of the venerable Hay ben Meqiṣ. With his help he tours the eight spheres of the Ptolemaic universe, including the sphere of the twelve constellations of the zodiac. Standing at the edge of the ninth sphere, the Primum Mobile, the poet asks his guide if there is more to be seen.

---

57. Poem #16.
58. Poem #41.
59. Poem #65.

He learns that beyond is the Empyrian, the "place" of God, hidden from view. It is accessible, he is told "when you get to know your soul" (we-teda' 'et ruhakha). Through "the power of the soul, which is wisdom," man can "know Him and see Him." [60]

THE SOUL'S ODYSSEY

Medievalists had a passion for order. Their geocentric universe was defined mathematically with sufficient refinement to explain the seasonal and diurnal movements of the planets and stars as seen with the naked eye. Ibn Ezra lauds Hay ben Meqis, personified Wisdom, whose ordered phrases resemble "arranged pearls." Moreover, there is confidence that the divinely ordered movement of the heavenly bodies is a reflection of their intelligence and obedience to their Maker. Yet, lurking behind this conviction were the nagging questions concerning the nature of the human spirit, or the soul. In his dialogue hymn, "'Imru beney 'elohim," [61] Ibn Ezra addressed this question.

The term "beney 'elohim" (literally, "sons of God") refers to the angels, the soul's interlocutors. Since the soul is of the same species as the angels ("If I am your kindred"), why is she forced to live among mortals. Ibn Ezra who employs the image of species, genus and individual in his characterization of world forms considers the soul to be from the species, "angel." [62] The angels' response to the soul is instructive:

> Although your roots are in the heavens, desire has driven you to
> Become involved [with the body]...[63]

Yet, not all is lost. The soul can use the agency of the body to redeem herself:

> Now let it be your agent for the needed

---

60. *Hay ben Meqis*, in I. Levin, *Yalqut*, p. 132; A. Ibn Ezra, *Sefer Ha-Moladot*, in Ms. Oxford, Bodley, Opp. 707, p. 65b ff; Langermann, "Astrological Themes," p. 53.
61. Poem #65.
62. Sirat, *A History of Jewish Philosophy*, p. 107; Ibn Ezra's comment on Ex. 3: 15.
63. See I. Levin, "'He'ahzi Be-Sullam Hokhmah'--Haspa'at Torat Ha-Nefeš Ha-Neoplatonit 'Al Širat Avraham Ibn Ezra," pp. 45–48. Poem #65.

Task; take the road that will lead you up
To the angels.... [64]

The soul is determined to learn about the sublunar world from the inside. Like Wisdom with which it is identified, the soul wishes to fully know herself, in order to know her God. Only by descending into the physical world can this happen:

Then take hold of Wisdom's ladder, lower yourself and ascend;
You will find a fountain of invention welling within you; with your
own effort draw from it. [65]

Only after its "holy indulgence" in the amusements of this world will the soul be convinced that "its content is illusion." [66]

Yet, there is a risk in making the descent. The soul may be overcome by her "indulgence" and be weighed down by her "impurity." The pure soul will easily advance through the four elements that encase the earth and the spheres of the upper world. The soul that is heavily burdened with sin will not be able to make the ascent. Her fate is uncertain. Following is a description of the soul's predicament by the first Jewish Neoplatonist, Isaac Israeli (b. 850), in his *Book of Definitions* (p. 26):

He who does not attach himself to the intellectual precepts which God has revealed to the elect among His creatures...and perseveres in his own injustice, sinfulness, coarseness, and in the evil of his ways, will be rendered unclean by his impurities, and they will weigh him down and prevent him from ascending to the world of truth.

To overcome this danger, Ibn Ezra, in his hymn "'Aṣulah mi-meqor ḥayyim," admonishes the soul (in language adapted from Ibn Gabirol's *Keter Malkhut*, 30):

Put away Time's delicacies. Why

---

64. Ibid.
65. Ibid.
66. For the Arabic sources of this conceit, see Levin. Ibid.

> Would you be a vagabond and outcast (*golah we–surah*)
> when you leave the body? [67]

However, there is hope for the impure soul, and the Tudelan poet would likely agree with Ibn Gabirol's judgment (paraphrasing Lev. 12: 4) in his *Keter Malkhut*, Ibid.

> She shall not touch any holy thing,
> Or come into the sanctuary,
> Until the days of her purification are completed.

The soul's reward is "adhesion" (*devequt*) "to God and His angels." Its punishment is alienation and banishment. The "perfected" soul does not have to wait for the death of the body to achieve "adhesion." In his hymn, "*Ṣam'ah lekha, 'el*," Ibn Ezra urges the soul:

> Renounce the honors that come from mortals and attach yourself
> To the angels on high and be joined to them. [68]

He is more explicit in his *Yesod Mora'*, 7. 12:

> Therefore it is advisable to seek that which will lead to the love of Him, to study the sciences...that will enable you to recognize God's hand in Creation. God will then open the eyes of his heart and give him a new understanding. He will be loved by his Maker in his lifetime and his soul will adhere to Him (*we–nafšo deveqah bo*). [69]

In this conceit, Ibn Ezra was presumably influenced by Ibn Gabirol who (in his *Meqor Ḥayyim*, 3. 56–57) refers to a state of ecstasy in which the purified intellect is united with the "spiritual essences" (*ha–'aṣamim ha–ruḥaniyim*) of the supernal world. The attainment of this goal was already suggested by Plotinus (in his

---

67. Poem #36.
68. Ibn Ezra, *Širey Ha–Qodeš*, 1: 119.
69. Levin, *Yalqut Ibn Ezra*, p. 332.

Enneads IV, 8, 1) and addressed in more detail by Isaac Israeli (in his *Book of Definitions*, pp. 25–26):

> [When] the truths of the subject of science...become clear to man; that he may distinguish between good and evil...[and] obtain the reward of his Creator, blessed be He, which is the union with the upper soul, and the illumination by the light of the intellect and by the beauty and splendor of wisdom. When attaining this rank, he becomes spiritual, and will be joined in union to the light which is created, without mediator, by the power of God...This then will be his paradise...

The focus of Ibn Ezra and his Jewish colleagues on the nature of the soul was motivated by their fascination with contemporary Neoplatonism, Sufi mysticism, and ascetic poetry (*zuhdiyyāt*). This prompted the emergence of new genres in which the center of attention was the individual and the fate of his soul. The tendency to compose personalized "confessions" (*widduyim*) and "supplications" (*baqqašot*) is already evident in the writings of the late ninth--early tenth century Babylonian poets, Nissi Nahrawani and Saʿadyah Gaon. The Andalusian treatment of the soul follows the model of the earlier Babylonians, even as it expands its thematic focus with the Neoplatonic myth of the soul's fall and ascent. Scheindlin notes that in this context the soul "yearning for restoration came to be seen as underlying the very impulse to pray. Prayer came to be understood...as a universal impulse stemming from the nature of the human soul itself." [70]

GOD IS ALL

In describing the nature of God, Ibn Ezra's choice of words borders on pantheism. In his commentary on Gen. 1: 26, he writes, "God is the One; He made all; He is all." In a comment on Ex. 23: 21, he adds, "He is all and from Him comes all." The theme is repeated in his hymn, "*Šem 'eli menat gorali*" (Poem #21) "All is contained in the One alone; He brought it out of nothing completed." This is followed by the personalized conceit: "Within me I can see God's wonders...He is with me" (ibid.). A bolder image appears in his "*Ahalay yikonu derakhay*" (Poem #22):

---

70. Scheindlin, *The Gazelle*, p. 143.

Wherever I turn I find You;
I am connected to You, for nothing separates us.

The first line is similar to Judah Halevi's, *"Yah 'anah 'emṣa'akha,"* [71]

When I go forth to meet You
I find You facing me.

The latter conceit in Ibn Ezra's *"'Aḥalay yikonu,"* however, has no parallel in Hispanic-Hebrew poetry. Ibn Ezra's writings on his relationship to God are exceptional in their stark intimacy. Scheindlin has observed that in this figure "the boundary of pantheism seems to be crossed" by Ibn Ezra, even though the "poet still speaks as if there is an 'I'." [72] The larger question of whether the "I" in synagogue poetry is reflective of the cantor-poet or of his congregation is relevant in this context. Scheindlin suggests that "ordinarily when the precentor uses the first person pronoun, he speaks in the name of the congregation." The only exception, in Scheindlin's view, is the genre known as *rešut*, a private prayer in which the synagogue poet asks for "eloquence" and "pleads that his prayer be heard so that the congregation not be disappointed in their trust in him." [73] However, Ibn Ezra's flirtation with pantheism can also be observed in his other writings where he speaks for himself, as in his commentary on Gen. 1: 26, and Ex. 23: 21, cited above and in his *Yesod Mora'* 10. 2: "God is the One, and there is no being but by cleaving to Him." Therefore it is likely that similar views in *"'Aḥalay yikonu derakhay"* reflect his personal opinion as well.

In figures adapted from Canticles and Arabic love poetry, God is the desired Beloved and the poet is the yearning and devoted lover, but with a difference:

Lovers are bound to part; or the beloved is wroth and the lover perishes;
But I lust after the Beloved who made me; there I will
        find every treasure;
I rest content that He will not depart; He repairs the broken spirit.

---

71. Halevi, *Širey Ha-Qodeš*, 1: 216.
72. See Scheindlin, *The Gazelle*, p. 224.
73. Ibid., p. 145.

Passion's lovers are plagued by jealousy; but the One I love can be trusted;
If, like me, others are enamoured of Him, I rejoice in their company. [74]

Unlike the flirtatious "fawn" or "gazelle" in the Arabic *ghazal* who is often bored and readily cruel, the beloved deity is dependable. Moreover, there is a balance in the divine-human relationship which is notably lacking in the Arabic love poem. A. Hamori gives a fitting description: "The lover's darling would try a sane man's patience. Promises are put off, and accusations founded on fancy torture the poor aspirant; he is forever in suspense." [75]

In his dialogue hymn, "'*Amut we-lo' met me-ḥoli ha-'ahavah*," Ibn Ezra elaborates on the contrast between sacred and profane love. The rhetoric displays both their polarity and parallel:

I am in mortal danger, but not from an erotic
Love-sickness of a desperate suitor;
My desire is to be with the mighty Monarch who has
No weakness; He is the fountain of my craving;
My anguish is hidden in the recess
Of my heart; my face does not show it,
  Lest they say of me: "His base passion killed him –
  Why does he put on airs?"

Love's token is faithful,
Though few are privy to its secret:
If you love a mortal, he will
Find a pretext to evade honor;
If you love the merciful Father,
His honor will stir him to compassion;

---

74. Poem #23.
75. Hamori, "Love Poetry (*Ghazal*)," p. 212.

Such is my Beloved and Friend whom I have chosen;
He stores up a reward for the upright. [76]

Although he parodies the obsession of the wretched lover in the *ghazal* and
boasts of Israel's (the lover's) own purified "desire," both suffer in equal measure. The
same Hebrew term, *heśeq*--adapted from Deut. 21: 11, "Suppose you see among the
captives a beautiful woman whom you desire (*we-ḥaśaqta bah)*"--applies to both.
Israel hides his anguish, "Lest they say of me, 'His base passion killed him.'" "They"
are the "fault-finders" (Hebrew, *merivim*) stock characters in the Arabic love poem
which Ibn Ezra co-opts for his rhetorical purpose. In the *ghazal*, the *merivim* often
intrude on the lovers' privacy out of jealousy, or they have good intentions and help
the lover overcome his obsession.

Israel insists that her "passion" is not "base," that is: erotic; but it is passion
nonetheless. Moreover, her obsession with the "mighty Monarch" will not lead to
disillusionment. Unlike the insensitive beloved in the *ghazal* who does not keep his
promise ("he will / Find a pretext to evade honor"), Israel's darling is dependable.

The manner in which the tropes of Arabic love poetry were absorbed and
transformed by the poetry of the synagogue is of special interest. Scheindlin has
noted that the Arabic *ghazal* had much in common with Canticles. Both sources
referred to the beloved by animal epithets, such as gazelle, deer and fawn, and
idealized the garden setting and the theme of nature's renewal. Moreover, the
"frustration" experienced by the hopelessly infatuated lover in Arabic love poetry
was easily adapted by synagogue poets in their treatment of Israel's often frustrated
hopes for national restoration. [77]

Paradox, along with polarity and parallel, is a dominant figure in the *ghazal*
and in its sacred counterpart. In both forms the lover chooses suffering over
detachment. The verse attributed to an anonymous Arab poet, "A wounded heart is
dearer to me than a calm mind without you," is matched by Israel's cry [in Ibn
Ezra's, *"Eykha levavi ya'amod,"*] "I am honored to bear the sweet pain for God's

---

76. Poem #62.
77. Scheindlin, *The Gazelle*, pp. 37-38.

sake," and in his "*Im yom peduti 'eyḥar*": "For my trust in You, my oppressor causes me grief; I treasure the sorrow." [78]

Ibn Ezra's hymn, "*Esbaʿ beʾ-ʿet 'erʿav*," highlights the several facets of paradox in the God–Israel relationship:

> When I yearn to praise You, I am satisfied;
> When I desire to adore You, I am refreshed;
> I rest secure in my fear of You;
> I wear terror like a garment.
> I am exalted when I bow before You;
> When I am humbled You are there to lift me up.
> Though I am in bondage to the sons of my brother and
>   of my maidservant,
> I am free whenever I worship You.
> The pain You bring me is sweetness
> To the spirit, the heart and the soul. [79]

ISRAEL: LOVER AND BELOVED

Ibn Ezra's synagogue poetry, like most medieval art, was didactic. His hymns for the Sabbath and festival morning *yoṣer* ("Praised are You...creating {*yoṣer*} light and fashioning darkness") cycle, included, among others, the *zulat*, chanted after "There is no God but You (*zulatekha*)" and before, "You were always the help of our ancestors"; the *'ahavah*, preceding the benediction, "Praised are You, Lord, who loves His people Israel" (*ha-boḥer be-ʿamo yisraʿel be-'ahavah*); and the *geʾullah*, prior to "Praised are You, Lord, Redeemer (*gaʾal*) of the people Israel." The dominant theme in the *zulat, 'ahavah*, and *geʾullah* is the certainty of God's faithfulness to Israel. Although Ibn Ezra's treatment is consistent with the hymn's mission, he invariably enhances its rhetorical impact with a dose of dramatic tension modeled after Canticles and the *ghazal*. The following is from his *geʾullah*, "*Yoʾel ʿod le–haviʾ 'el*":

---

78. Hamori, "Love Poetry (*Ghazal*)," p. 212; Poems #49 and #50.
79. Poem #19.

Abused in their lifetime, scattered among islands, they are helpless.

Driven, dispersed, scorned and ostracized by all,

While the ignorant laugh and hiss and agitate against them in their torment;

They think that God has left them and their hope vanished...[80]

Israel, like the despondent lover in the *ghazal*, is at times uncertain if her Beloved can be trusted. She suspects that He is now attracted to the other maidens [namely, the nations], "leav[ing] me for distant places." She vows, "I will never be attracted to a stranger," and is "confident that His promise will be kept." [81] However, the suspense heightens as the years of Israel's exile lengthen and she is unable to be reunited with her Beloved in their national home. The poet pictures the agony she endures in her sleepless nights:

> ....now she scoured the highways asking, "When will he return?"
> At night she stands watch with Orion and Pleiades inquiring
> About him; although he is late in arriving, she waits
> in silence and hopes. [82]

In her desperation she cries out:

> Would that God were my enemy! [83]

That would be preferable to neglect.

In Arabic love poetry, the humiliated lover may venture an argument in his attempt to persuade the pitiless beloved. The following from Ibn al-Rūmī (d. 896) is a paradoxical argument designed to promote an illicit love affair:

> How can it have happened that she is a sword held over me though
> I found my love when I entered her door?

---

80. Poem #43.

81. Poem #50.

82. Poem #60.

83. Poem #44.

Lord, if there must be retribution make me her shield; let me suffer
for her sins. [84]

Israel's argument is also directed to her Lord. It urges Him to be consistent:

Why do You let them tread upon her until she dies in exile?
If she be Your servant, redeem her; if your daughter, let her live! [85]

She is asking that He obey his own law (in Lev. 25: 47-54), which requires
that Israelite slaves sold to aliens be redeemed. Adding sarcasm to the argument, she
hopes that God will be as compassionate as Pharaoh, the slavemaster, who (in Ex. 1:
22) spared the infant daughters of Israel from death by drowning. In a variation on
this rhetoric Israel again reminds God that His ordinances apply to Him as well:

How could He sell the nobleman's [Abraham] daughter to a stranger?
I remember His instruction in the Torah (Ex. 21: 8),
"When a man sells his daughter as a slave and she displeases [her master],
He shall have no right to sell her to a stranger!" [86]

Ibn Ezra's treatment of Israel as God's beloved is primarily rooted in biblical
and rabbinic sources. Israel is referred to as the blessed younger brother, in contrast
to the cursed Esau, or as the son of the lady Sarah, rivaling Ishmael, the offspring of
Hagar the maidservant. Israel is named God's loyal betrothed who followed Him
into an unsown wilderness (Jer. 2: 2), His dedicated servant (Lev. 25: 55), His elegant
daughter (Cant. 7: 2), and His first-born son (Ex. 4: 22).

In his hymns where Israel is the beloved, Ibn Ezra again employs the
occasional argument as a rhetorical device. Adding to its dramatic impact is an irony
of situation as in the following from his "*Eres mah lakh 'od*":

How is it that the studious son [Jacob] who by his wits (*be-sikhlo*)

---

84. Ibn al-Rūmī, *Dīwān*, ed. H. Nassar, I, 315; Hamori, "Love Poetry (*Ghazal*)," p. 213.
85. Poem #48.
86. Poem #54.

Won his brother's blessing and his inheritance,
And the father [Isaac] agreed that he [Jacob] should rule his
    kindred (Ex. 27: 37),
Finds the blessing reversed and sovereignty passed on to
    him (my brother). [87]

In the following from his "*Ašpil lekha libi we-'eyni*," the argument is more emphatic in pointing to the contrast between promise and commitment:

[Israel:]

Will You now prefer the son of the disliked [Hagar] over the
    son of the beloved!
My Lord, how can You go back on Your word while I am
    burning with fever
Seeing my city and sanctuary in the hands of the slave [Ishmael]
    and brother [Esau]. [88]

The argument in his "*Eliyyah li-ševuyah*," appeals to God's sense of justice. If Israel is God's "first-born" then "the right of the first-born is his" (*ha-lo' mišpat ha-bekhorah*) according to law. The citation from Deut. 21: 17 is instructive in that it reveals the likely model for the poet's rhetoric. The Hebrew *mišpat* is used by Abraham in his intercession for Sodom and Gemorah [in Gen. 18: 25], "Shall not the judge of all the earth do what is just?" (*ha-šofet kol ha-'areṣ lo' ya'aseh mišpat*). In arguing for the just rights of his people, Ibn Ezra is following Abraham the patriarch who questioned the justice of God in allowing innocent people to be punished with the guilty. [89]

COURTING ISRAEL

It is likely that in his travels through Europe, Ibn Ezra encountered Christian monks determined to convince the Jews to abandon their faith. In Ibn Ezra's time, Western

---

87. Ibn Ezra, *Širey Ha-Qodeš*, 1: 329.
88. Ibid., 1: 334.
89. Ibn Ezra, *Širey Ha-Qodeš*, 1: 298.

Europe witnessed dynamic changes in economic progress, population growth, and the revival of classical learning. Jewish translators of Greek and Latin texts from antiquity were partly responsible for the cultural and intellectual ferment which C. H. Haskins called a "twelfth-century renaissance." These developments brought unease to some Church leaders who were apprehensive of the "Judaising" elements in the new thinking.

Adding to the fears of Churchmen was the widening influence of Islam coming from the south. These perceived threats to the stability of the Church brought about a determined effort to win Jews (and Muslims) to the Christian faith. In line with these efforts is the statement made by the twelfth-century cleric Odo, from the school of Peter Abelard, "For, if it is proper for us to exhort those who are fashioned in the faith to live better, surely we should recall the Jews from their erroneous disbelieving sect." Seconding a proselytizing mission to the Jews was Joachim da Fiora, known for his messianic speculation, and Peter the Venerable whose more sophisticated anti-Jewish polemic included selections from the Talmud as well as from Scripture. The latter focused his argument by comparing the worldly success of Christendom to the lowly status of Jewry in exile. [90]

Ibn Ezra's hymns reflect some of the agitation in the Jewish community when faced with Christian polemics. The following is from his *"Eheru pa'amey mešihi"*:

> What do I say to them who taunt me; I fear to answer.
> Though my enemy has prospered and I have lost, I can pour
> out to God my heart...[91]

Presumably, Ibn Ezra was not impressed with the skills of the Christian monks. In his *"Im koah 'avanim kohi"* [92] he denigrates their efforts: "...a fool would shut me off from light into darkness," and in *"Az me-'eres misrayim bekhori kinnitikha"* [93] he calls them "foolish people who pursue the useless." The monks'

---

90. See C. H. Haskins, *The Renaissance of the Twelfth Century*; R. Chazan, *Daggers of Faith*, 21-23.

91. Poem #45.

92. Poem #44.

93. Poem #52.

persistence and Jewry's refusal is recorded by the poet in his "*Eykha levavi ya'amod*":

> Pursuing me and breaking down my walls, they intend to abolish me;
> They fancy themselves learned in God's ways while abusing Him.
> They broke His laws and forsook [God] the source of life,
>   and the dead man they divided [into father and son].
> I will not be drawn to the stranger; God almighty alone I trust.
> I vow never to exchange the glory of the living God for
>   a corpse on a crucifix. [94]

In their debate with Jewish leaders, Christian missionaries would point to Israel's long exile implying that God had abandoned them. Ibn Ezra's "*Im yom peduti 'eyhar*" echoes this charge and the response given to it:

> Why do my enemies rejoice at my plight
> When my Beloved leaves me for distant places?
> It matters not if He is near or distant,
> I will never be attracted to a stranger! [95]

Among the disputed issues in the Jewish–Christian debate was the question of the Messiah's arrival. Both camps supported their positions with citations from the Israelite prophets. In his dialogue "*Amrah ṣiyyon: 'eykh šekheḥuni vanay?*" Ibn Ezra replicates the arguments of the two parties:

> The foe:

> "The prophecies have already been fulfilled:
> If the early seers were indeed faithful and true
> Then their comforting words were realized in the Second Temple.

---

94. Poem #49.
95. Poem #50.

A thousand years have passed, what more can you hope for?
Why do you persist in saying: He will come and save you?" [96]

The foe, that is, the monk, in his argument that the statements of the
prophets are to be read in their historical context may have been familiar with the
second century *tanna*, Rabbi Nathan, who championed this view. Following is his
response [in *bSan* 97b] to colleagues who recontextualized prophetic teachings as
predictors of future events: "The following verse [from Hab. 2: 3] goes to the heart
of the matter, 'For there is still a vision for the appointed time; it speaks of the end
and does not lie. If it seems to tarry, wait for it; it will surely come; it will not
delay.' (This means that we are to do) not like the rabbis who interpret (the verse in
Dan. 7: 25), 'until a time and times and the dividing of time' (as holding a Messianic
date for the future), and not like Rabbi Simlai who interpreted (the verse in Ps. 80:
6), 'You have fed them with the bread of tears and given them tears to drink in full
measure (*šališ*),' nor like (R.) Aqiva, who interpreted, 'Once again, in a little while, I
will shake the heavens and the earth (Hag. 2: 6).' But (we are to take these passages
as referring to events now past), the first kingdom (Hasmonean) lasted seventy years;
the second kingdom (Herod) fifty two years, and the kingdom of Ben Kosiba, two
and a half years." [97]

Ibn Ezra, however, is not persuaded. He takes the monks' argument, "The
prophecies have already been fulfilled," to be all inclusive. Pointing to the pervasive
hostility among the nations in his day, he is convinced that Isaiah's vision [in 2: 4] of
an age of peace has not, as yet, arrived:

Zion:

"Be still, my foe who roars like a lion;
The prophets spoke of the future. Tell me
Have the nations broken their swords into plowshares?"....[98]

Occasionally the exchange between the two became abusive. The Christian

---

96. Poem #58.
97. See Silver, *Messianic Speculation in Israel*, p. 198.
98. Poem #58.

monk was convinced that the new covenant made the old one "obsolete," [99] a view which his Jewish respondent vehemently opposed:

The foe:

"I have seen my wish
Come true; My creed is just and my power unlimited;
How do you, Zion's sons, expect to oppose me?
Your Torah is flawed, why obey it!
Was not God's hand against you and your fathers?"

Zion:

"Enemies of God, have you not heard
The words of His prophets? Why do you defame His Torah
And praise your creed which you stole from Him?
Now He will raise up His right arm and destroy you
Because you have put to death God's people." [100]

TRANSCENDENCE AND FAMILIARITY

We have seen the use of dramatic paradox in Ibn Ezra's hymnography in which the faithful lover finds relief in suffering. Another rhetorical device favored by the poet in designing the God-Israel relationship is the perceptual paradox: "While dwelling in the heights, You provide for the lowly," and "You are highly exalted, but I find You near at hand." [101] Seeing the divine Beloved as both transcendent and immanent evokes a response of mixed awe and familiarity.

Israel holds her God in highest esteem. In the poet's vision, He is "awesome in splendor; all greatness is [His] due! An army [in the heavens] proclaims it making haste on its rounds." He is the "master of the prevailing winds, There in the lightning we see His conversation. The earth confirms it and the hills agree...the work of God

---

99. See Heb. 8: 13.
100. Poem #58.
101. Poems #29 and #30.

is in the flowering tree" and in every living form. [102] Peering behind the supernal curtain, Ibn Ezra reveals the inner workings of the celestial landscape:

> His radiance kindles the lights in heaven; his galaxies sing to Him;
> Armed by His might, they are faithful in doing His will;
> Their course is steady as they race carrying His chariot throne;
> Awe and terror follow the throne, and God's seat bears its bearers! [103]

Inspired by Ezekiel's [in 1: 4ff] vision of the divine chariot throne, identified with the Empyrian, the tenth sphere, Ibn Ezra adds a notable paradox. "God's seat bears its bearers" affirms the transcendent deity's absolute independence.

Collateral with the feeling of awe in the presence of divinity is a sense of compatibility and intimacy between God and Israel. The poet, speaking for the latter, is "connected" to God: "Wherever I turn I find You...Whatever I say is within Your hearing." "Your beauty is all that my eyes can see; My ears hear only Your command." [104] From this familiarity the relationship achieves a balance in which both parties feel free to reveal their thoughts. God repeatedly chastizes Israel for her unfaithfulness and obstinacy. Israel, for her part, ventures to question God's judgment and His compassion. [105] In the boldest exchange between the pair, Israel appears to be giving her Beloved an ultimatum:

> Generations come and go,
> But the pain of God's people endures;
> For a thousand years their decline was
> A source of amazement; in their agony,
>> They cried, "If You intend to redeem us, do it, and
>> If You will not, tell us!" [106]

---

102. Poems #24 and #25.
103. Poem #27.
104. Poem #22.
105. Poems #48 and #54.
106. Poem #56.

Israel's argument, based on Ruth 4: 4, is suggestive of a threat: "If You, God, will not keep Your promise, then have the decency to inform us and we will make other plans." The alternative is not stated. In this courageous response, the poet, representing his people, makes clear that unlike the timid and resigned lover in the Arabic *ghazal*, Israel's uncommon familiarity with her Beloved permits her to be assertive. Their balanced relationship allows the parties to speak their minds.

What is Israel's motive in laying down this challenge? Has the lover become the flirtateous coquette? Here, as in the *ghazal*, we are left in suspense. The provocative language in addressing deity is not uncommon. The Psalmist [44: 24] urges God, "Rouse yourself. Why do You sleep, O Lord," and likewise Isaiah [51: 9], "Awake, awake, put on strength, O arm of the Lord! Awake, as in days of old, the generations of long ago."

ISRAEL'S DIARY

Israel kept a selective record of life with her Beloved. Ibn Ezra's interpretation of this record is preserved in his commentaries on the Pentateuch, Isaiah, the Twelve Minor Prophets, Psalms, Job, the Five Megillot, and Daniel. These works were completed during the last twenty-four years of the poet's life and reflect his sense of mission. Particularly instructive are his comments on the Five Books of Moses written at age sixty-four in Lucca following a crisis in his personal life. He writes about it in a poem dedicated to his patron Rabbi Moses ben Meir:

Praised be God...
Who endowed Abraham son of Meir with vigor...
At the age of sixty-four
When in his declining years his sins delivered him
Into the hands of a familiar malady...

In my illness I made a vow to God
To explain the Torah given on Mount Sinai. [107]

In his introduction to the Pentateuch he reviews the several methods of interpreting the biblical text and finds them unworthy. He faults the Geonim for their lengthy excursuses and needless digressions. He is critical of Sa'adyah Gaon's commentary for its excessive reliance on teachings in astronomy. He then blames the Karaites for their vacillation in interpreting Scripture. "They change their views from moment to moment." He derides the Christian exegetes for "inventing mysteries in their analysis" of the Bible. He adds that "the Torah was not given to the ignorant and that the intermediary [lit. the angel] between God and the man is the intellect."

Next to be blamed are the Italian and Franco–German Bible interpreters for neglecting Hebrew grammar. Moreover, they depend on rabbinic legends and neglect the logical sense of the text. Ibn Ezra's commentary will hew to the plain meaning of Scripture with special attention to the subtle nuances of its languages, Hebrew and Aramaic. His devotion to Hebrew, the "sacred tongue," and the shades and colors of its grammar is evident in his writings on the subject and forms a major part of his mission. He makes this clear in the introductory poem to the Book of Genesis:

With the help of God, mighty and awesome
I begin to explain the Torah...
This righteous book by master Abraham
Is encased by the rules of grammar;
The intelligent will approve it;
They who support it will be happy. [108]

In line with his sense of mission as an emissary of Hispano–Hebrew culture to European Jewry was his translation from the Arabic into Hebrew of three pioneering works on Hebrew grammar by the influential Judah ben David Hayyuj. His strident criticism (in his commentary on Eccles. 5: 1) against the renowned Eres Yisrael liturgical poet Eleazar Qillir included the allegation that the latter abused the Hebrew language with his ungrammatical constructions. Nahum Sarna notes that the

---

107. Kahane, *Avraham Ibn Ezra,* 1: 69–70, Poem #46.
108. *Ibn Ezra 'Al Ha–Torah,* 1: 1.

"Spanish Bible texts and Talmud editions early acquired enviable reputations for exactitude." [109] This was undoubtedly due to the influence of Abraham Ibn Ezra and his passion for precision and accuracy in preserving the language of the Bible. Revealing in this regard is his comment on Ex. 25: 31: "The base and the shaft of the lampstand shall be made (*tey'aseh*) of hammered work":

> I have seen copies which the scholars of Tiberias examined, and fifteen of their elders swore that they thrice inspected every word and dot, every full (*plene*) and defective (spelling) and lo, the word *tey'aseh* is written with a *yod* (y); but I have not found the like in the books of Spain, France, and England (lit. "beyond the sea).

His attention to style and usage enabled Ibn Ezra to make sense of biblical passages heretofore obscure. He assumed that there are ellipses in the Bible. Relying on the rabbinic comment [in *bBM* 31b] that the Torah speaks in human language, he found that there are places in the narrative where missing words are understood though not stated. He gave the following examples from Deut. 33: 6, "May Reuben live and not die, and may his numbers [not] be few," and from Gen. 24: 67, "Isaac brought her to the tent, [the tent of] Sarah his mother."

Ibn Ezra's views on rabbinic interpretation of Scripture are a mixture of esteem and caution. He is critical of the exegetes in Christian Europe for their excessive use of rabbinic homiletics in interpreting Scripture. At the same time, he condemns the Karaites for their failure to consider the oral traditions in the understanding of the Written Torah. He is unambiguous in his reliance on rabbinic teaching in matters relating to Jewish law (*halakhah*) and says so in the introduction to his Bible commentary. After asserting his independence in interpreting the text in its plain meaning, he adds, "However, when it comes to the statutes and ordinances, I shall rely upon our ancient [Sages]." In his dealings with rabbinic analysis of Scripture he differentiated between a tradition (*qabbalah*) received by them which

---

109. See N. Sarna, "Ibn Ezra as an Exegete," p. 7.

he accepts and their use of logical inference (*sevarah*) from the text which he may reject. [110]

He does not make this distinction when he finds that the rabbis have not interpreted the text in its plain meaning. In his comment on Gen. 22: 19, "So Abraham returned to his young men," he writes, "Isaac is not mentioned because he was [still under thirteen years of age and therefore] under the jurisdiction of his father. Whoever says that [Abraham] killed him and left him and later he [Isaac] was resurrected are perverting the text [in Gen. 22: 12 which reads, 'Do not lay your hand on the boy or do anything to him']." In his criticism Ibn Ezra has in mind the rabbinic discussion [in *Genesis Rabbah* 56. 11] on the verses, "And they [Abraham and Isaac] went both of them together [to Mount Moriah]" (Gen. 22: 6-8) and "So Abraham (in the singular) returned to his young men." "And where was Isaac?" ask the Rabbis. [111]

Even as he acknowledges rabbinic authority in *halakhah* and accepts its judgment when supported by tradition, he boldly proclaims [in his introduction to Genesis], "God alone I fear, and I will be impartial in explaining the Torah." This intellectual honesty probably led him to hint at some discrepancies in the biblical text itself. With characteristic caution in approaching the sensitive subject, he notes [in his comment on Deut. 1: 2]:

> If you understand the secret (*sod*) of the "twelve" (last verses in Deut. 34: 1-12), and also "That day Moses wrote down this poem" (Ibid., 31: 22); "The Canaanites were then in the land" (Gen. 12: 6); "In the mountain of the Lord it will be seen" (Ibid., 22: 14); "His bedspread is an iron bedspread" (Deut. 3: 11), you will recognize the truth.

If according to tradition the Pentateuch was written by Moses, the twelve verses in Deut. 34: 1-12 and the one in Deut. 31: 22 which refer to Moses in the third person may be a later interpolation. The verse in Gen. 12: 6 may have been written after Moses at a time when the Canaanites *were no longer in the land*. Commenting

---

110. Ibn Ezra, *Commentary on the Torah*: Gen. 22: 4; Ex. 9: 10.
111. Ibid., Gen. 22: 4; S. Spiegel, *The Last Trial*, pp. 4-8.

on the verse Ibn Ezra writes, "The prudent one will keep silent." Genesis 22: 14 states that Abraham called the site where the binding of Isaac took place, *'Adonay-yir'eh.* As a result people were accustomed to say, "on the mountain of the Lord there is a vision." However, such a reference would apply only after Solomon built the Temple there. [112] The note in Deut. 3: 11 that the king of Bashan's "iron bedspread" remained in Rabbah of the Ammonites is likely to have been made by a later writer since in the time of Moses the city was in hostile hands and the Israelites would not have placed it there. The perceptive Ibn Ezra, anticipating modern historical criticism, also argued that the Book of Isaiah was not the work of one author. The first thirty-nine chapters were composed by the eighth-century B.C.E. prophet whereas chapters forty and following were the work of an unnamed prophet who "refers to a period yet to come." [113]

Anticipating as well Ralph Waldo Emerson's observation that "a foolish consistency is the hobgoblin of little minds," Ibn Ezra's practice is at times contrary to his preachment. He excoriates Eleazar Qillir for his use of rabbinic legends in writing for the synagogue liturgy and is himself guilty of this practice. [114] He faults the Geonim for introducing subjects in botany and other types of "foreign learning" (*hokhmot nokhriyot*) into their biblical studies while he loads his own commentaries with mathematics, astronomy, and astrology. [115] He disagrees with the rabbis [in *bNed* 32a] that Scripture can be interpreted through the use of *gematri'a* (numerical values) yet does the very same thing in explaining the divine name YHWH. [116]

In all fairness to Ibn Ezra, A. Mondschein argues that his resistance to the use of *gematri'a* may have been motivated by a fear that the device would be exploited

---

112. These problems were already familiar to the rabbis. See *bBB* 15a; *bMen* 30a; *Sifre Deut.* ed. Horovitz-Finkelstein, 34. 357. 15 (p. 427).

113. Ibn Ezra commentary on Is. 40: 1. There he credits R. Moses ha-Kohen Ibn Gikatilla with the view that the Book of Isaiah comprises two parts.

114. See A. Mirsky, "Ha-Ziqah Še-Bayn Širat Sefarad Li-Drašot ḤaZaL," *Sinai* 64 (1969), pp. 248-53.

115. Ibn Ezra commentary on Gen. 1: 14; Lev. 25: 9; Is. 14: 12; cf. Sarna, "Ibn Ezra as an Exegete," p. 20.

116. Ibn Ezra commentary on Gen. 14: 14; Ex. 33: 21 and Sarna, "Ibn Ezra as an Exegete," pp. 19-20.

by Muslims in their anti-Jewish polemics. He lists several such attempts:

1. God's promise to Abraham [in Gen. 17: 2], "And I will make my covenant between me and you, and will make you exceedingly numerous (*bi-m'od me'od*)." The numerical value of the latter two words equals "Muhammad" *MHMD* = 92.

2. The verse in Gen. 1: 16, "God made the two great (*ha-gedolim*) lights." *Ha-gedolim* which equals 98 refers to Muhammad and the sixth day of the week, Friday, sacred to Muslims.

3. "And Abram journeyed on by stages toward the Negeb" (Gen. 12: 9). Since the numerical values of *Ha-Negbah* (the Negeb) and of Mecca (*MKH*) equal 65, Muslims could find support for their belief that the Ka'bah was built by Abraham. Other Muslim polemicists cited the verse [in Gen. 21: 21], "He (Ishmael) lived in the wilderness of Paran," and equated the latter with Mecca. [117]

Ibn Ezra's strong opinions on how Scripture is to be interpreted often led him to disparage those with whom he disagreed. The errant were called "stupid," "mindless," "lacking in faith," "dull-witted," and "empty-headed." [118] Choice epithets were reserved for the heretic Hiwi Al-Balkhi whom he called "Ha-Kalbi" [= the dog] and added [in Ex. 14: 22], "may the bones of the dog be crushed," and [in Ex. 16: 13], "may the name of Hiwi rot." He is equally vehement in denouncing Anan ben David, founder of the Karaites, whom he scorns in his introduction to Genesis. He curses Anan [in Ex. 34: 21] with, "May his name be blotted out." Bearing the brunt of Ibn Ezra's invective is an otherwise unknown Hispanic writer named, Yishaqi. In his note to Gen. 36: 31-32, Ibn Ezra asks derisively, "Was he given the name Yishaqi so that all who hear [his comment] will laugh at him" [119] and recommends [in Num. 24: 17] that "his books be burned."

---

117. See A. Mondschein, "Le-Yahaso Šel RAB"E 'El Ha-Šimuš Ha-Paršani Be-Middat Ha-Gematriah," pp. 147-48; M. Perlmann, "Polemics Between Islam and Judaism," p. 121.

118. Gen. 32: 33; 15: 13; 20: 19; Deut. 33: 2; Gen. 25: 34; 31: 18.

119. A play on the Hebrew ṢHQ, after Gen. 21: 6.

Nor were more prominent figures spared his barbed arrows. As Uriel Simon has shown, Ibn Ezra's diatribes were also directed against R. Jonah b. Janah, illustrious Hispanic–Hebrew grammarian and lexicographer whom he called "prater," "madman," and "dreamer." Disagreeing with Dunaš ben Labrat—the gifted Hispanic poet who introduced quantitative meters to Hebrew verse—on the interpretation of Ps. 139: 17, he urges that his books be destroyed. Even the venerable Sa'adyah Gaon is castigated for a contrary opinion and "anyone who agrees with him should be flogged." [120]

There is little reason to suspect that in his invective Ibn Ezra meant to be taken at his word. It is likely that his stridency is reflective of mannerisms common to court poets hired to heap abuse on the patron's enemies. It should also be noted that Ibn Ezra's emphatic defense of his interpretation of the Torah in its plain meaning is linked to Christian and Muslim attempts to read into the sacred text more than is warranted. Following is part of his criticism in the introduction to Genesis:

> The third way of [commenting on Scripture] is dark and dismal and far from the truth. They invent allegorical meanings for all things...Why change the obvious into a mystery?

While it is possible that Ibn Ezra was opposed to *gematri'a* fearing its use by Christians and Muslims, it is clear that he saw a danger in confusing plain meaning with allegory. From the sizable body of Christian and Muslim polemical literature there is evidence that he had good reason to be apprehensive. For example, Muslims read Ishmael's Paran [in Gen. 21: 21] as an allegory for Mecca (see above) and the comment on Is. 21: 7, "riders on donkeys, riders on camels," as a reference to the prophethood of Jesus and Muhammad respectively. [121]

One of the early anti-Jewish polemicists was the Muslim author Ahmad Ibn Hazm (994-1064). Living in Spain, he was a contemporary of Samuel Ibn Nagrela whom he admired as "the most learned and skilled in disputations" and despised

---

120. See U. Simon, "Lešono Ha-Harifah Ve-Ha-Šenunah Šel RAB"E," pp. 111-14.
121. See Mondschein, "Le-Yahaso...Gematriah," p. 148; Perlmann, "Polemics Between Islam and Judaism," p. 121.

because he was "a heretic, a Jew," and "filled with hatred toward the Prophet [Muhammad]." Ibn Hazm's outburst was prompted by an allegation that Nagrela wrote a tract critical of the Koran. Ibn Ḥazm's *Refutation* was designed to aid Muslims in their disputations with the Jews. Presumably, Abraham Ibn Ezra was familiar with Ibn Hazm's writings and his allegorical interpretations of Scripture. Following are examples of the latter's effort to read hidden meanings into the text which Ibn Ezra would find objectionable:

> The Lord came from Sinai
> And dawned from Seir upon them;
> He shone forth from mount Paran (Deut. 33: 2).

Ibn Hazm sees in this verse a reference to three successive revelations. Beginning at Sinai to the Jews, continuing at Seir [= Edom] to the Christians, God's word was "sealed" at Paran, the home of Ishmael (Gen. 21: 21) and a metonymy for Mecca, the birthplace of Islam's Prophet. A citation from Deut. 18: 18 was also suggestive to Ibn Hazm of a deeper meaning:

[God:]

> "I will raise up for them a prophet like you [Moses] from among their own people."

"From among their own people," was perceived as a reference to Ishmael's descendents, and "the prophet like you" was meant for Muḥammad. The likelihood that Ibn Ezra was acquainted with Ibn Hazm's *Refutation* and the alleged Nagrela tract critical of the Koran may be seen in the way each dealt with Jacob's blessings in Gen. 49: 10, "The sceptre shall not depart from Judah."

Since there is no longer a Judean ruler, this verse proved to Ibn Hazm that due to Jewish sinfulness there occurred an abrogation (Arab. *naskh*) of their covenant with God. Whereupon God made a new commitment to Christians and Muslims. When Ibn Nagrela observed that the exilarchs remained the Jewish rulers from the House of David, Ibn Hazm answered:

That is incorrect. The exilarch has no ruling power over any Jew or anyone else. His office is merely a title with no substance or authority, nor does he wield a sceptre. [122]

Ibn Ezra, presumably mindful that Gen. 49: 10 served a polemical purpose for Ibn Hazm, interpreted the verse in its historical context:

> The sceptre of prominence shall not depart from the tribe of Judah until the time of David who was at first king of Judah. (The prominence of Judah is evident in that its tribe led the others in the wilderness journey {Num. 10: 14} and was the first to do battle with Canaan {Jud. 1: 2}).

THE PLAYFUL SIDE

The reverse side of the exacting grammarian and uncompromising Bible comentator revealed an exceptional talent for play and entertainment. Three of his poems on the game of chess have survived. Presumably he wrote others on this "battle of wits." Added to the intellectual challenge that the game presented was the certainty of its peacefully eternal renewal:

> When the king is seized in an ambush, without mercy he is placed in a net;
> Unable to save himself, there is no fortified city to which he can flee!
> Condemned by the enemy, he submits; he is now without hope and is
>   taken to his death;
> His soldiers have perished fighting for his cause; their lives a ransom for his own;
> Seeing their leader stricken, they leave the field, their glory vanished;
> And yet, these mortally wounded will rise again,
> And once more they will do battle. [123]

Other forms of play that appealed to Ibn Ezra were the staged debates. The

---

122. Perlmann, "Polemics Between Islam and Judaism," pp. 113–14. Recent scholarship questions whether Nagrela ever wrote a tract that was critical of the Koran. See D. Wasserstein, *The Rise and Fall of the Party-Kings*, pp. 202–05, and S. Stroumsa, "From Muslim Heresy to Jewish-Muslim Polemics: Ibn al-Rāwandī's *Kitāb al-Dāmigh*," pp. 767–82.

123. Poem #18.

parties in the dialogue arguing their special merits included man and the animals;
winter and summer; Sabbath and the festivals; wine and bread; the sailor and sea;
and the limbs of the body. The latter in *qaṣīdah* style, "*Ḥadašim maʿaseh ʾel*," Ibn
Ezra intended as a tribute to his patron, Rabbi Menaḥem and his son Rabbi Moses.
The poem opens with an imaginary debate between tongue, eye, and ear with each
claiming that it is indispensable to the general welfare of the body. The poet must
now resolve their differences:

> I awoke and found my inner body at war;
> Hostile camps faced each other fully armed.
> Then a voice emerged from the heavens: Why are you fighting?
> Find an agreeable way to resolve your dispute:
> Seek out Rabbi Menaḥem, who brings comfort
> To the soul and restores the body. [124]

In Ibn Ezra's skilled treatment the poem combines both entertainment and
panegyric. The debate between the sailor and the sea, "*Efros kaf, ʾaf ʾikaf*," may
have resulted from the poet's personal experience during his travels on the
Mediterranean Sea and the English Channel:

> Tempting fate upon the faithless waters,
> I risked my life;
> Reassured (strange though the day appeared),
> I thought: I trust the waters this time of the year.
> Resolute, I left my house,
> I boarded the ship, now my home,
> And to my sorrow, I fell asleep.
>> "Why, O Sea, do you frighten the meek; I am strange to your ways;
>> Why does your anger rage, why is your temper uncontrolled?".....

> Then the sea spoke up, "Do not ask why,
> Consider the wisdom of treading upon me
> And how stupid it is to trust a wooden boat;
> Remember, every sailor is seasoned by disaster....

---

124. Poem #11.

I cannot be becalmed when winds come over me!"

"Be still, O sea, for my faith is firm;
The Rock, my Master, will rebuke the storm...

The sea answered, "Your speech is mindless;
Remaining here confined in close quarters,
You persist in your sin and insolence.
Now you will be unwittingly consumed
Like the fish you devoured with pleasure.
This, covetous man, is measure for measure.
Do you not know? Have you not heard?
  God's eye is on His creatures, requiting deeds;
  Your blood be on your own head; death to you, not life!"

God exalted, Your majesty be revealed;
Redeem and regard one broken by Your wrath...[125]

As in the previous debate, a third party—God in this case—is summoned to arbitrate the dispute. The contest between summer and winter, "*El 'ehad, mah rabbu 'eydekha*," opens with the conventional praise of God and His world of orderly seasonal change in contrast to man and his pursuit of folly. However, there are rumblings of discord between the two seasons, summer and winter.

In a mock-serious tone the poet has the two antagonists standing before the bar of judgment with each pleading his cause. As in his didactic poem on the months of the year, "*Šim'u na' 'el divrey ha-rofe*" (above), the following comprises sets of longer opening strophes followed by shorter summaries:

[Summer:]

"Winter's name (*horef*) is derived from [the word] disgrace (*herpah*);
Men become bald (*yiqrah*) from the bitter cold (*ba-qerah ha-nora'*);
Even the houses crumble from the frost;

---

125. Poem #15A.

The man who works to earn his bread has to keep his hands hidden
And no foot will dare to make a journey;
Nary a bird can be seen in the heavens,

Except to the men who stand
Huddled around a fire;
Were it not for its warmth
They would surely perish."

[Winter:]

Every living creature hates the summer;
You fear to go outdoors because of the heat,
And you feel a chill in your bowels. [126]
It is known that the heart does not tolerate (summer) days,
You are warned not to imbibe sweets [127]
And fear to eat them even when the sun goes down.

The time of dusk is revered,
Men race to the shade it brings;
Even the strongest
Run to the cold springs."

Again the dispute is given over to arbitration by a higher authority. God is summoned to render a verdict:

I will put this weighty matter to the One
Who heals the broken-hearted and endows the weak
With courage and patience, lest the frail
Suffer and perish before their time.

---

126. This is in line with the view in medieval physiology that summer's heat causes an imbalance in the four fluids of the body resulting in the dominance of black bile and melancholy. See M. Yishaqi, "Megamot Didaqtiyot Be-Širat Ha-Ḥol Šel Avraham Ibn Ezra," p. 26.
127. Sweets tend to increase bodily heat.

He anticipated both the good and evil to come,
And each season He arranged in order;
Even as He gave me the talent to tell you.

My lips praise His name
Loving-kindness rests with Him;
I crave His company always;
In it I rejoice each day. [128]

The contrived debate, a popular form of entertainment in Ibn Ezra's day, was the benign equivalent of the more serious and equally engaging religious disputation. The latter could vary from Judah Halevi's, *Kuzari*, a literary fiction, based on the conversion of the King of the Khazars to Judaism after hearing Christian and Muslim advocates, to the staged debates by Christian monks in Barcelona (1263) and Tortosa (1413-14). Ibn Ezra's mock counterparts had none of their solemnities. Designed as a diversion for the patron and his company, the combatants, having fought bravely, would, like the chessmen, "rise again / And once more...do battle." [129]

While admiring the play of intellectual energy required for a debating contest, Ibn Ezra was not kindly disposed to games of chance. Such play, devoid of any mental skill, he found abhorrent, as he relates in the following diatribe against gamblers:

The dice player
Is like an open wound;
He will come to ruin
And be despised in the city.

He squanders his money
And adds to his burden;
He rebels against his Maker
By the telling of lies.

---

128. Yiṣhaqi, "Megamot," pp. 15-19.
129. Poem #18.

He hopes to profit
And never succeeds;
There is no bloom to his years;
His days are mostly frustration.

He wanders from city to city,
Never recognizing any one place;
He is poor and immature,
Trying to reach the heights...

His hair is unkempt
And his clothes are tattered;
He persists in harming
Himself and others.

He eats in haste
Without giving thanks;
But is not slim from fasting
On the Day of Atonement.

Every one in his family
Despises him;
The day of his death
Is a time for song and joy...[130]

FOLK HERO

Of the five celebrated scholar-poets in "Golden Age" Spain, only Abraham Ibn Ezra
inspired in the public mind the kind of legend generally associated with a Moses or
Elijah the Prophet. Surpassing his contemporaries in his wide range of interests, the
Tudelan polymath who wrote extensively on the many subjects he studied was
perceived as a heroic figure. He became famous as the penniless itinerant poet armed
only with his wits and an astrolabe. This image cultivated by his admirers added to
his charisma.

---

130. Kahane, *Rabbi Avraham Ibn Ezra*, 1: 161.

In legends from Egypt, where Ibn Ezra was warmly received, he is portrayed as a saviour of Jews condemned to death by governmental decrees. Other traditions remember him as one privy to the secret of the Divine Name which he employed on his several missions of rescue. Following is a translation from Egyptian Judeo-Arabic of an Ibn Ezra folk-tale:

It is told that in a land ruled by Christians it was the practice on one of their festivals to sacrifice a Jew in their worship service. The Jews cast lots to determine which one of their children will be the victim for the year...One year the lot fell on the sagely Rabbi's only child, a son, age twenty. The lad was exceptionally bright and knowledgeable in the Torah, and when word of his fate became known there was much weeping and mourning. It was determined that he would be sacrificed on the first night of Passover. The Sage now turned to his students and asked, "Would you be willing to travel to Cairo to Rabbi Abraham Ibn Ezra...and deliver this letter to him and explain the situation...?" They replied, "Our Master, we hear and obey." He wrote the letter and they were off to Cairo.

After a journey of three months they arrived in Cairo where they chanced upon a poor vagabond. When they asked him, "Where is the home of Rabbi Abraham Ibn Ezra?" he replied, "I am he." They gave him the letter, and he said to them, "Do not worry. With God's help I will go with you and we will solve this problem, and it will be good." He took them to his home and they stayed with him.

When a month had passed, they said to him, "Master, we should like to return and have this matter resolved." He replied, "Do not speak to me about it. When I will be ready, we will go." They remained until the night before Passover, and after the Rabbi cleared the leaven from the house, they went to the synagogue. There they sat for four hours until the service was completed and cookies mixed with oil were distributed. After the Rabbi and students had eaten two cookies each, they left. Rabbi Abraham Ibn Ezra showed them the way and they followed. However, instead of taking the main highway they took a detour through the wilderness. "Master, where are we headed in this wasteland?" they asked. He replied, "Take hold of the edge of my garment." They did as he ordered. He then pronounced the Divine Name and before dawn they were back home.

When the students saw their city, they were amazed. One of them said, "This is our city." Another replied, "This is not where we live. We are still in Cairo." Then Rabbi Abraham went before them until he came to the home of the local Sage. When he knocked on the door, the latter found Rabbi Abraham standing there and thought him to be a beggar. "What do you want? Are you not aware of the crisis we face?" asked the Sage. "I know your situation; but with faith in God, may He be praised and exalted, a miracle will happen," replied Rabbi Abraham. The Sage greeted his students and said to them, "Tell me what happened." They answered, "Master, the man you see standing before you is Rabbi Abraham Ibn Ezra." The Sage drew near to him and invited [Rabbi Abraham] to his home. When they finished praying in the synagogue, the students told their story to the Sage and to his great amazement they showed him the cookies that they had not eaten.

Then Rabbi Abraham Ibn Ezra spoke to the lad who was to be taken for sacrifice at the heathen altar, "When their procession comes for you, tell them that I am your guest; and when they ask if you have a [last] request, say that you want your guest at your side." "I hear and obey," replied the lad.

Before two hours had passed, a large procession of Christians arrived to take the lad into the city. He said to them, "Take me and my associate. He will be a part of whatever happens to me." They replied, "We need only one, but if you give us two, all the better." Now that Rabbi Abraham and the lad were seated in the canopy, they were asked if they had any requests to make. "Yes," said Rabbi Abraham, "I should like it if you would place the archbishop in a barrel and tie it to the canopy until the procession is completed." They agreed, set the archbishop in the barrel, tied it to the canopy, and allowed it to be dragged in the procession around the city until it reached the church.

The canopy arrived at the church and Rabbi Abraham and the lad were asked what they would like to eat. Rabbi Abraham requested two young hens. When the hens were brought the Rabbi ascended the church altar and called out to the large crucifix above it, "O cunning one, come down from your pedestal and sharpen this knife." The figure obeyed and sharpened the knife. All were in a panic and shaken with fear. Then the Rabbi called out to the figure of the woman (the Virgin Mary), "Come down and start the fire [to cook the hens]." She did as ordered. When the churchmen saw this their hearts sank and they shut their eyes [in disbelief]. "Master of the Jews," they cried, "Remove your anger from upon us and return the figures to their places. Take the [young] Jew with you and leave. We will issue a decree that henceforth we will never require from you a sacrifice each year." They wrote the decree, sealed it, delivered it, and urged them to leave. The [two] returned to their homes and celebrated the Passover as never before. And Rabbi [Abraham], may his merit preserve us, returned to his city. [131]

The fable that Christians require the blood of a Jew for their worship service is the reverse side of the blood libel leveled against Jews in Christian Europe. In the latter charge, Jews were falsely accused of requiring the blood of Christian children for Passover use. [132] Abraham Ibn Ezra's reputation as master of the Divine Name derives from his book *Sefer Ha-Šem*, on this subject. In this work, written in Béziers in 1147, he notes [8: 3], "The Tetragrammaton (*YHWH*) was known only to a few righteous individuals, until Moses our master came [and revealed it to all]." [133] The following Ibn Ezra folk tale from Egypt reveals the poet's talent as a matchmaker:

Once when Rabbi Abraham Ibn Ezra was seated and surrounded by his students, he raised his eyes heavenward and laughed and cried. His students asked him, "Master, why do you laugh and cry?" He replied, "I had a vision of an exceptionally beautiful girl, the daughter of a rabbi in a certain city. She is gracious and learned in the reading of the Torah. To every suitor who comes to ask for her hand, she lays down a challenge, 'If you can improve on my reading of the Torah, I will marry you. If you cannot, I refuse.' Not one of the young men could surpass her. However, it has

---

131. See Y. Avishur, "Sippurey 'Am Ḥadašim 'al Avraham Ibn Ezra (U-Veno) Mi-Miṣrayim U-Me-'Iraq," pp. 167–70.

132. Cf. *JE*, 4: 1120–1131.

133. Levin, *Yalquṭ Avraham Ibn Ezra*, pp. 427, 438.

been decreed that she is to marry a farmer who does not know how to recite, 'Hear O Israel etc.' (Deut. 6: 4). This problem can be solved only by me."

Rabbi Abraham set out to visit this farmer and found him plowing his field. He greeted him in Hebrew, "Šalom 'Aleykhem" (Peace be to you). The farmer replied, "Sir, I do not understand what you said." "My son," said the Rabbi, "Leave this work, the plowing, the effort, and the frustration. Come and work for me as one of my agents. I will pay you adequately, feed you to your satisfaction, and dress you in admirable clothes. The farmer agreed, left his farm, and went with the Rabbi. The latter dressed the farmer to look like a rabbi, complete with cloak and turban. He also designated the farmer as "the sage" while he, the Rabbi, would serve as his beadle. Then they went to the city where the girl lived.

Rabbi Abraham wrote a learned letter of introduction stating that an eminent scholar from a certain city will soon be arriving. The letter he sent to the several elders of the city. Upon reading it, they were amazed at its elegant style and consummate wisdom. They agreed that never in their lives had they read a letter with such eloquence. The elders now called together the prominent men of the city and all went out to greet the sage who was to arrive by boat. Meanwhile, Rabbi Abraham instructed the farmer–sage that he not utter even one word.

The elders and the prominent men of the city came in a large procession to welcome the sage. One of them even ran to kiss his hand. They headed toward the synagogue and there they sat in silence waiting for the sage to speak. Rabbi Abraham, the beadle, spoke up, "Why do you not speak? Why does not someone begin with words from the Torah?" "Let the sage begin and we will follow," they answered. Said the beadle, "You should speak to the issues that concern you, and he will respond in his turn." Then when one of the elders rose and held forth on a matter of Jewish law, he was asked a question from one of the men in the gathering, which the elder was unable to answer. Others among the elders attempted to answer this question without success. Now the beadle (Rabbi Abraham) stood up and easily disposed of the problem. The elders were astonished and proceeded to put to him a host of other questions which he handily resolved, and added, "The answers to these problems I have heard from my master, the rabbi." The elders looked at each and said, "If the beadle is superior to everyone among us, how much more so must be his rabbi."

Toward evening the sage and his beadle came to the home of the girl's father. The sage was seated in a place of honor and no one was allowed to approach him. He did not eat with the others nor did he pray in their company. In the morning the elders gathered in the synagogue to study the Torah, together with the beadle and the sage. The latter did not speak a word, as ordered by Rabbi Abraham.

After several days had passed, the elders requested that the beadle ask the sage if he would consent to give a lecture on the Sabbath. "I will inquire of him," said the beadle, "and I am hopeful that he will agree." That evening Rabbi Abraham instructed the sage, "Tomorrow I will hand you a letter that I have written. Open it and make believe that you are reading it. Then begin to cry, hand the letter to me and make a hasty exit out of the room." The sage agreed.

While they were in the synagogue Rabbi Abraham wrote the letter, sealed it and gave it to the sage. The latter opened it as instructed, appeared to be reading it, cried, and quickly left the room. The elders were left wondering and asked the beadle, "Why was the sage in tears and why did he leave suddenly?" "Here is the letter which he received from home," replied the beadle, "Read it and you will have the answer to your questions. The elders read the letter and everything became clear. From it they learned the sage's wife and son had died. Calculating from the date of the letter the tragedy occurred during the past week. The sage now began his period of thirty days mourning, never leaving his lodging during this time. At the end of the thirty days the beadle taught the sage to read three words from the Torah, and gave him the following instructions: "On the Sabbath when you ascend the pulpit to read from the Torah you should cough, wipe your brow, expectorate, and read the first word I taught you. Then you need to pause, repeat this practice, and read the second word. Pause again, cough, wipe the brow, expectorate, and read the third word and then fall down in a dead faint." The sage replied, "I hear and obey." Without hesitation the beadle informed the elders that the sage wishes to lecture on the coming Sabbath. A public announcement was made in the synagogue inviting every Jew to hear the sage's lecture.

Meanwhile, the girl learned from her father about the visiting sage and his learned beadle. Like the others the father concluded that if the beadle is uncommonly gifted how much more so the sage. However, the daughter insisted, "Let him come and read the Torah for me. If he can improve on my reading I will marry him." After scolding her, the father announced, "On the Sabbath he is to lecture..." "I am willing," replied the daughter. "On the Sabbath I will come and listen to him."

On the said day, the congregation gathered in the synagogue and the girl sat by the window to hear the sage speak. He stepped up to the pulpit, coughed, wiped his brow, and expectorated. After a pause, he spoke one word. He repeated the practice, paused, and uttered a second word. After saying the third word, he fainted and fell to the ground. His beadle rushed to him, raised him up and sat him on his chair. The beadle now reassured the congregation, "Do not fear. Since you have come together to hear the sage's lecture, I will repeat it to you. Last night I was awakened from my sleep and happened to hear the sage rehearsing the lecture he was to give today." The beadle then proceeding to impress the congregation with words of uncommon wisdom and insight.

When the girl was asked by her father, "Did you hear the beadle repeat the sage's lecture," she replied, "It appears to me that the beadle is the sage. If the beadle wishes to marry me, I am his." Again the father scolded her, "Fool, why would you take the servant when you could have the master. Furthermore, the sage is available whereas the beadle is married." This made sense to the young lady and she was persuaded. When her father approached the beadle asking whether the sage would be willing to marry his daughter, he was told to wait for an answer. On the following day the beadle informed the father that the sage was prepared to take his daughter for a wife. Terms of the marriage and the wedding document (*ketubah*) were written by the beadle. On the day when the Seven Blessings [for Bride and Groom] were recited, the whole congregation joined in the celebration and feasted late into the night. That night when the sage was about to consummate the nuptials with his spouse, Rabbi Abraham Ibn Ezra looked up to the heavens and prayed, "Master of the Universe, I have done what was required of me. Now You do what is required of You." Then Rabbi Abraham pronounced the Divine Name and returned home.

Alone in their bedroom, the sage tried to express the love he felt for his bride. She soon discovered that she had been duped and kicked him in the chest. He fell from the bed and rolled down the flight of stairs. He lay flat, afraid to move, motionless, blood streaming from his face and tears in his eyes.

God, praised and exalted, took one of his tears and sent it to the learned Elijah [the prophet] of blessed memory who kept teaching him the Torah until he became as proficient as Moses son of Amram, may he rest in peace. The young man regained consciousness, picked himself up, and sat in the vestibule singing hymns of thanksgiving until the dawn. His father-in-law awoke and sat next to him proudly listening to his songs. They then went to the synagogue for the morning prayers, and the young bridegroom delivered a sermon of surpassing eloquence.

Meanwhile, the bride's mother queried her daughter, "How did the sage conduct himself last night?" The girl told how she kicked her spouse, and he fell down the stairs and did not sleep with her. When mother and daughter were informed that he is to lecture in the synagogue, they hastened to go there and heard his impressive talk. That night when the young man entered the chamber of his wife, she said, "Master, tell me about yourself. When you came to me last night it was as though the gates of hell had opened. Tonight when you came through the door you brought the gates of paradise with you." He told her his story, and the elders of the city knew that the beadle was Rabbi Abraham Ibn Ezra, may his merit protect us. Amen..."[134]

The success of Abraham Ibn Ezra as matchmaker was no small accomplishment. The rabbis [in *Gen. Rabbah* 68. 4] tell the story of a Roman matron who asked what God had been doing since the creation of the world. "He sits and makes matches," was the answer, "[and] it is as difficult...as the dividing of the Sea of Reeds." In synagogue hymnography a dominant theme for the Pentecost service portrays God seeking to find a suitable mate for the Torah. [135] The legend above adds to Ibn Ezra's character in the folk imagination. He is not only a master of the Divine Name and a heroic saviour in times of distress, but also a humble figure willing to play the role of a lowly beadle. Moreover, he is clever and imaginative in resolving problems. Although he is well versed in the Torah, he does not make a

---

134. Avishur, "Sippurey 'Am," pp. 179–81.
135. See L. J. Weinberger, "God as Matchmaker," pp. 238–44.

display of his learning and allows the sage to take the credit. Characteristically, Ibn Ezra is on intimate terms with his Maker and having carried out his mission he addresses his Maker in knowing language, "I have done what is required of me. Now You do what is required of You."

SECULAR POETRY

1. THE PATRON

Early I set out for the patron's home;
They say: He is off riding;
I return toward evening,
They say: He is already sleeping;
He either mounts a horse or climbs into bed;
Woe to the wretched man who is unlucky! [1]

$$--/\text{ס}--/--/-\text{ס}--//--/-\text{ס}--/--/-\text{ס}--$$

אַשְׁכִּים לְבֵית הַשַּׂר--אוֹמְרִים: כְּבָר רָכַב,
אָבוֹא לְעֵת עֶרֶב--אוֹמְרִים כְּבָר שָׁכַב.
אוֹ יַעֲלֶה מֶרְכָּב אוֹ יַעֲלֶה מִשְׁכָּב--
אוֹיָה לְאִישׁ עָנִי נוֹלַד בְּלִי כּוֹכָב!

This poem, and the three following, is a *telunah* [=complaint], a common genre in Hispano-Hebrew poetry. Ibn Ezra blunts his rage by blaming the stars for his ill-fortune. Notable is the poet's dependence on the patron in the courtly culture of the day. A patron like Ḥasday Ibn Šaprut, physician to the Ummayad caliph, 'Abd-al-Raḥmān III of Cordoba, set the standards for Jewish courtier society in Andalusia. The penniless Ibn Ezra undoubtedly sought the support of one of the rich and influential members of the Jewish courtier class in his day. [2]

The four-line poem effectively conveys the futility of the poet's efforts to gain support from an unresponsive patron. The anaphora in the response from the patrons' servants, *'omerim kevar rakhav...'omerim kevar šakhav* (They say: he is off riding...They say: he is already sleeping) is balanced in the poet's reaction with its

---

1. Schirmann, *Ha-Širah Ha-'Ivrit*, 1: 575; Levin, *Yalqut Avraham Ibn Ezra*, pp. 108–09. Preceding each poem is its scansion listing long and short syllables: -, ס.
2. Cf. A. Ibn Daud, *Sefer Ha-Qabbalah*, pp. 276–78; Profiat Duran (ca. 1350—ca. 1415) in his *Ma'aseh 'Efod*, p. 23 writes that Ibn Ezra did not have even "two *prutot*" to his name.

complementary phrasing: '*o ya'aleh merkav, 'o ya'aleh miškav* (He either mounts a horse, or climbs into bed).

When Ibn Ezra speaks of himself as "unlucky," lit. "starless born" (*beli kokhav*), he means that his birth occurred in a defective stellar configuration. He refers to this phenomenon in his *Sefer Ha-Mivḥarim*: [3]

> We know that "everything that God makes is eternal; nothing may be added or subtracted from it" (Eccles. 3: 14). Solomon has spoken [here] of the laws of heaven. He who was born in a [stellar] configuration which is defective relative to the perfect thing cannot become like the one who was born in a perfect configuration. This is the meaning of "That which is crooked cannot be made straight; and that which is wanting cannot be numbered" (Eccles. 1: 15). Therefore, he who has it in his configuration to be poor and without wealth cannot become rich, except for this: because man's soul comes from a place higher than all the stars, man can by means of his mind (*da'ato*) mitigate his misfortune somewhat.

However, the mock-serious tone in the last line suggests that the object of the poet's complaint is the hard-hearted patron and not the "crooked" stars.

2.   MISFORTUNE

> At my birth the spheres and planets strayed in their orbits;
> Were I a merchant of candles the sun would not set until I died!
> In vain I strive for success, for my stars have played false with me;
> Were I to trade in shrouds, men would not die in my lifetime!
> Were I to market a furnace, its fire would go out and remain unignited!
> Were I to seek on a rainy day some water from the sea, it would dry up!

---

3. Ms. Jewish Theological Seminary, New York, Mic 2625, fol. 131a and Langermann, "Astrological Themes in the Thought of Abraham Ibn Ezra," pp. 51-52.

Were I to sell armaments, all enemies would be reconciled
and not make war! [4]

--/-ס--/-ס--//--/-ס--/-ס--
-ס--/-ס--/-ס--//-ס--/-ס--/-ס--

גַּלְגַּל וּמַזָּלוֹת בְּמַעֲמָדָם/ נָטוּ בְמַהֲלָכָם לְמוֹלַדְתִּי,
לוּ יִהְיוּ נֵרוֹת סְחוֹרָתִי--/ לֹא יֶחֱשַׁךְ שֶׁמֶשׁ עֲדֵי מוֹתִי.

אִיגַע לְהַצְלִיחַ וְלֹא אוּכַל/ כִּי עִוְּתוּנִי כוֹכְבֵי שָׁמַי,
לוּ אֶהְיֶה סוֹחֵר בְּתַכְרִיכִין--/ לֹא יִגְוְעוּן אִישִׁים בְּכָל יָמָי.

5   לוּ אֶשְׁלְחָה יָדִי בְּכִבְשָׁן אֵשׁ וָאוּד,
כָּבָה וְסָר חֻמּוֹ וְלֹא נִמְצָא צָרֵב.
אִלּוּ בְּיוֹם גֶּשֶׁם בְּיָם גָּדוֹל אָקוּ/ לִשְׁאָב מְעַט מַיִם--הֲלֹא אָז יֶחֱרַב
לוּ אֶמְצָאָה חֵפֶץ בְּמִלְחָמָה--אֲזַי/ כָּל שׂוֹנְאִים שָׁלְמוּ וְלֹא נִמְצָא קְרָב.

The line, "For my stars have played false with me," translates literally, "My
stars made me crooked" ('*iwwetuni*). The same term is used in Eccles. 1: 15, "That
which is crooked (*me'uwwat*) cannot be made straight," and in Eccles. 7: 13, "Who can
make straight what he has made crooked?" ('*iwweto*). Commenting on the latter
verse, Ibn Ezra writes:

> The sage who is penniless should rejoice in God's wisdom and not rage
> against his poverty. His fate has been decreed from the time of creation. The
> wise astrologers understand the verse [in Gen. 2: 3], "And God rested from all
> the work that he had done in creation" that God delegated to the created
> [stars] governance of the sublunar world. Therefore if one's stellar
> configuration [at birth] is crooked (*me'uwwetat*) in matters of wealth or other
> [misfortunes] there is no remedy for him.

In his plaint the poet tempers his sarcasm with self-effacing mock-serious
hyperbole. Unlike the plaint in *The Patron* (above) where the real culprit is the

---

4. Levin, *Avraham Ibn Ezra*, pp. 199–200.

uncaring Maecenas, here the poet focuses his attack at the personified stars who purposely "strayed in their orbit" and followed the "crooked" path in order to do him harm.

3. ON HIS TORN GARMENT

> I have a mantle; it resembles a sieve
> For sifting wheat or barley;
> In the dark of night I unfurl it like a tent
> And heavens starry radiance filters through;
> I behold the moon and the Pleiades,
> Even Orion's lustre is reflected;
> I grow weary counting its holes
> Like the many teeth of a giant saw;
> To attempt to sew its shreds
> Crosswise is hopeless;
> Were a fly to descend on it compulsively
> Like a fool, he would soon regret it!
> O God, convert this rag to one worthy of praise and repair. [5]

ס---/ס---/ס--//ס---/ס---/ס--

מְעִיל יֶשׁ לִי וְהוּא כִּדְמוּת כְּבָרָה
לְחִטָּה לַהֲנָפָה אוֹ שְׂעוֹרָה,
כְּאֹהֶל אֶפְרְשֶׁנּוּ לֵיל בְּאִישׁוֹן--
וְכוֹכְבֵי רוֹם יְשִׂימוּן בּוֹ מְאוֹרָה,
5   בְּתוֹכוֹ אֶחֱזֶה סַהַר וְכִימָה
וְיוֹפִיעַ כְּסִיל עָלָיו נְהָרָה.
וְאֵלֶּה מִסְפֹּר אֶת כָּל נְקָבָיו
אֲשֶׁר דּוֹמִים לְשִׁנֵּי הַמְּגֵרָה,
וְתִקְוַת חוּט תְּפִירַת כָּל קְרוּעָיו--
10   עֲלֵי שְׁתִי וָעֵרֶב--הִיא יְתֵרָה,
וְאִם יִפֹּל זְבוּב עָלָיו בְּחָזְקָה
כְּמוֹ פֶתִי--יְהִי נִמְלָךְ מְהֵרָה.

---

5. Schirmann, Ha-Širah Ha-'Ivrit, 1: 576; Levin, Yalqut Avraham Ibn Ezra, p. 111.

אֱלוֹהַי, הַחֲלִיפֵהוּ לִי בְּמַעֲטֶה
תְּהִלָּה וְתֵיטִיב הַתְּפִירָה.

In this poem and the following, Ibn Ezra pioneers the new realism in mid-twelfth century Hispanic-Hebrew prosody. Following the conquest of Andalusia by the reform-minded Moslem Almohades in 1148-49 and the decline of Jewish courtly society, the poet's thematic focus shifted to the trials of everyday life. The mock-serious tone of Ibn Ezra's complaint about his torn garment is characteristic of this poet who found comic relief in a predicament. However, the abrupt transition in the closing couplet from a jesting hyperbole ("Were a fly to descend on it etc.") to a solemn plea for divine aid ("God, convert this rag etc.") suggests that the poet was barely able to conceal his discomfort. Adding to the hardships of the poet's vagabond life was the need to use his garment as a cover in the cold outdoor night (line 3).

Yet, in his prayer, Ibn Ezra does not ask for another more stylish garment. He merely wants the one he owns repaired ("and repair its tears"). He wants to be able to praise his coat, but not to be praised for it. The poet had little use for the boor who covered his ignorance with opulent clothes. In his gnomic verse Ibn Ezra warns that men should be judged by their actions, not their garments. [6]

4.   THE FLIES

Where can I find refuge from my oppressors?
I cry for help from the robber flies
Who give me no respite.
Like arch-enemies they tyrannize me with a vengeance;
They run races on my eyes and eyelids,
They croon lusty lyrics at my ears.
I had planned to eat my bread alone,
But there they were, like wolves, feeding on it;
And then, as if invited, like friends or relations
There they were, draining the wine from my cup;

---

6. Levin, *Avraham Ibn Ezra*, pp. 209-10.

Even so they were not satisfied, for I found them
In the choice liquor and the tender fatted lamb;
But it was not enough; they lusted only to eat what was before me:
The wine I drink and the morsel I eat!
Were I to invite friends to dine,
They would be ever-present at the head table!
I yearn for winter and windy rains and icy snows
To put an end to them;
Were it not for this, they would drive me to despair,
And so I give thanks to God who dwells among the cherubim. [7]

--ס/---ס/---ס//--ס/---ס/---ס

לְמִי אָנוּס לְעֶזְרָה מֵחֲמָסִי?/ אֲשַׁוַּע מִפְּנֵי שֹׁד הַזְּבוּבִים!
אֲשֶׁר לֹא יִתְּנוּ הָשֵׁב לְרוּחִי,/ בְּכָל כֹּחָם יְעִיקוּנִי כְאוֹיְבִים,
וְעַל עֵינַי וְעַפְעַפַּי יְרוּצוּן,/ בְּאָזְנַי יֹאמְרוּ שִׁירֵי עֲנָבִים.
אֲדַמֶּה לֶאֱכֹל פִּתִּי לְבַדִּי--/ וְהֵם בּוֹ יֹאכְלוּ כִּדְמוּת זְאֵבִים,
5   וְעוֹד יִשְׁתּוּ בְכוֹס יֵינִי, כְּאִלּוּ/ קְרָאתִים כַּאֲהוּבִים אוֹ קְרוֹבִים.
וְלֹא יִרְצוּ לְבַד חֶלְקָם; פְּקַדְתִּים/ בְּיֵין עַתִּיק וּמִשְׁמַן שֶׂה כְשָׂבִים--
וְיִמְעַט, רַק אָכֹל מֵאֲשֶׁר לְפָנַי/ לֵיֵין מִשְׁתִּי וּפַת אָכְלִי תְאֵבִים.
וְכִי אֶקְרָא מְיֻדָּעַי לְאָכְלָה--/ וְהִנָּם יוֹשְׁבִים רֹאשׁ הַמְסֻבִּים.
יִקַּו לְבִי סְתָו, כִּי הוּא יְכַלֵּם/ בְּקֹר רוּחַ שְׁלָגִים אוֹ רְבִיבִים--
10   וְלוּלֵי זֹאת אֲנִי קָץ מִפְּנֵיהֶם--/ בְּכֵן אוֹדֶה לְיוֹשֵׁב הַכְּרוּבִים.

When hearing the opening line in this *qaṣīdah*-style poem in *ha-merubbeh* meter, "Where can I find refuge from my oppressors?" the listener is unprepared for what follows, "I cry for help from the robber flies." From the alarming beginning, one expects to hear that the poet is in danger of his life. The happy surprise that comes with learning that the enemy is the pesky fly brings only slight relief. Having engaged the listener, the poet personifies the wayward insect and endows him with the character of an unwelcome intruder. The fly's persistence in "lusting...to eat what was before me" not only adds humor to the predicament, but evokes remembrance of human gluttony.

---

7. Schirmann, *Ha-Širah Ha-'Ivrit*, 1: 576–77; Levin, *Yalqut Avraham Ibn Ezra*, p. 110.

In the closing lines the poet's mock–heroic efforts to protect himself against his winged invader gives way to a prayer for winter's icy blast. "It will put an end to them," he hopes. H. Schirmann suggests that Ibn Ezra's older contemporary, Joseph Ibn Sahl (d. in Cordoba in 1123/24) was the first Hispanic-Hebrew poet to write about the outrageous antics of the little insects in his "Racing like stallions, the flies, like vultures, hasten to eat my flesh." It is likely that Ibn Ezra, who lived in Andalusia for a time, was familiar with Ibn Sahl's work. [8]

5.   MY HONOR

My honor is intact—though I humble myself
And choose not to sit among those whose reputation is flawed
But who like to think that they occupy the head table,
Hoping that the dais will cover their disgrace;
As for me, I define my place, while the Omnipresent is with me,
While they use it to conceal their blemishes! [9]

$$--/---\text{ס}//--/---\text{ס}$$

כְּבוֹדִי בִּמְקוֹמִי--וְאִם אַשְׁפִּיל שִׁבְתִּי--
וְלֹא אֶבְחַר מָקוֹם כְּקַלִּים בְּגְאוֹנָם,
אֲשֶׁר הֵמָּה חוֹשְׁבִים הֱיוֹתָם רֹאשׁ מוֹשָׁב--
וְהַמּוֹשָׁב לָהֶם יְכַסֶּה עֶלְבּוֹנָם.
5   אֲנִי הוּא הַמָּקוֹם וְהַמָּקוֹם אִתִּי,
וְהֵמָּה--הַמָּקוֹם יְמַלֵּא חֶסְרוֹנָם!

The tone of the poem reveals that Ibn Ezra takes seriously his position in the Jewish community. It is likely that the poet saw himself as the surviving representative of a once illustrious and rapidly fading Hispano-Hebrew civilization. The poem which bears the inscription, "Written by the sage Abraham ben Ezra when he was seated by his host in a place not befitting his station," was probably composed during the poet's travels in Christian Europe.

This satirical epigram is the poet's reaction to his insensitive host. Feeling

---

8. Schirmann, Širim Hadašim Min Ha-Geniza, pp. 209–12.
9. Schirmann, Ha-Širah Ha-'Ivrit, 1: 577.

slighted at being seated in a place beneath his dignity, Ibn Ezra ridicules his host and the assembled guests "who like to think that they occupy the head table, / Hoping that the dais will cover their disgrace." Ibn Ezra prefers to remain distant from the men seated at the head table, confident that his character defines the pride of place (Heb. *maqom*; the term is used five times in the poem). The poet's boast, "I define my place" is in line with rabbinic teaching [in *bTan* 21b]: "It is not the place that honors the man, but it is the man who honors the place." Extending the pun, the poet adds, "while the Omnipresent (*maqom*, cf. *mEdu* 5. 6) is with me."

Here, as in the poem that follows, Ibn Ezra, following Arabic models, combines lampoon (*hijā'*) with boasting (*fakhr*). [10] In the closing line, Ibn Ezra returns to lampooning the head table guests. The word *maqom* may be read as the "place (that conceals their blemishes)" or "May the Omnipresent (*ha-maqom*) replenish their loss." In the latter sense it is a condolence to those who have suffered the loss of an ox or an ass, according to the rabbis (in *bBer* 16b). The use, in close proximity, of paronomasia: "my place" (*ha-maqom*) and "the Omnipresent" (*ha-maqom*) is a common mannerism in Arabic and Hispano-Hebrew poetry. [11]

6.   THE DENIZENS OF MORAH

No wine is to be found in the emptied flask,
The cheese is missing,--stolen as it were--
And the hostess is blind in one eye;
Limping and bent she hobbles toward the well;
The natives are kin to Cain,
Barely superior to beasts;
Were I not to live among them
I would turn an [evil] eye against it! [12]

---

10. Cf. G. Schoeler, "Bashshār b. Burd, Abū 'l-'Atāhiyah and Abū Nuwās," pp. 278–79.
11. Cf. A. Arberry, *Arabic Poetry*, pp. 21–22.
12. Schirmann, *Ha-Širah Ha-'Ivrit*, 1: 578; see also Trachtenberg, *Jewish Magic and Superstitions*, pp. 54–56 on the "evil eye".

הַקַּנְקָן רֵיקָן בְּלִי יַיִן,
וְהַגְּבִינָה גְּנוּבָה בְּלִי זַיִן,
וְהַגְּבֶרֶת עִוֶּרֶת בְּלִי עַיִן--
חִגֶּרֶת וְנִשְׁבֶּרֶת צָעֲדָה עֲלֵי עַיִן.
וְאַנְשֵׁי הַמָּקוֹם אֲחֵי קַיִן,   5
וּמוֹתַר הָאָדָם אֲשֶׁר בּוֹ אַיִן.
אִם אֵין אֲנִי דָר שָׁם--
אָשִׂים בְּרֹאשָׁהּ הָעַיִן.

The lack of metrical structure heightens the tone of spontaneity in the poem,
which, he may have hastily constructed during his stay in the city of Morah. Its
location is not known. Despite the absence of meter there is much alliteration and
assonance revolving around the letters, *nun, gimel, bet, lamed reš,* and paronomasia,
as in the following opening lines:

> *Ha-qanqan reqan beli yayin;*
> *We-ha-gevinah genuvah beli zayin;*
> *We-ha-geveret 'iwweret beli 'ayin;*
> *Higgeret we-nišberet sa'adah 'ale 'ayin.*

As in the previous poem, Ibn Ezra combines satirical invective directed at the
discourteous host with self-praise in the closing two lines. The limping hostess, blind
in one eye (*'ayin*) who barely manages to reach the well (*'ayin*) adds a touch of the
grotesque to the bizzare banquet of gluttons who consume the wine and cheese
before the distinguished poet has tasted them. In characterizing the gluttons as
kinsmen of Cain, the poet is charging that they are empty boors, devoid of learning.
The Hebrew term, *hevel,* Abel, Cain's brother (Gen. 4: 2) is also used to designate,
"vanity" or "emptiness" as in Eccles. 1: 2. Continuing his invective, Ibn Ezra calls the
denizens of Morah, "Barely superior to beasts." Here, as well, he summons a verse
from Eccles. (3: 19), "Men have no advantage over the animals." Schirmann interprets
the last line, "Were I not to live there [in Morah] / I would place the letter
'ayin before it." *'Ayin* before Morah, spells 'Amorah, or Gemorah, the city destroyed
by fire because of its sins (Gen. 19: 24).

7. SONG OF THE NATIONS

The Arabs sing of love and lust,
The Romans, of war and vengeance,
The Greeks, of wisdom and cunning,
The Persians, of proverbs and riddles,
And Israel sings hymns in praise of the Lord of hosts. [13]

הַיִּשְׁמְעֵאלִים--שִׁירֵיהֶם בַּאֲהָבִים וַעֲגָבִים,
וְהָאֲדוֹמִים--בְּמִלְחָמוֹת וּנְקָמוֹת,
וְהַיְּוָנִים--בְּחָכְמוֹת וּמְזִמּוֹת,
וְהַהֲדִיִּים--בִּמְשָׁלִים וְחִדוֹת,
וְהַיִּשְׂרְאֵלִים--בְּשִׁירִים וְתִשְׁבָּחוֹת לַיְיָ צְבָאוֹת!   5

This is another unstructured poem devoid of meter and of consistent rhyme.
In this practice, Ibn Ezra, differs from his Hispanic–Hebrew colleagues, who
generally embellished their secular poetry with meter and rhyme. The unfavorable
comparison between the poetry of the Hebrews and that of other nations is echoed
in Ibn Ezra's liturgical *qerovah* for the afternoon service on the Day of Atonement:

The songs of all nations are built on lies;
But my songs are for God's possession. [14]

8. FOR JOSEPH B. AMRAM

The image that revived me,
Can it now hasten my death?

The face of my choicest love
Is like the cherub's flaming sword
Standing guard over Eden;
His gaze barring my approach
Keeps me at bay.

---

13. Schirmann, *Ha–Širah Ha–'Ivrit*, 1: 578.
14. Levin, *Širey Ha–Qodeš...Ibn Ezra*, 2: 111

Though rejected, I do not detest him;
What can I do? I love him!
[In his absence I am like the moon, pale with grief],
He makes me glow like the sun;
The lustre in his eye excites me.

May his love for me endure
Even now when he hates me;
A slight motion of his lips
Would lift my spirits
Like an enchantress calling.

Will the cloud forever settle
On the face of the moon;
He beckoned me and said:
I was singed by the sun
And I sought refuge in the shade.

How compelling is he and gracious;
Even God has to love him!
Heaven's voice is his witness [saying]:
"You little one, my son,
How God loves you!" [15]

--ס-/--//--ס-/--

צוּרָה הֶחֱיַתְנִי--/ אֵיךְ מֹתִי בְשֶׁלָּהּ?
צוּרַת רֹאשׁ אֲהָבִים--
לַהַט עִם כְּרוּבִים
עַל עֵדֶן נְצִיבִים,
5   כָּכָה רְחַקְתְּנִי/ עֵינוֹ עֵינוֹ מִקְרֹב לָהּ!

---

15. Schirmann, *Ha-Širah Ha-'Ivrit*, 1: 579–80; Stern, "The Muwashshahs of Abraham
Ibn Ezra," p. 372.

נִמְאָס לֹא מְאַסְתִּיו,

מָה אַעֲשׂ? אֲהַבְתִּיו

[.............תִּיו]

כְּשֶׁמֶשׁ לְהַטַתְנִי/ אוֹר עֵינוֹ בְּהִלָּה.

10   תּוֹסִיף אַהֲבָתוֹ

בְּי עֵת גַּעֲרָתוֹ.

הֵנַע לִי שְׂפָתוֹ,

הִיא הִיא הֶעֱלָתְנִי--/ "בַּעֲלַת אוֹב" עֲנוּ לָהּ!

עַל צוּרַת לְבָנֶה

אֵיךְ תִּשְׁכֹּן עֲנָנֶה?

רָמַז לִי וְעָנֶה

"שֶׁמֶשׁ שֶׁזָפַתְנִי/ וְאֶחֱסֶה בְצִלָּהּ."

מַה תָּקְפּוֹ וְטוּבוֹ,

עַל כִּי אֵל אֲהֵבוֹ!

20   בַּת קוֹל תַּעֲנֶה בוֹ:

יָא צְגִיר, יָא אַבְנִי,/ וָאִישׁ יַחבֵּךְ אללה!

Ibn Ezra's *muwashshaḥ* encomium, dedicated to his patron, Joseph ben Amram of Sijilmasa, Morocco, employs stock figures from the Arabic *ghazal* (love poetry) reconfigured in a Hebrew idiom. In the opening belt couplet, the poet laments that the relationship with his patron–friend has soured. His friend's fobidding gaze which keeps the poet at bay is an image borrowed from 'Abbasid love poetry. Here is Abū Nuwās' (756–810) description of the beloved:

His face, a goblet next his lip,

  looks like a moon lit with a lamp;

Armed with love's weaponry, he rides

  on beauty's steed, squares up eye's steel--

> Which is his smile, the bow his brow,
> the shafts his eyes, his lashes lances. [16]

Ibn Ezra now reconstructs the imagery in a biblical setting by comparing the face of his "choicest love" to the "cherub's flaming sword / Standing guard over Eden," after Gen. 3: 24. The poet waits for a word from his friend, "A slight motion of his lips / Would lift my spirits." That the beloved's lips have the power to heal is a familiar conceit in the Arabic *ghazal*; [17] however, the Hebrew poet, would add a biblical simile to the image:

> Like an enchantress calling.

The reference is to the medium at Endor who is able to consult a spirit and call up the dead Samuel, after I Sam. 28: 7ff.

The moon is a prominent figure in the poem. In line ten, the bereft poet, pale from sleepless nights--a common image in the love poem--[18] is compared to the moon. In line 19, the patron-friend is the smiling moon, now obscured by a cloud, due to the current strained relations between the pair. In the lines following, the poet celebrates their reconciliation, but not without adding a note of self-praise. Comparing himself to the sun, Ibn Ezra puts into the mouth of his friend an excuse for their estrangement. The latter was probably offended ("singed") by some unknown action of the poet and therefore withdrew from his company ("sought refuge in the shade").

Following a common practice, Ibn Ezra closes his *muwashshah* with a *kharjah* in colloquial Arabic. Among the conventions of this form is that it be close to the language of the common people, and that the strophe preceding the *kharjah* must contain an expression like, "he said," "I said." [19] In his encomium, Ibn Ezra meets both of these requirements.

---

16. The poem is translated in G. Schoeler, "Bashshār b. Burd...Abū Nuwās," p. 298.
17. See Arberry, *Arabic Poetry*, pp. 20–21.
18. See Pagis, *Širat Ha-Ḥol We-Torat Ha-Šir*, p. 268.
19. See Stern, *Hispano-Arabic Strophic Poetry*, p. 33.

9   TRIBUTE TO SAMUEL IBN JĀMI'

Did the heavens submit to an earthling,
Or did the soil–bound reach the heights?
A mortal drew near the angels and was
Privy to their council and they were unaware;
It was the esteemed Samuel, scion of the wise;
Without him they (the wise) are bellowing oxen;
He is the Lord's staff, a prodigy and model
For his generation, while the staves of idolaters are felled;
Gates of wisdom open effortlessly with
His mouth, but without him they labor in vain;
He guides the wayfarer to his
Destination, but without him they stray like sheep;
O men, enter the garden of Eden and touch
The tree of knowledge and the tree of life and do not fear.
Those who hasten to enter will find his insights a source
Of strength, but without him there is calamity.
You who are hungry come and feed on his grain;
Fill up with rich bread until you have had enough.
You who are thirsty, draw from the well of his
Intellect flowing in all directions.
Justice comes from his lips and his truthful breath
Kills the wicked, and he remains innocent.
Men content by nature rejoice in him,
While the mournful at the mere mention of his name take pleasure.
His generosity is gracious and benefits friends
Afflicted by Time, and I among them much sinned against.
Why has Time made my flesh a target
And directed its bow and arrows to pierce me?
The years of famine arrived in place of the days
Of plenty and they were devoured like ears of grain.
I wander afar because of the forces arrayed against me;
They make camp about my heart and do not budge;
Furiously, they wage war upon me, and I timidly retreat
Lest I die before they do.

They take up the ax in anger to torture me;

They set fire to my home and its guardians tremble.

My children weep when I am forced to take the rugged road;

I am a stranger whose name and city are forgotten.

My oppressors are as numerous as the sea and

Can its waters overcome me and I not drown?

Alas, my eyes are torrents of tears

Descending on my heart unable to quench its flame.

My family is disabled and I am ignorant of what lies ahead;

I ask others who have suffered--

I am told there is no record or report

Of anyone having endured as much.

I can forgive the sins that Time commits

If only it would keep the promise it made

To be gracious and permit me to see the face

Of the Rabbi [Samuel], then would I rejoice as would Time itself.

[Rabbi], be not offended by my limited gifts of speech;

My ears tremble from fear and my eyes grow dim.

What can I do, being powerless?

I am a vagabond, therefore my words stray. [20]

$$---/-\circ--/-\circ--//-\circ--/-\circ--/-\circ--$$

גָּבְהֵי שְׁחָקִים אֶל הֲדֹם נִכְנָעוּ/ אוֹ הָאֲדָמוֹת אֶל זְבֻל נָגָעוּ?

קָרַב אֱנוֹשׁ אֶל מַלְאֲכֵי עֶלְיוֹן, עָדַי/ עָמַד עֲלֵי סוֹדָם וְלֹא יָדָעוּ.

הַהוּא שְׁמוּאֵל בֵּין מְתֵי חָכְמָה לְאִישׁ/ נֶחְשָׁב--וּבִלְעָדָיו שׁוֹרִים גָּעוּ.

מַטֵּה אֱלֹהִים הוּא וְהוּא מוֹפֵת וְאוֹת/ בַּדּוֹר--וּמַטּוֹת הָאֱלִיל נִגְדָעוּ.

דַּלְתֵי תְבוּנוֹת נִפְתְּחוּ עַל פִּיו בְּלִי/ יִיגָע--וּבִלְעָדָיו לְרִיק יָגָעוּ.   5

הַהוּא מֵאֲשֶׁר עוֹבְרֵי דֶרֶךְ עֲלֵי/ יֹשֶׁר--וּבִלְעָדָיו כְּשֵׁיוֹת תָּעוּ.

בֹּאוּ לְגַן עֶדֶן, מְתִים, וּגְעוּ בְּעֵץ/ דַּעַת וְעֵץ חַיִּים, וְאַל תִּשְׁתָּעוּ.

עוֹשׁוּ וָבֹאוּ, תִּמְצְאוּ דַעְתּוֹ מְקוֹר/ חַיִּים--וּבִלְעָדָיו כְּדֹב תִּפְגָּעוּ.

בֹּאוּ, רְעֵבִים, לַתְּבוּאוֹת, לַחֲמוּ/ לֶחֶם חֲמֻדוֹת עַד אֲשֶׁר תִּשְׂבָּעוּ!

בֹּאוּ, צְמֵאִים, שַׁאֲבוּ מִמַּעְיָנוֹת/ שִׂכְלוֹ, לְיָמִין גַּם שְׂמֹאל נָבָעוּ.   10

צָדְקוּ שְׂפָתַי, כִּי בְרוּחָם בֶּאֱמֶת/ יָמִית בְּנֵי רֶשַׁע, וְלֹא רָשָׁעוּ;

20. Levin, *Yalqut Avraham Ibn Ezra*, pp. 111–13.

בּוֹ יִשְׂמְחוּ אַנְשֵׁי שְׂמָחוֹת, אִם שְׁמוֹ/ שָׁמְעוּ אֲבֵלֵי לֵב--וְהִשְׁתַּעְשָׁעוּ.

טוֹבוּ וְהֵטִיבוּ בְמִנְעַמָּיו בְּנֵי/ יָמִים לְכָל רֵעַי, וּבִי פָשָׁעוּ.

לָמָּה לְמַטָּרָה בְּשָׂרִי נָתְנוּ/ וַיִּדְרְכוּ קֶשֶׁת וְחֵץ תָּקָעוּ?

15 בָּאוּ שְׁנוֹת רָעָה וְחָלְפוּ כָל יָמַי/ אֹכֶל וְהֵם כַּשִּׁבֳּלִים נִבְלָעוּ.

הִתְחַבְּרוּ עָלַי גְּדוּדֵי הַנָּדוֹד,/ חָנוּ סְבִיב לִבִּי וְלֹא נָסָעוּ,

עַמִּי בְּחָזְקָה נִלְחֲמוּ, וָאֲזַחֲלָה,/ פֶּן אֶגְוָעָה טֶרֶם אֲשֶׁר יְגְוָעוּ,

וַיֹּאחֲזוּ גָרֶז לְעַוּוֹתִי בְאַף/ וַיִּתְצוּ בֵיתִי וְשׁוֹמְרָיו זָעוּ.

יִפְעוּ יְלָדַי עֵת הַדּוּרִים אֶהֱלֹךְ,/ נֶהְפַּךְ שְׁמִי לַהֲדַר וְעִירִי פָעוּ.

20 כָּבְדוּ מְצוּקוֹתַי כְּחוֹל הַיָּם, וְאֵיךְ/ עָבְרוּ עָלֵי יַמִּים וְלֹא טָבָעוּ?

אֵיךְ יֵרְדוּ עֵינַי נְהָרוֹת מִבְּכִי/ עַל לַהֲבֵי לִבִּי וְלֹא יִשְׁקָעוּ

כָּלָה שְׁאֵר גּוּפִי וְנַפְשִׁי נִבְעָרָה/ וָאֶשְׁאֲלָה אִישִׁים אֲשֶׁר נָגָעוּ--

לֹא יָדְעוּ כִדְמוּת תְּלָאוֹתַי בְּכָל/ קוֹרוֹת, וְלֹא נִרְאוּ וְלֹא נִשְׁמָעוּ.

חַטַּאת בְּנֵי יָמִים וּפִשְׁעָם אֶסְלָחָה/ אִם קִימוּ נֶדֶר אֲשֶׁר נִשְׁבָּעוּ:

25 כִּי יַעֲשׂוּ חֶסֶד וְיִרְאוּנִי פְנֵי/ הָרָב, וְאָרִיעַ--וְיִתְרוֹעָעוּ.

קָצֵר שְׂפָתַי אַל לְעָוֹן יַחֲשֹׁב/ כִּי צָלְלוּ אָזְנַי וְעֵינַי שָׁעוּ.

מָה אֶעֱשֶׂה עַתָּה--וְיָדִי אֵין לְאֵל?/ טָרוּד אֲנִי, עַל כֵּן דְּבָרַי לָעוּ.

The panegyric in honor of Ibn Ezra's friend and patron Samuel Ibn Jāmiʿ of Gabes, Tunisia is in the form of a *qaṣīdah* with hemistichs in balanced meter. In line with the conventions of the genre, the poem exudes hyperbole and stock images. The honoree, like Moses, attains heavens' heights and is privy to the secrets of angels. He has no peers worthy of mention and is generous to a fault. Employing a contrasting rhetoric, Ibn Ezra argues that compared to Samuel all the wise are "bellowing oxen." His patron is "the Lord's staff," while the staves of the idolaters are worthless; even the fortress, Wisdom, closed to others, is opened for him. Unlike the *laudes*, above, to Joseph ben Amram, the poet here personalized the ode mentioning the "esteemed Samuel" (line 5) by name.

As in the earlier tribute, Ibn Ezra subtly injects himself into the poem. While praising the kindness of his patron to the wretched "afflicted by Time," he adds, "and I among them." This opening allows him to blame personified Time for his troubles. In this practice, Ibn Ezra follows a contemporary convention by faulting Time and the World for the ills that afflict humankind. [21] Time, in contrast to the consistently generous patron, may favor man at the outset, only to disappoint him later. Time's most pernicious sin is causing friends to be separated. Ibn Ezra laments that he has to "wander afar" and "take the rugged road." He has become a stranger to himself "whose name and city are forgotten." Characteristically, Time has not kept its promise that the friends would be reunited (line 48).

Prominent in Ibn Ezra's poetry is the use of biblical imagery. In his *laudes*, the poet invites Samuel's contemporaries to join the patron's company, "Enter the Garden of Eden and touch / The Tree of Knowledge and the Tree of Life," after Gen. 2: 9. More subtle is the reference in the following stich, "Those who hasten to enter will find...a source of strength, but without him there is calamity." The literal translation of the latter hemistich, "but without him it is as if they encountered a bear (*ke-dov tifga'u*)." The source of the poet's conceit is the extended metaphor in Amos 5: 18-19: "Why do you want the day of the Lord? It is darkness not light; as if someone fled from a lion, and was met by a bear (*u-fga'o ha-dov*), and went into a house resting his hand against the wall and a serpent bit him." Later, when the poet regrets that "the days of plenty [during the heydey of courtly life in Andalusia] were devoured like ears of grain" he has in mind Joseph interpreting Pharaoh's dream in Gen. 41: 24ff.

10.   IN HONOR OF BARUKH IBN JAU

> You who reproach me with complaints and quarrels,
> I beg you to cease
> Now that my beloved has deserted me
> And taken with him my heart and my good sense.
>
> Have mercy on one who suffers from pain;
> Take pity on his condition.
> From anguish, gray hairs hasten upon his head
> Almost as fast as the bird flies.
> The wretched man, his heart melting from love's fever
> Is reluctant to show his face.

---

21. See Levin, "'Zeman' We-'Tevel' Be-Širat Ha-Ḥol Ha-'Ivrit Be-Sefarad," pp. 68-79.

His lover's parting has made his hair white
Before its time;
It has ordered his eyelids
To disdain sleep.

My soul longs for my lover;
His praises are most fitting.
He is faithful and not malicious;
His friendship is cherished by his brothers.
My heart aches
When I remember his choice verses.
   When he set out on his journey and left me,
   Clouds covered the day;
   Alas, the separation has left me
   Sorrowful and broken-hearted.

Nevertheless, if the days
Were to make peace with me,
I would travel the desert and the seas
To see his face before I die,
While the faces of my enemies
Would be shamed from jealousy.
   O that I had wings like a dove,
   I would fly away and rest
   When I set my eyes
   Upon the gazelle who puts the moon to shame.

Long have I known my beloved;
He would not break off our friendship.
A charming man, praised by his peers;
His name, Barukh is known far and wide.
My love for him is more precious
Than pearls. I hold him
   Dear to me as a gift
   Of earth's choicest wealth.

Even as the One (God) is unique, without equal
So is he esteemed beyond measure or form.

God, exalted and concealed,
His mercies by lips proclaimed,
Restore Your children in their land;
Bring them together as in the past.
Then will the poet sing as in the days of old
And as in former years:
  We have been through much and sorely tried;
  What do not people say about us!
  Come here, O light of my eye,
  Let us turn suspicion into certainty. [22]

-ס--/-(ס)/--/-ס-/--(ס)/--.

בַּעֲלֵי רִיבִי, שְׁעוּ נָא/ מִמְּרִיבָה וּתְלוּנָה,
כִּי נְדוֹד דּוֹדִי שָׁמַנִי/ מִבְּלִי לֵבָב וּבִינָה.

רַחֲמוּ אֱנוֹשׁ גַּם נִכְאֶה/ וַחֲמֹלוּ עַל מַעְצְבוֹ,
קַל--וּכְמְעַט כָּעוֹף יִדְאֶה/ מִיגוֹן שֵׂיבָה זָרְקָה בּוֹ,
5   דַּל, עֲדֵי כִּי לֹא יֵרָאֶה/ מֵחֲלִי הֵמֵס לְבָבוֹ--
כִּי פְרֵידָתוֹ הַלְּבִינָה/ שַׂעֲרָה עַד לֹא הִזְקִינָה
וַתְּצַוֶּה עַל אִישׁוֹנִי/ לִהְיוֹת מֹאֵס בְּשֵׁנָה.

כָּלְתָה נַפְשִׁי לָרֵעַ/ נָעֲמוּ לִמְאֹד שְׁבָחָיו,
נֶאֱמָן חָדַל הָרֵעַ/ מָתְקוּ דוֹדָיו לְאָחָיו,
10 אַךְ לְבָבִי יִקָּרֵעַ/ עֵת זְכוֹר מַנְעַמֵּי שִׁירָיו.
יוֹם אֲשֶׁר נָסַע וּפָנָה/ תַּחֲנֶה עָלָיו עֲנָנָה!
הֵהּ לְפֵרוּד הִנְחִילַנִי/ נַחֲלַת יָגוֹן וּמַגֵּנָּה.

וַעֲלֵי כָל זֹאת, לוּא יָמִים/ יִהְיוּ מַשְׁלִימִים אִתִּי--
אֲרַכְּבָה מִדְבָּר וְיַמִּים/ לַחֲזוֹתוֹ טֶרֶם מוֹתִי,

22. Levin, *Yalqut Avraham Ibn Ezra*, pp. 115–16; Stern, "The Muwashshahs of Abraham Ibn Ezra," p. 376.

15 וּפְנֵי צָרִים וְקָמִים/ יִפְּלוּ מֵחֲמְדָּם אוֹתִי.
לוּ יְהִי אֵבֶר כְּיוֹנָה/ לִי אָעוּפָה וְאֶשְׁכּֽנָה
עַד אֲשֶׁר אָשִׂימָה עֵינִי/ עַל צְבִי מַחְפִּיר לְבָנָה.

דּוֹד יְדַעְתִּיו מִלְּפָנִים/ חָק אֲהָבִים לֹא יְשַׁנֶּה,
נֶחְמַד בָּרוּךְ מִבָּנִים/ זֶה שְׁמוֹ, כִּי לֹא אֲכַנֶּה.
20 יָקְרָה לִי מִפְּנִינִים/ אֲהַבְתִּי בוֹ, וְהִנֵּה
לִי לְקַחְתִּיהוּ לְמָנָה/ מִיקַר אֶרֶץ וְהוֹנָהּ--
כִּי כְאֶחָד מֵאֵין שֵׁנִי/ הוּא בְּלִי עֵרֶךְ וּתְמוּנָה.

אֵל אֲשֶׁר נִשָּׂא וְנֶעְלָם/ וַחֲסָדָיו יוֹדוּן פִּיּוֹת,
שׁוֹבְבָה בָנִים לִגְבוּלָם/ וּכְקֶדֶם יַחַד לִהְיוֹת;
25 עַד לְשׁוֹרֵר כִּימֵי עוֹלָם/ וּכְשָׁנִים קַדְמוֹנִיּוֹת:
ובלאונה ואבתלינה/ ואיש יקול אלנאס פינא;
קום בנא יא נור עיני/ נגעל אלשך יקינא.

In his tribute to Barukh Ibn Jau, member of the prominent Andalusian family, [23] Ibn Ezra employs the *muwashshah* complete with *kharjah*. In the opening "belt" he introduces his "reproachers" (*merivim*), stock figures in the love poem, who rebuke the desperate lover for his reckless behavior. [24] In responding to the meddlesome moralists, the poet, now separated from his friend, begs for relief. In describing his despair, Ibn Ezra summons the conventional images of the genre. His heart melts with "love's fever," his hair has become white before its time and his nights are spent without sleep.

Seeking to explain his strange conduct, the poet lists the choice qualities of his patron-friend "Barukh...known far and wide" who "puts the moon to shame," and, like God, "is he esteemed beyond measure or form." Despite the hardships of travel, the poet vows to be reunited with his friend, Time permitting ("If the days were to make peace with me" {lu' yamim yihyu maslimim 'iti}). The Hebrew conveys the sense that Time is an agressor and the poet prays for relief.

In the closing *kharjah*, Ibn Ezra departs from defined conventions. The

23. See Abraham Ibn Daud, *Sefer Ha-Qabbalah*, pp. 68ff.
24. See Pagis, *Širat Ha-Hol*, p. 269.

strophe immediately preceding does not have expressions like: "he said...I said" (see above). Moreover, the closing strophe, instead of reciting the charms of the beloved, as is customary, is an appeal to God for national restoration. S. M. Stern notes that Ibn Ezra's poem is an imitation of a *muwashshah* by the Andalusian Arab poet, Abū Bakr Ibn Baqī (d. 1150). Both poets use the same *kharjah*. I. Levin observes that the colloquial Arabic of an earlier form of this *kharjah* was "starkly erotic," and was sanitized in its present form. [25]

11. FOR R. MENAHEM OF ROME AND HIS SON MOSES

The works of the Lord are new every morning;
Yet His thoughts are weighty to the wise.
He made lips for speech
And created eyes for men to behold other creatures.
He planted the ear that it not move
And receive the words that approach it.
Though I am asleep, my heart is awake and observes
My limbs taking a hostile stand like warriors:
The eye attacks the ear, and the tongue
Raises its voice in alarm.

The eye speaks: I am the one who sees and perceives
I search out the innermost chambers,
Even the heavens and the earth in an instant
I scan without having to move.
With one glance I appraise forms of all shapes and sizes,
However many and in fractions unlimited.
I discern the distant from the nearby
And separate the bright from darkness.
I am wise to the laws of geometry
And am privy to the number of stars and planets.
Though I move about without the benefit of wings
I know all that men have achieved.

---

25. Levin, *Yalqut Avraham Ibn Ezra*, p. 116; Stern, "The Muwashshahs of Abraham Ibn Ezra," p. 376; idem, *Hispano-Arabic Strophic Poetry*, p. 33.

Said the ear to the eye: Please be still.
Is not your ability limited by the presence of light?
You can see only that which is before you,
Whereas my power extends in all six directions.
You are like the blind when a veil bars your view
While I can listen behind a wall or a mountain top.
I can hear the word of God both by day and at night
When you lock up your gates.
I can enjoy the singers and musicians
And can appreciate the voices of men and women.

Said the tongue to the eye and the ear:
Do you think that the body is yours to rule?
It is I who am likened to a king dwelling in the palace
While you are mere servants under my command.
Life and death is in my power;
My words can delight or embitter.
I am unique and have no peers as you do;
I alone have the power of speech.
I am an advocate for reconciliation between the estranged;
With wisdom's help I reveal the unknown;
I also help my teeth to chew
Food in manageable portions.

I awoke and found my inner body at war;
Hostile camps faced each other fully armed.
Then a voice emerged from the heavens: Why are you fighting?
Find an agreeable way to resolve your dispute:
Seek out Rabbi Menahem, who brings comfort
To the soul and restores the body.
Happy the man whose eye sees his splendor.
Even the ear which hears his words;
Every tongue speaks his praise,
Even scrolls are unable to contain its volume.
His eye has seen the wonders of his God

And his ears have heard His voice that spoke to the Fathers.

His tongue utters words of Torah,

The six orders of the Mishnah issue from his mouth;

He is considerate of both rich and poor

Like a shepherd mindful of his flock.

He stops his ear from hearing falsehoods

And his speech restores life to the body.

While only one gate opens for the wise,

One hundred gates open for him.

His hands are generous like bountiful rain

Changing the desert into rivulets.

I appeal to the One who listens to prayer

And who knows my wishes, and those of all men:

Preserve the Rabbi [Menaḥem] and his son Rabbi Moses

In life until the concealed Redeemer arrives;

May they go up to the Temple of the Lord together

With Judah, Benjamin and Israel. [26]

--ס/---ס/---ס//--ס---ס/---ס

חֲדָשִׁים מַעֲשֵׂי אֵל לַבְּקָרִים,/ וְאִם רֵעָיו לְמַשְׂכִּילִים יְקָרִים,

אֲשֶׁר בָּרָא שְׂפָתַיִם וְשָׂם פֶּה,/ וְיָצַר עַיִן אֱנוֹשׁ לִרְאוֹת יְצוּרִים,

וְשָׁת אֹזֶן בְּלִי נוֹעַ נְטוּעָה,/ וְאֵלֶיהָ יָבֹאוּ כָּל דְּבָרִים.

אֲנִי יָשֵׁן וְלִבִּי עֵר--וְהִנֵּה/ נְתָחַי נִצְּבוּ לָרִיב כְּצָרִים,

5   וְקָם עַיִן עֲלֵי אֹזֶן וְלָשׁוֹן/ וְהִרְחִיב פֶּה וְנָשָׂא קוֹל וְהָרִים--;

נְאֻם עַיִן: אֲנִי רוֹאֶה וְחוֹזֶה,/ מְחַפֵּשׂ מַה בְּחַדְרֵי הַחֲדָרִים,

וְשָׁמַיִם לְפִי רֶגַע וְאֶרֶץ,/ אֲשׁוּרֵמוֹ בְּלִי צַעַד אֲשׁוּרִים,

וְיַחַד אֶחֱזֶה צוּרוֹת מְשֻׁנּוֹת,/ וְאִם רַבּוּ בְּלִי חֶלְקֵי שְׁבָרִים,

וְאַפְרִישׁ הָרְחוֹקִים מִקְּרוֹבִים/ וְאַבְדִּיל הַלְּבָנִים מִשְּׁחוֹרִים,

10   וּבִי חָכְמוּ בְּנֵי מִדּוֹת וְעָלוּ/ לְמַזָּלוֹת וְכוֹכָבִים סְפוּרִים,

וְכָל רֶגַע בְּלִי כָנָף אֲהַלֵּךְ/ וּבִי תִכּוֹן מְלֶאכֶת כָּל גְּבָרִים.

---

26. Levin, *Yalqut Avraham Ibn Ezra*, pp. 116-18. On the conceit, "His hands are generous like bountiful rain etc.," see Pagis, *Ḥidduš U-Masoret Be-Širat Ha-Ḥol*, p. 18-19.

נְאָם אֹזֶן לְעָיִן: הַחֲרֵשׁ נָא,/ וּמַה תּוֹכַל--וְלָךְ צֹרֶךְ לְאוֹרִים?

וְלֹא תִרְאֶה לְבַד מַה יֵּשׁ לְנֹכַח--/ וּמֶמְשַׁלְתִּי בְּכָל שִׁשָּׁה עֲבָרִים,

וְאִם מָסָךְ לְנֶגְדֶּךָ, אַף בְּעִוֵּר--/ וְאֶשְׁמַע אַחֲרֵי קִירוֹת וְהָרִים.

15 וְדַת אֵל אַאֲזִין יוֹמָם וְלָיִל--/ וּבַלַּיְלָה שְׁעָרֶיךָ סְגוּרִים,

וְכָל שָׁרִים וְנוֹגְנִים בִּי יְבִינוּן/ וְאַכִּיר הַנְּקֵבוֹת מִזְּכָרִים.

נְאָם לָשׁוֹן לְעָיִן גַּם לְאֹזֶן:/ חֲשַׁבְתֶּם לִהְיוֹת לְשָׂרִים?

אֲנִי נִמְשָׁל לְמֶלֶךְ דָּר בְּאַרְמוֹן--/ וְאַתֶּם כַּעֲבָדִים לִי מְסוּרִים;

וְהַחַיִּים וְהַמָּוֶת בְּיָדִי/ וּבִי טַעַם מְתוּקִים מִמְּרוֹרִים.

20 אֲנִי יָחִיד בְּלִי רֵעַ כְּמוֹכֶם/ וְאָנֹכִי לְבַדִּי אִישׁ דְּבָרִים.

אֲנִי מֵלִיץ בְּצֶדֶק בֵּין לְבָבוֹת/ וְאוֹדִיעַ בְּחָכְמָתִי סְתָרִים

וְאֶהְפֹּךְ מַאֲכָל לִהְיוֹת לְעֶזֶר/ לְשֹׁנַיִם, וְיִגְזֹר גְּזֵרִים.

הֲקִצוֹתִי וּבְקִרְבִּי קְרָבִים,/ וּמַחֲנוֹת זֶה וְזֶה כֻּלָּם אֲזוּרִים--

וְקוֹל נָתְנוּ שְׁחָקִים: מַה תְּרִיבוּן?/ לְכוּ נָא, בַּחֲרוּ מִשְׁפַּט יְשָׁרִים!

25 לְכוּ אֶל רַב מְנַחֵם, הַמְנַחֵם,/ נְפָשִׁים עַד יְשִׁיבֵם לַפְּגָרִים

וְאַשְׁרֵי עַיִן אֱנוֹשׁ רוֹאֶה הֲדָרוֹ,/ וְאֹזֶן תַּאֲזִין מִפִּיו אֲמָרִים,

וְכָל לָשׁוֹן תְּסַפֵּר מַהֲלָלָיו--/ וְנִלְאוּ לְהַכִילָם הַסְּפָרִים.

וְעֵינוֹ רָאֲתָה פְלָאוֹת אֱלֹהָיו/ וְאָזְנָיו יִשְׁמְעוּ בַּת קוֹל כְּהוֹרִים.

לְשׁוֹנוֹ תַעֲנֶה מַעֲנֶה תְעוּדָה/ בְּפִיו שִׁשָּׁה סְדָרִים הֵם סְדוּרִים.

30 וְעֵינוֹ שָׁם עֲלֵי עָשִׁיר וְאֶבְיוֹן/ כְּמוֹ רוֹעֶה יְבַקֵּר הָעֲדָרִים,

וְאָזְנוֹ מִשְּׁמוֹעַ שָׁוְא אֲטוּמָה/ וּמִדַּבְּרוֹ וּפִיו חַיֵּי בְשָׂרִים,

וְאִם שַׁעַר לְכָל מֵבִין בְּחָכְמָה--/ לְפָנָיו נִפְתְּחוּ מֵאָה שְׁעָרִים,

וְיָדָיו יִזְלוּ גִּשְׁמֵי נְדָבוֹת/ עֲדֵי בִמְקוֹם חֲרֵרִים שָׁם נְהָרִים.

תְּפִלָּתִי לְשׁוֹמֵעַ תְּפִלּוֹת/ וְכָל חֶפְצִי וְחֵפֶץ כָּל בְּרוּרִים--

35 הֱיוֹת הָרַב וְרַב מֹשֶׁה יְחִידוֹ/ בְּחַיִּים עַד עֲמוֹד גּוֹאֵל שְׁמוּרִים

וְעָלוּ בֵית אֲדֹנָי עִם יְהוּדָה/ וּבְנִימִן וְיִשְׂרָאֵל חֲבֵרִים.

In this *qaṣīdah*-style panegyric, Ibn Ezra sings the praises of Rabbi Menahem and his son Rabbi Moses. The tribute, written during the poet's stay in Rome, is divided into the standard introductory section in which the honorees are not mentioned followed by a linking triad leading into the *laudes*. In the opening the poet dreams that his limbs are engaged in a debate with each claiming superiority over the others. [27] Listed among their virtues is the eye's ability to understand the laws of geometry and the marvels of astronomy, while the ear boasts that it can appreciate the tone of musical instruments and the voices of a mixed choir. Not to be outdone, the tongue, a third party in the debate, argues its merits by asserting that it alone has the power of life and death, according to Prov. 18: 21.

When the poet awakens to the clamor of the warring limbs, he skillfully connects the debate theme in the introduction to the panegyric by advising the competing parties to consult the wise rabbis Menaḥem and Moses. This clever rhetorical device, characteristic of Ibn Ezra and his contemporaries, was admired for its ingenuity in paying tribute to patrons whose "hands are generous like bountiful rain / Changing the desert into rivulets." As in his other panegyrics, the poet employs a figure of contrast:

> While only one gate opens for the wise,
> One hundred gates open for him.

Closing the ode is a prayer for Israel's national restoration which the poet's patrons will be priviliged to witness.

12.   TO HIS BELOVED

> O sun which does not set by day or night,
> Arise upon us!
>
> O sun-like man let the light of your face shine
> Upon them that love you; do it with your favor
> And let not the arrows in your eyes harm them!
>   Why must you kill a heart in anger
>   When it is yours for the taking?
>
> The stars in heaven envy you,
> They desire a shade of light like yours;

---

27. On the debate in Hispanic–Hebrew poetry, see Schirmann, *Le–Toledot Ha–Širah Ve–Ha–Drama Ha–'Ivrit*, 1: 372–73.

With your radiance the earth outshines the sky.
  Arise, O gazelle, go up and triumph
  And in your majesty, prosper.

The eye that sees you is happy –
Now if only the heart would resist the attraction.
What am I to do in this case?
  Although the eye should be a teacher to man's heart,
  She has become a snare.

I find myself at present a captive of my affection;
I plead with you, but you are unresponsive;
Shall I remain silent? Will you answer me then?
  I am prepared to die if only you would speak,
  Be it in praise or blame.

The choice honey from your lips is sweet;
It is God's work, unblemished.
Your breath radiates the fragrance of apples.
  My beloved, where have you eaten the apple?
  Come and say to me: ah! [28]

$$\text{--ס/-ס--/-ס--//--/-ס-}$$
$$\text{--ס/-ס---/--}$$

שֶׁמֶשׁ בְּיוֹם וְלֵיל לֹא יִזַּח,
עָלֵינוּ זְרַח!

שֶׁמֶשׁ אֱנוֹשׁ, נְסָה אוֹר פָּנֶיךָ
עַל אוֹהֲבִים, עֲשֵׂה בִרְצוֹנֶךָ--
5   אַל תִּגְּמֵם בְּחִצֵּי עֵינֶיךָ!
לָמָּה בְזַעְפְּךָ לֵב תִּרְצַח?
הוֹאֵל נָא וְקַח!

28. Levin, *Yalqut Abvraham Ibn Ezra*, pp. 113–14; Stern, "The Muwashshahs of
Abraham Ibn Ezra," p. 371.

כּוֹכְבֵי זְבוּל יְקַנְאוּ אוֹתָכָה,
כִּי חָמְדוּ הֱיוֹת אוֹרָם כָּכָה,
10 הִנֵּה בָךְ אֲדָמָה מָלָכָה.
קוּם, הַצְּבִי, עֲלֵה גַם הַצְלַח
וַהֲדָרְךָ צְלַח!

עַיִן אֲשֶׁר תְּשׁוּרְךָ אַשְׁרֶיהָ--
לוּלֵי מְשׁוֹךְ לְבָבִים אַחֲרֶיהָ;
15 מָה אֶעֱשֶׂה אֲנִי בִדְבָרֶיהָ?
הַעֵין אֱנוֹשׁ לְבָבוֹ תוֹכַח--
הִיא הָיְתָה לְפַח.

עַתָּה אֲסִיר יְדִידוּת הִנְנִי,
אֶתְחַנְּנָה לָךְ--לֹא תַעֲנֵנִי,
20 אֵיךְ תֶּחֱשֶׂה עֵדֶן וּתְעַנֵּנִי?
לוּ אֶגְוָעָה וּפִיךָ תִּפְתַּח
בִּגְנַאי אוֹ שֶׁבַח.

נֹפֶת וְצוּף בְּפִיךָ מְמֻלְחִים,
מַעֲשֵׂה אֱלֹהִים--לֹא מְרֻקָּחִים,
25 רֵיחַ בְּאַפְּךָ כַּתַּפּוּחִים--
חביבי אן אכלת אלתפאח
קם אעמל לי אח.

This *muwashshah* panegyric to an unnamed patron employs the standard figures of contemporary love poetry. The beloved Maecenas, luminous like a never failing sun, is petitioned in words associated with divine worship. "Let the light of your face shine upon them that love you" is a paraphrase of the Psalmist's (4: 7) prayer to God. Likewise, the plea, "Do it with your favor" (*bi-rsonekha*) is borrowed from Isaiah (60: 10) speaking in God's name, "In my favor (*u-virsoni*) I have had mercy on you."

Characteristic of Ibn Ezra is his rhetorical argument with the "gazelle:"

> Why must you kill a heart in anger
> When it is yours for the taking?

In his sacred poetry (Poem #54, below), Ibn Ezra will argue with God, addressing him in the third person:

> How could He sell the nobleman's [Abraham] daughter to a stranger?

In the third strophe, the poet designs a rhetoric of helplessness. He is caught in a double bind: seeing the "gazelle" makes him both happy and addicted. The eye should know better, but it fails him, and his heart is unable to resist. The extended conceit closes with the hyperbole that the "captive" poet is prepared to give his life for a mere word from his beloved.

Ibn Ezra closes the *muwashshaḥ* with a *kharjah* which, S. M. Stern suggests, the poet (and the Hispanic–Hebrew writer, Todros Abulafia, b. 1247) might have borrowed from the Arabic poet, Ibn Quzmān (d. 1160). [29]

13.   ELEGY ON THE DEATH OF HIS SON ISAAC

> Father to the child, approach and mourn
> For God has removed from you
> Your son, your only son
> Whom you loved, even Isaac.

> I am the man who saw
> Disaster, whose joy was banished;
> I am deprived of my child,
> I never believed it possible;
> In my declining years I had hoped
> That he would bring me relief and deliverance;
> Alas, I labored in vain
> And sired a son to dismay me!

---

29. See Stern, *Hispano–Arabic Strophic Poetry*, pp. 187–88.

How can I ever be cheerful
Now he breathed his last and died, my Isaac.

I shall surely weep each moment
And raise a bitter lament
When I recall, three years past,
His death among foreigners,
And his vagabond life,
And my longing for him,
While I cried night and day,
Until I brought him home;
How much sorrow befell me;
Such is the chronicle of Isaac!

Hold back, my friend,
If you comfort me, you bring me grief;
Do not make me recall the love of my life,
Do not force me to hear his name;
Fate has doused the ember remaining within me,
Will I be harmed again?
Fate has shocked me with endless horror;
Fate has removed the apple of my eye;
My flesh and my heart fail
Since Fate put an end to Isaac!

God who contains all in His hand
And does His will in every creature,
Comfort the aching heart of a father
Who from his youth did fear Your name;
Quicken within him a feeling of consolation
That it may enter his broken heart;
This man who taught his loved one to fear You;
To walk in the way of his fathers,

You who from his youth

Decreed the way for your servant, Isaac. [30]

אָבִי הַבֵּן, קְרַב לִסְפֹּד, כִּי אֵל מִמְּךָ רָחַק
אֶת בִּנְךָ אֶת יְחִידְךָ אֲשֶׁר אָהַבְתָּ אֶת יִצְחָק.

אֲנִי הַגֶּבֶר רָאָה שֶׁבֶר וּמְשׂוֹשׂוֹ גֻלָה.
הָהּ, פָּקַדְתִּי פְּרִי בִטְנִי וְעַל לִבִּי לֹא עָלָה!
כִּי חָשַׁבְתִּי לְעֵת זִקְנָה הֱיוֹתוֹ לְרֶוַח וְהַצָּלָה--   5
אַךְ לָרִיק יָגַעְתִּי וְיָלַדְתִּי לַבֶּהָלָה,
כִּי אֵיךְ יִשְׂמַח לִבִּי--וַיִּגְוַע וַיָּמָת יִצְחָק!

בָּכֹה אֶבְכֶּה בְּכָל רֶגַע וְאֶשָּׂא נְהִי נִהְיָה,
בְּזָכְרִי זֶה שָׁלֹשׁ שָׁנִים מוֹתוֹ בְּאֶרֶץ נָכְרִיָּה
וְצֵאתוֹ מִמָּקוֹם לְמָקוֹם; וְנַפְשִׁי עָלָיו הוֹמִיָּה   10
עַד שֶׁהֲבֵאתִיו אֶל בֵּיתִי, לַיְלָה וְיוֹמָם בּוֹכִיָּה,
כַּמָּה תְלָאוֹת מְצָאוּנִי--וְאֵלֶּה תּוֹלְדוֹת יִצְחָק!

רֵעִי, הַרְפֵּה מִמֶּנִּי! אִם תְּנַחֲמֵנִי--תְּנִיעֵנִי
מַחְמַל נַפְשִׁי אַל תִּזְכֹּר וּשְׁמוֹ אַל תַּשְׁמִיעֵנִי,
גַּחַלְתִּי אֲשֶׁר נִשְׁאֲרָה לִי כִּבָּה זְמָן--וְאִם יִרְ'עֵנִי?   15
שִׁמְמוֹת עוֹלָם הֱשִׁמַּנִי וַיִּקַּח מַחְמַד עֵינִי--
כָּלָה שְׁאֵרִי וּלְבָבִי כַּאֲשֶׁר כָּלָה יִצְחָק.

מָעוֹן, אֲשֶׁר הַכֹּל בְּיָדוֹ וְחֶפְצוֹ עוֹשֶׂה בְּכָל יְצוּרָיו,
דַּבֶּר עֲלֵי לֵב אָב נִכְאָב יָרֵא שְׁמֶךָ מִנְּעוּרָיו,
רוּחַ תַּנְחוּמִים עוֹרֵר עָלָיו וְיַעֲבֹר בֵּין בְּתָרָיו.   20
הוֹרָה חֲמוּדוֹ יִרְאָתְךָ לָלֶכֶת בְּדֶרֶךְ הוֹרָיו--
עוֹדֶנּוּ נַעַר אֹתָהּ הוֹכַחְתָּ לְעַבְדְּךָ לְיִצְחָק.

This is the longer of the two elegies in memory of Isaac Ibn Ezra and was

---

30. Schirmann, *Ha-Širah Ha-'Ivrit*, 1: 580–81; Levin, *Yalqut Avraham Ibn Ezra*, pp. 103–04.

written three years after his death. [31] Written in the form of a *muwashshah*, the work is remarkably free from the stock images of the conventional lament on the death of a patron. There is no hyperbole in eulogizing the virtues of the deceased and no call to sun and stars to cover their faces and join in the mourning. The only concession to forms in the traditional elegy is the poet's blaming Time and the World for the tragedy they caused ("Fate has shocked me with endless horror").

The father's lament in unembellished phrasing is deeply personal. Its pervasive theme is the "Binding of Isaac" story in the Pentateuch. Beginning with the opening "belt," taken from Gen. 22: 2 ("[Take] your son, your only son Isaac whom you love...[and offer him there as a burnt offering]") each of the following strophes closes with the name "Isaac", based on biblical sources. Presumably, Abraham Ibn Ezra felt himself put under trial like the patriarch Abraham. A secondary theme is the destruction of the Temple. The openings in the first and second strophes are borrowed from Lam. 3: 1 and 1: 2, respectively. Isaac's death prompts his father to recall the most tragic event in Israelite history.

Although Isaac Ibn Ezra was a gifted poet in his own right, [32] in the elegy he is remembered only as "my child" who "I thought...would bring me relief..." A reference to Isaac's vagabond life ("When I recall...His wandering from place to place") is the scant biographical information the father is willing to reveal about his son. The mere mention of Isaac's name evokes bitter memories and prompts the father to refuse the comfort of friends. Only God can "quicken within him a feeling of consolation" and soothe his broken heart. In the final strophe, the poet refers to himself in the third person when he asks the Heavenly Father to "comfort the aching heart of a[n earthly] father." In the closing couplet, Ibn Ezra points to the irony of his predicament in a bold conceit. He reminds God that even as Isaac was taught "to fear You," "You...decreed" that he should die in his youth!

---

31. See B. Dinur, *Yisra'el Ba-Golah*, 2: 3, pp. 79, 328, n. 55 for the text of the shorter elegy where the father remembers that he hastened to his son's bedside hoping to save him (*'ašer 'aṣti le-vaqqeš-na' 'arukha lo*).

32. See I. Ibn Ezra, *Yiṣḥaq ben Avraham Ibn Ezra: Širim*, pp. 3–50.

14.   LAMENT ON THE DESTRUCTION OF ANDALUSIAN AND NORTH AFRICAN JEWRY

From the heavens troubles descended upon Spain!
My eyes flow with tears!

I weep like an ostrich for Lucena.
Her remnant dwelt innocent and secure,
Unchanged for a thousand and seventy years;
Then came her day and her people were exiled and she a widow
Forbidden to study the Torah, the Prophets and the Mishnah;
Even the Talmud was lonely; its glory departed.
The killers took over and fugitives sought shelter;
The house of prayer and praise became a mosque.
For this I weep and strike hand against hand in lament without respite;
  I cannot keep silent; O that my head were a spring of water.

I will shave my head and cry bitterly over the exiles from Seville,
Over its noble men that were slain and their sons enslaved,
Over refined daughters converted to the foreign faith.
Alas, the city of Cordoba is forsaken, her ruin as vast as the sea!
Her sages and learned men perished from hunger and thirst.
Not a single Jew was left in Jaen or Almeria;
Majorca and Málaga struggle to survive.
The Jews who remained are a beaten bleeding wound.
For this I mourn and learn a dirge and wail with bitter lamentation;
  I shout in my distress: They have vanished like water.

I cry out like a woman in labor for the congregations of Sijilmasa—
A city where genius and wisdom flourished; their brilliance obscured
    the darkness.
The pillar of learning was bent and the edifice crumbled;
The Mishnah became an object of scorn trampled underfoot;
The enemy had no mercy; the nobles they cut down.
Woe, the congregation of Fez is no more; this day they are
    given to the plunderer;

Where is the protection for the congregation of Tlemsan?
  Its glory is melted away.
A bitter voice I raise over the fate of Ceuta and Meknes;
I rend my garments for Dar'ī already vanquished;
  On one Sabbath day, the blood of sons and daughters was spilled
    like water.

How shall I explain it? On account of my sin I was afflicted.
By my God's decree, my rock and strength, destruction has been
    determined against me.
For whom can I hope? What can I say? It is all my fault.
My heart becomes hot within me on account of my sinful soul;
She (my soul) is exiled from her country, her desired haven, to a
    polluted land;
Ashamed and dumbfounded she is unable to speak of her hardship;
With pain in her heart she hopes for mercy from her Rock;
That He may bring redemption from slavery; she seeks shelter under
    His wings.
Each moment in prison, she survives by the mention of His name.
Only tears are upon her cheek while the sons of Hagar cast
  Their arrows and until the Lord will look down from the heavens! [33]

6/3/3

אֲהָהּ יָרַד/ עַל סְפָרַד/ רָע מִן הַשָּׁמַיִם!
עֵינִי עֵינִי יֹרְדָה מַיִם!

בִּכוֹת עֵינִי/ כִּיָּעֵנִי/ עַל עִיר אֶלְיסַאנָה!
בְּאֵין אָשָׁם/ בְּדָד שָׁם/ הַגּוֹלָה שָׁכְנָה
5   בְּאֵין חֵלֶף/ עַד אֶלֶף/ שָׁנִים וְשִׁבְעִים שָׁנָה--
וּבָא יוֹמָהּ/ וְנָד עַמָּהּ/ וְגַם הָיְתָה כְּאַלְמָנָה,
בְּאֵין תּוֹרָה/ וְאֵין מִקְרָא/ וְהַמִּשְׁנָה נִטְמָנָה,

---

33. Levin, *Yalqut Avraham Ibn Ezra*, pp. 101–02. The scansion includes only the long syllables which are listed by number above the Hebrew text; see Mark Cohen, *Under Crescent and Cross*, p. 183 on the historical background of this poem.

וְהַתַּלְמוּד/ כְּמוֹ גַלְמוּד/ כִּי כָל הוֹדוֹ פָנָה.

וְיֵשׁ הוֹרְגִים / וְגַם עוֹרְגִים/ מְקוֹם אָנֶה וָאָנָה.

10 מְקוֹם תְּפִלָּה/ וּתְהִלָּה/ לְבֵית תְּפִלָּה נִתְכְּנָה.

לְזֹאת אֶבְכֶּה/ וְכַף אַכֶּה/ וּבְפִי תָמִיד קִינָה

וְאֵין לִי דָמִי/ לֵאמֹר: מִי/ יִתֵּן רֹאשִׁי רֹאשֵׁי מָיִם.

רֹאשׁ אֶקְרַח/ וּמַר אֶצְרַח/ עַל גּוֹלַת אַשְׁבִּילְיָה--

עַל אֲצִילִים/ הֵם חֲלָלִים/ וּבְנֵיהֶם בַּשִּׁבְיָה,

15 וְעַל בָּנוֹת/ מְעֻדָּנוֹת/ נִמְסְרוּ לְדָת נָכְרִיָּה.

אֵיךְ עֻזְּבָה/ עִיר קוֹרְטְבָה/ וַתְּהִי כַיָּם שְׁאִיָּה?--

וְשָׁם חֲכָמִים/ וַעֲצוּמִים/ מֵתוּ בְּרָעָב וְצִיָּה.

וְאֵין יְהוּדִי/ גַּם יְחִידִי/ בְּגִיָּאן גַּם אַלְמְרִיָּה.

וּמַיּוֹרְקָה/ וְעִיר מָאלְקָה/ לֹא נִשְׁאַר שָׁם מִחְיָה

20 וְהַיְּהוּדִים/ הַשְּׂרִידִים/ הֻכּוּ מַכָּה טְרִיָּה.

לְזֹאת אֶסְפְּדָה/ וּמַר אֶלְמְדָה/ וְאֶנְהֶה עוֹד נְהִי נִהְיָה

לְשַׁאֲגוֹתָי/ בְּתוּגוֹתָי/ וַיִּמָּאֲסוּ כְּמוֹ מָיִם.

הוֹי אֶקְרָא/ כְּמִצְרָה/ עַל קָהִלּוֹת סְגַלְמָאסָה--

עִיר גְּאוֹנִים/ וּנְבוֹנִים/ מְאוֹרָם חֹשֶׁךְ כִּסָּה

25 וְשַׁח עַמּוּד/ הַתַּלְמוּד/ וְהַבִּנְיָה נֶהֱרָסָה

וְהַמִּשְׁנָה/ לִשְׁנִינָה/ בְּרַגְלַיִם נִרְמָסָה

וְעַל יְקָרִים/ מְדֻקָּרִים/ עֵין אוֹיֵב לֹא חָסָה.

אֲהָהּ, אָפֵס/ כָּל קְהַל פָאס/ יוֹם נִתְּנוּ לִמְשִׁסָּה.

אֵי חֹסֶן/ קְהַל תִּלֶמְסֶן?/ --וְהַדְרָתָהּ נָמַסָּה.

30 וְקוֹל אָרִים/ בְּתַמְרוּרִים/ עֲלֵי סַבְתָּה וּמִכְּנָאסָה.

וְסוּת אֶקְרָעָה/ עַל דַּרְעָה/ אֲשֶׁר לְפָנִים נִתְפְּשָׂה--

בְּיוֹם שַׁבָּת/ בֵּן עִם בַּת/ שָׁפְכוּ דָמָם כַּמָּיִם.

מָה אַעַן?/--כִּי לְמַעַן/ חַטָּאתִי זֹאת הָיְתָה,

וּמֵאֵלִי/ צוּר חֵילִי/ רָעָה אֵלַי כָּלְתָה.

35 לְמִי אֲשַׁבֵּר?/ וּמָה אֲדַבֵּר?/--וְהַכֹּל יָדִי עָשָׂתָה!

חַם לִבִּי/ בְּתוֹךְ קִרְבִּי/ עַל נַפְשִׁי אֲשֶׁר עֻוְתָה,

וּמֵאַרְצָהּ/ מְחוֹז חֶפְצָהּ/ לְאֶרֶץ טְמֵאָה גָלְתָה

וְנִכְלְמָה/ וְנֶאֱלְמָה/ לְסַפֵּר תְּלָאוֹת לָאָתָה.

וְעִם כְּאֵבָהּ/ בִּלְבָבָהּ/ לְחַסְדֵּי צוּרָהּ קִוְּתָה

40 לְצַוּוֹת פְּדוּת/ מֵעַבְדוּת/ כִּי בְצֵל כְּנָפָיו חָסָתָה.

בְּבֵית כִּלְאִים/ בְּכָל עֵת, אִם/ זָכְרָה שְׁמוֹ--אָז חָיְתָה,
רַק בִּכְיָה/ עֲלֵי לְחָיָהּ/ בְּיַד אָמָה אֲשֶׁר קַשְׁתָּהּ
מְאֹד תּוֹרֶה-;/ עֲדֵי יֵרֵא/ אֲדֹנָי מִשָּׁמָיִם.

The Moslem revival under Muhammad Ibn Tumart, founder in ca. 1121 of the uncompromising unitarian Almohade dynasty, brought much destruction to Jewish communities in the Maghreb and Andalusia in 1146/47. Ibn Ezra lists the Jewish communities destroyed by the onslaught, beginning with Lucena where the study of the Torah and Talmud was forbidden. Despite the accepted status of Jews as a protected minority (dhimmis) in Moslem lands, 'Abd al-Mu'min, successor to Ibn Tumart, invoked a "tradition" which stated that if the Jewish Messiah did not arrive five hundred years after Muhammad's flight (hegira) in 622 they would be required to become Muslims. Since that period had already expired, 'Abd al-Mu'min was unrestrained in dealing with the Jews who, in 1146, were forced to acknowledge Muhammad as God's preeminent messenger and seal of the prophets. [34]

Here, as in the previous elegy on the death of Isaac, Ibn Ezra avoids the use of topical embellishments. The sense of urgency and crisis is enhanced by the short staccato rhyme scheme in the strophes:

> Bekhot 'eyni/ ka-ye'eni/ 'al 'ir 'elisa'nah
> Be-'eyn 'asam/ badad sam/ ha-golah sakhanah   (lines 3–4)

The rapid pace of devastation is conveyed in the list of fallen cities sounded in swift succession:

> Not a single Jew was left in Jaen or Almeria;
> Majorca and Málaga struggle to survive.

As expected, the prominent source of referral is the book of Lamentations. The opening couplet is based on Lam. 1: 16 as are lines 6 and 42–43. "From the heavens troubles descended on Spain" is an inversion of the rabbinic comment (in Gen. Rabbah 51. 3), "Nothing evil descends from above." In the closing strophe, after naming some fourteen cities destroyed, the poet blames his sinful generation for the

---

34. Cf. Baron, A Social and Religious History of the Jews, 3: 124–25.

calamity. Despite the presence of "noble men" and "refined daughters" of Seville; "sages and learned men" of Cordoba; and the "genius and wisdom" of Sijilmasa, Ibn Ezra will protect the traditional theodicy as expressed in Israel's prayer book, "Because of our sins were we exiled from our land."

15.   A SEA VOYAGE

A.

To my God I reach out my hand, even as I bow before my Lord;
In my distress He is my strength, my firm fortress;
I pay Him homage for His power, made of wonders;
Because of my sins I came adrift upon the sea
And said, "Woe is me, woe is me."
From His palace He heard my plea.
　　Tossed about among the waves, I said, "I am lost!"
　　He, the Rock of Ages said, "I will still the roaring sea."

Tempting fate upon the faithless waters,
I risked my life;
Reassured (though the day appeared strange),
I thought: I trust the waters this time of the year.
Resolute, I left my house,
I boarded the ship, now my home,
And to my sorrow, I fell asleep.
　　"Why, O Sea, do you frighten the meek; I am a stranger to your ways;
　　Why does your anger rage, why is your temper uncontrolled?"

My soul was troubled within me.
Then the sea spoke up, "Do not ask why,
Consider the wisdom of treading upon me
And how stupid it is to trust a wooden boat;
Remember, every sailor is seasoned by disaster;
The captain is anguished, ruled by misfortune;
And aboard ship there is grief.
　　Intruder, do not grieve against me in my realm,
　　I cannot be becalmed when winds come over me!"

"Be still, O sea, for my faith is firm;
The Rock, my Master, will rebuke the storm;
My movements are made not by my choice;
By His written decree I come to you;
In the beginning He set a limit to my life;
Who then can avert his fate?
When He established the heavens I was there!
    How can I fathom His secrets or be hidden from His gaze?
    In His hand is the sea and dry land; where can I flee?"

The sea answered, "Your speech is mindless;
Remaining here confined in close quarters,
You persist in your sin and insolence.
Now you will be unwittingly consumed
Like the fish you devoured with pleasure.
This, covetous man, is measure for measure.
Do you not know? Have you not heard?
    God's eye is on His creatures, requiting deeds;
    Your blood be on your own head; death to you, not life!"

God exalted, Your majesty be revealed;
Redeem and regard one broken by Your wrath,
Raise Yourself up from Your throne of mercy;
Come out and save Your handmaid's son
Who seeks entrance into Your land.
I shall worship You and give You praise among Your flock,
To the ages, I will make known Your faithfulness.
    This I will reveal wherever I go, repaying my debt to You;
    I shall sing in my rhyme: deliverance is the Lord's! [35]

---

35. Schirmann, *Ha-Širah Ha-'Ivrit*, 1: 581–84; Levin, *Yalqut Avraham Ibn Ezra*, pp. 105–07.

3/3/3

6

אֶפְרֹשׁ כַּף/ אַף אֶכַּף/ אֶל אֵלִי,
הוּא חֵילִי/ מִגְדָּלִי/ בַּצַּר לִי.
אָקֹד לוֹ/ עַל גָּדְלוֹ/ שֶׁהִפְלִיא.
בִּדְבַר תֹּךְ/ מָטָה תוֹךְ/ יָם רַגְלִי

5 וָאֹמַר:/ "רָזִי לִי/ רָזִי לִי"--
וַיִּשְׁמַע/ מֵהֵיכָ-/ לוֹ קוֹלִי.
בֵּין גַּלִּים עָבַרְתִּי,
אָמַרְתִּי: "נִגְזָרְתִּי!"
אָמַר צוּר עוֹלָמִים:
10 "אַשְׁבִּיחַ שְׁאוֹן יַמִּים."

בְּיָם בּוֹגֵד/ מִנֶּגֶד/ הִשְׁלַכְתִּי
אֶת נַפְשִׁי/ וּלְמוֹקְשִׁי/ דָּרַשְׁתִּי:
וּבְשׁוּרִי/ יוֹם נָכְרִי--/ נִחַמְתִּי,
וְיָם בִּזְמָן/ זֶה נֶאֱמָן/ חָשַׁבְתִּי

15 וּבִיגוֹנִי/ עַל פָּנַי/ נִרְדַּמְתִּי
וּבַסְּפִינָה/ כַּמְּדִינָה/ עָבַרְתִּי,
עָזַבְתִּי/ אֶת בֵּיתִי/ נָטַשְׁתִּי.
מַה לָּךְ, יָם, תַּבְהִיל מָךְ?
גֵּר אָנֹכִי עִמָּךְ.
20 לָמָּה אַפְּךָ חָרָה?
מַה זֶּה רוּחֲךָ סָרָה?

רוּחִי בִי/ בְּלִבָבִי/ הוֹמִיָּה,
וְיָם אָמַר:/ "אַל תֹּאמַר:/ מֶה הָיָה?
הֲלָדְרֹךְ בִּי/ וּבְקָרְבִּי/ תּוּשִׁיָּה?
25 וּלְיוֹעֵץ/ לוּחַ עֵץ/ אֵין מִחְיָה,
וְכָל מַלָּח/ הֵן נִמְלָח/ בְּשַׂאֲיָּה,
וְרַב חוֹבֵל/ רַב חֶבֶל/ רַב בְּכִיָּה,
וְהָאֳנִיָּה--/ תַּאֲנִיָּה/ וַאֲנִיָּה.
אַל נָא תָלוֹן עָלַי,
30 כִּי אַתָּה בָא אֵלַי--
וַאֲנִי אֵיךְ אָנוּחַ?

וַתָּבוֹא בִי רוּחַ!"

"הֶחָרֵשׁ, יָם,/ כִּי קַיָּם,/ בִּטְחוֹנִי
וּבְסַעַר/ הֵן יִגְעַר/ צוּר קוֹנִי.
35 וְאֵין שָׁבְתִּי/ אוֹ לֶכְתִּי/ בִּרְצוֹנִי
וּבִכְתָבוֹ/ בְּךָ לָבוֹא/ צִוַּנִי
וּבְרֵאשִׁית/ קֵץ הֵשִׁית/ אֵל אוֹנִי,
גַּם קִצִּים/ נֶחֱרָצִים/ מִי יָנִיא?
בַּהֲכִינוֹ/ שָׁמַיִם/ שָׁם אָנִי!
40 סוֹדוֹ אֵיךְ אֲבִינֶנּוּ
וְאֶסָּתֵר מִמֶּנּוּ?
בְּיָדוֹ יָם וְחָרָבָה--
וַאֲנִי אָנָה אֲנִי בָא?"

מֵשִׁיב לִי,/ יָם: "בִּבְלִי/ לֵב שָׁחַתָּ
45 וּבְאוֹנְךָ/ וּזְדוֹנְךָ/ הָלַכְתָּ--
וְאַתְּ עָצוּר/ וְאַף נָצוּר/ נוֹתַרְתָּ!
זְכֹר דָּגִים/ תַּעֲנוּגִים/ אָכַלְתָּ--
בְּלִי שֵׂכֶל/ תֵּאָכֵל/ גַּם אַתָּה!
אִישׁ חֶמְדָּה/ קַח מִדָּה/ מָדַדְתָּ!
50 הֲלוֹא יָדַע-/ תָּ אִם לֹא/ שָׁמַעְתָּ?--
עֵין אֵל עַל מִפְעָלוֹ,
גְּמוּל יָדוֹ יָשִׁיב לוֹ.
בְּרֹאשְׁךָ דָּמְךָ יִהְיֶה,
מֵת אַתָּה וְלֹא תִחְיֶה!"

55 אֵל גֵּאֶה,/ תֵּרָאֶה/ גַּאֲוָתְךָ,
פְּדֵה וּרְאֵה/ הַנִּכְאֶה/ בְּחֶמְלָתְךָ,
הַנָּשֵׂא/ עַל כִּסֵּא/ חֶמְלָתְךָ!
הוֹפִיעָה/ וְהוֹשִׁיעָה/ בֶּן אֲמָתְךָ
הַשּׁוֹאֵל/ לָצֵאת אֵל/ אַדְמָתְךָ.
60 אֶעֶבְדְךָ/ גַּם אוֹדְךָ/ בַּעֲבָדְתָּ,
לְדוֹר וָדוֹר/ אוֹדִיעַ/ אֱמוּנָתְךָ.
אַגִּיד זֹאת בְּכָל מַהֲלָךְ
וַאֲשַׁלֵּם תּוֹדוֹת לָךְ.

אָשִׁירָה בְּרָנְנַי
יְשׁוּעָתָה לַהּ!

B.

You rescued me from the mighty waters;
You led me with Your gracious kindness.
Will rest come to a restless vagrant?
I fear the wind and the mire,
The flood sweeps over me.
   Arise O Lord, deliver me:
   Let not the deep overwhelm me!

The time [of my rescue] is in Your hand, though I am
Of little worth on land or sea;
A mere beast in Your sight.
   Guide my life with Your counsel,
   And having gained this honor, take me.

On the day Your sea raged against me
As I strengthened my hand by Your name
My hands were weak from fear of You:
   If you will not preserve me
   My sin will cast me into the pit.

I will remember this all my days:
When the north wind came
Bringing affliction upon me in a blast at sea,
   I called out and You answered,
      Saying, "Here I am, I am here!" [36]

8/8

מִמַּיִם רַבִּים תַּמְשֵׁנִי, /
רוּחַ טוֹבָה, תַּנִּיחֵנִי!

36. Schirmann, Ha-Širah Ha-'Ivrit, 1: 584–85.

אֵיךְ לֵב נָע וָנָד יִנָּפֵשׁ?
יִירָא מֵרוּחַ וָרֶפֶשׁ,
5   כִּי בָאוּ מַיִם עַד נֶפֶשׁ.
קוּמָה, אֵלִי, הוֹשִׁיעֵנִי
וּמְצוּלָה אַל תִּבְלָעֵנִי!

בְּיָדְךָ עִתּוֹתַי--וַאֲנִי מָה
אֶחֱשֵׁב בַּיָּם אוֹ בַאֲדָמָה,
10   וְעִמְּךָ הָיִיתִי כַבְּהֵמָה.
בְּחֶלְדִּי בַּעֲצָתְךָ תַנְחֵנִי
וְאַחַר כָּבוֹד תִּקָּחֵנִי.

רְפוּ יָדַי מֵאֵימֶיךָ
יוֹם סָעַר עָלַי יַמֶּךָ,
15   וָאֲחַזֵּק יָדַי בְּשִׁמֶךָ:
אִם אַתָּה לֹא תַעֲמִידֵנִי,
חֶטְאִי אֶל בּוֹר יוֹרִידֵנִי.

מִדֵּי הֱיוֹתִי זֹאת אֶזְכֹּרָה
בְּבוֹא רוּחַ צָפוֹן בִּסְעָרָה
וְעָבַר עָלַי בַּיָּם צָרָה
יוֹם קָרָאתִי וַתַּעֲנֵנִי
לֵאמֹר, "הִנֶּנִי, הִנֵּנִי!"

Travel by sea, an often dangerous enterprise in the Middle Ages, inspired Hispanic-Hebrew poets to relive their experience. Samuel Ibn Nagrela wrote a *qasīdah*-style poem about his near death encounter with a sea mammoth and his miraculous rescue. [37] Ibn Ezra's seascape favored the *muwashshah*, with a short, staccato, internal rhyme making for a heightened sense of crisis and urgency. In addition, the latter injected the dialogue as a rhetorical embellishment.

Innocent to the ways of the wayward sea, Ibn Ezra sets out on his voyage hopeful of reaching dry land (line 59) without incident. Like Jonah, he falls asleep feeling secure. The turbulent waters awaken him and he is fearful that his sins will

---

37. See Weinberger, *Jewish Prince in Moslem Spain*, pp. 85-88.

bring down God's judgment upon him. To relieve his distress, he images a dialogue with the roaring waves and asks that they control their "temper."

In reply, the sea blames the winds for its anger and adds that the seasoned sailor who treads upon the ocean's domain should expect disaster. Now the poet invokes God's authority and argues that this voyage is ordained by divine order ("By His written decree I come to you"). The sea is not impressed charging that she is the instrument of God's judgment upon the poet, measure for measure:

> Now you will be unwittingly consumed
> Like the fish you devoured with pleasure.   (lines 47–48)

The poet gives up the effort to win an argument with the angry sea and turns to God, pleading for mercy and a safe "entrance into Your land." Behind the dialogue is the assumption that God delegates the governance of the sublunar world to natural forces like the stars ("When He established the heavens, I was there [i. e. my fate was decreed]"), the wind and the sea ("I cannot be becalmed when winds come over me"). Moreover, there is a natural kinship among the life forms in the sublunar world and man is forbidden to exploit the lower life forms (like the fish) for his mere pleasure.

In this all–embracing reverence for living beings, Ibn Ezra echoes the view of Samuel Ibn Nagrela who exhorted the butchers and fishmongers of Granada to show compassion to their brute creatures:

> "Even as you, they breathe and have a heart...
> [Like you] there is never a time when one among them does not
>   die [or give] birth." [38]

Only after Noah had saved the animals from the flood were they permitted

---

38. Weinberger, *Jewish Prince*, pp. 96–97.

to be eaten, but only to satisfy the appetite and not for random slaughter. [39] The second of Ibn Ezra's thanksgiving hymns celebrates his rescue from a storm–tossed sea. The longer lines in this *muwashshah* convey a lesser sense of urgency, and it is likely that this work, unlike the previous, was composed some time after the poet was safely put on shore. A literal translation of the opening "belt" couplet, based on Ps. 143: 10, reads: "You rescued me from the mighty waters; / You led me with Your good wind (*ruhakha tovah*)." The poet is thankful that he survived as he recalls his fears "on the day Your sea raged against me" and his answered prayer.

Ibn Ezra's reference to himself as a "restless vagrant" (*na' wa–nad*) is based on Cain's confession [in Gen. 4: 14], "I shall be a fugitive and wanderer on the earth." His comment, "[I] am a mere beast in Your sight" taken from Ps. 73: 22, may be understood in light of his commentary on this verse, "I was like a brute beast because I did not understand why the wicked prosper until You rescued me." In the closing strophe, when the poet repeats God's reassurance, "Here I am" he is quoting Abraham's readiness to sacrifice his son, after Gen. 22: 1. In this reference, he is suggesting that God has not forgotten the Merit of the Fathers (*zekhut 'avot*).

16.   IN A LIFETIME

Child of earth, remember your motherland
For at your time's end you'll return to its womb.

"Grow and prosper," they exhort the lad of five
Whose virtues surpass the rising sun;
He does not stir from mother's bosom;
    He makes father's nape his riding coach.

Why do you hurry to condemn a boy of ten?
He'll grow soon enough to learn from his mistakes!
Speak kindly to him; that he may hear your advice,
    He plays games with his parents and kin.

To the youth of twenty life is pleasant;

---

39. Gen. 9: 3; *Gen. Rabbah*, 34. 13; *bSan* 59b.

He's fleet as a roe deer and romps the hills;
He scorns reproof, he mocks his teacher's voice;
   The net of a beautiful girl keeps him in bonds.

At age thirty he falls into a woman's hands.
Coming to, he finds himself entrapped,
Harried on all sides by a host of arrows:
   The needs of his wife and children.

Shaken and humbled at forty he must
Be content with his lot, - whether good or bad.
He hastens on his way; forsakes his friends;
   Dutifully, he stands at his post.

At fifty, remembering the wasted years,
He laments that death's day is approaching.
He holds the world's riches in contempt,
   He fears that his end is at hand.

They ask, "What has happened to this man of sixty?
He is a tree without root or branch;
His sinews are weak and flabby,
   They will not support him in his struggle."

If he lives to the age of seventy
No one pays attention to him;
He is a burden to himself and his cane,
   A mere encumbrance to his friends.

A hardship to his children at eighty
He cannot see or think.
Mocked and scorned by neighbor and kin,
   His cup is gall; wormwood his bread.

Later he is thought of as dead;
The man who thinks himself a stranger,

Who has no care or design for himself, save

His soul's fate and reward, that man is happy. [40]

--/-ס-/--/-ס-

בֶּן אֲדָמָה יִזְכֹּר בְּמוֹלַדְתּוֹ,
כִּי לְעֵת קֵץ יָשׁוּב לְיוֹלַדְתּוֹ.

"קוּם וְהַצְלַח!" יֹאמְרוּ לְבֶן חָמֵשׁ,
מַעֲלוֹתָיו עוֹלִים עֲלוֹת שֶׁמֶשׁ.
5   בֵּין שָׁדֵי אִם יִשְׁכַּב וְאַל יָמֵשׁ,
צַוְּארֵי אָב יִקַּח לְמֶרְכַּבְתּוֹ.

מַה תְּאִיצוּן מוּסָר לְבֶן עֶשֶׂר--
עוֹד מְעַט קָט יִגְדַּל וְיִוָּסֵר!
דַּבְּרוּ לוֹ חֵן חֵן וְיִתְבַּשָּׂר,
10   שַׁעֲשׁוּעָיו יוֹלְדָיו וּמִשְׁפַּחְתּוֹ.

מַה נְּעִימִים יָמִים לְבֶן עֶשְׂרִים,
קַל כְּעֹפֶר דּוֹלֵג עֲלֵי הָרִים,
בָּז לְמוּסָר, לוֹעֵג לְקוֹל מוֹרִים,
יַעֲלַת חֵן חֶבְלוֹ וּמַלְכֻּדְתּוֹ.

15   בֶּן שְׁלֹשִׁים נָפַל בְּיַד אֵשֶׁת,
קָם וְהִבִּיט--הִנּוּ בְּתוֹךְ רֶשֶׁת!
אִלְּצוּהוּ סָבִיב בְּנֵי קֶשֶׁת--
מִשְׁאֲלוֹת לֵב בָּנָיו וְלֵב אִשְׁתּוֹ.

נָע וְנִכְנַע מַשִּׂיג לְאַרְבָּעִים,
20   שָׂשׂ בְּחֶלְקוֹ--אִם רַע וְאִם נָעִים,
רָץ לְדָרְכּוֹ וַיַּעֲזֹב רֵעִים,

---

40. Schirmann, *Ha-Širah Ha-'Ivrit*, 1: 588–90; Levin, *Širey Ha-Qodeš...Ibn Ezra*, 2: 542–45. Schirmann in his *Širim Hadašim Min Ha-Geniza*, p. 235, suggests that on the basis of recently discovered documents from the Cairo Geniza, the above poem which he and Levin published in their Ibn Ezra collections may have been written by Judah Halevi.

עַל עֲמָלוֹ יַעֲמֹד בְּמִשְׁמַרְתּוֹ.

בֶּן חֲמִשִּׁים יִזְכֹּר יְמֵי הֶבֶל--
יֶאֱבַל כִּי קָרְבוּ יְמֵי אֵבֶל,
25   בָּז בְּעֵינָיו אֶת כָּל יְקָר תֵּבֵל,
כִּי יְפַחֵד פֶּן קָרְבָה עִתּוֹ.

שָׁאֲלוּ: מֶה הָיָה לְבֶן שִׁשִּׁים?
אֵין בְּעֵצָיו בַּדִּים וְשָׁרָשִׁים,
כִּי שְׂרִידָיו דַּלִּים וְנֶחֱלָשִׁים
30   לֹא יְקוּמוּן אִתּוֹ בְּמִלְחַמְתּוֹ.

אִם שְׁנוֹתָיו נָגְעוּ אֱלֵי שִׁבְעִים,
אֵין דְּבָרָיו נִרְאִים וְנִשְׁמָעִים--
רַק לְמַשָּׂא יִהְיֶה עֲלֵי רֵעִים,
מַעֲמָס עַל נַפְשׁוֹ וּמִשְׁעַנְתּוֹ.

35   בֶּן שְׁמֹנִים טֹרַח עֲלֵי בָנָיו,
אֵין לְבָבוֹ עִמּוֹ וְלֹא עֵינָיו,
בּוּז וְלַעַג לִבְנוֹ וְלִשְׁכֵנָיו,
רֹאשׁ בְּכוֹסוֹ גַּם לַעֲנָה פִתּוֹ.

אַחֲרֵי זֹאת כַּמֶּת יְהִי נֶחְשָׁב.
40   אַשְׁרֵי אִישׁ נֶחְשָׁב לְגֵר תּוֹשָׁב
אֵין בְּלִבּוֹ רַעְיוֹן וְלֹא מַחְשָׁב--
רַק בְּאַחֲרִית נַפְשׁוֹ וּמַשְׂכֻּרְתּוֹ.

Ibn Ezra's meditation on the ages of man belongs both to the gnomic verse genre of Hispano-Hebrew poetry and to the writings for the synagogue. In the Spanish liturgy, the poem was chanted as an "self-rebuke" (*tokhehah*) during the concluding service on the Day of Atonement. Samuel Ibn Nagrela treats this theme in his collections of aphorisms. [41] The early second century treatment of the theme by Rabbi Judah ben Temah [in *'Avot* 5. 24] qualifies as a prescription for the several ages, rather than an admonition: "At five, the study of Torah...At thirteen: fulfillment of the commandments...At eighteen: marriage...At twenty: seeking a livelihood..."

The somewhat later observation on man's life stages given in *Eccles. Rabbah* 1. 3 introduces a didactic element. Commenting on the seven "vanities" mentioned in Ecclesiastes, R. Samuel b. R. Isaac in the name of R. Samuel b. Eleazar is of the opinion that they refer to the seven worlds which a man beholds. [42] "At a year old he is like a king seated in a canopied litter, fondled and kissed by all. At two and three he is like a pig, sticking his hands in the gutters. At ten he skips like a kid. At twenty he is like a neighing horse, adorning his person and longing for a wife. Having married, he is like an ass [working for a livelihood]. When he has begotten children, he grows brazen like a dog to supply their food and wants. When he has become old, he is [bent] like an ape." Expanding on this rabbinic note, Ibn Nagrela [in his *Ben Qohelet*, #79] empowers the subject with an opportunity for dispensing stark *sententiae* on the gloomy fate that awaits all living creatures:

> The terrors of time come upon man...when he reaches sixty;
> From sixty to seventy he groans from the pain of age...[43]

In his presentation, Ibn Ezra combines the gnomic *mememto mori* character of the ages of man with an admonition to repentance. There is melancholy and regret in the swift transition from the "pleasant" twenties to the "entrapped" and "harried" thirties and the "shaken and humbled" forties. Reflecting the experiences of his own unhappy life, Ibn Ezra has a sullen view of human existence. Ibn Nagrela who fared much better than Ibn Ezra could celebrate the man of thirty who took "pride in his strength...youth and beauty" and rejoice with the one who at forty was "attached to the company of his old time friends." [44]

The misogyny in Ibn Ezra's, "At age thirty he falls into a woman's hands, /

---

41. Ibn Nagrela, *Ben Qohelet*, #79.
42. Cf. the seven stages of life in W. Shakespeare's *As You Like It*, Act II, scene 7.
43. Weinberger, *Jewish Prince*, p. 127.
44. Ibid.

Coming to, he finds himself entrapped," is not unfamiliar in Andalusian-Hebrew prosody. His younger contemporary, Judah Ibn Šabbetai, wrote a *maqāmah* in 1188 with the provocative title, *A Gift of Judah, the Misogynist* (*Minhat Yehudah, Soneh Ha-Našim*). In the mock-serious narrative, the protagonist, Zerah, hears his father Tahkemoni expatiate on the wiles of women ("Who can free himself from their chains?") [45] and resolves not to marry. Unrelieved dejection follows the man of fifty who remembers his "wasted years" leading to the eighty year old who "cannot see or think."

He who is a "stranger" in the present World, indifferent to its vanities, and is focused on winning the World to Come for his soul, will prosper. Again, the contrast between Ibn Ezra and Nagrela is significant in that the latter ends his account of human development with a lament for "my heart and flesh!" Nagrela had better reasons to mourn his successful career in the present world.

17. SELECTIONS FROM *HAY BEN MEQIS*

A. THE ENCOUNTER

Wise men, listen to me; scholars, hear my speech; young and old, take heed; lads and fools, pay attention. What I say is true, my argument is reasonable; I left home, I gave up my property, I abandoned my job, my relations, my country, because my mother's sons quarrelled with me; they made me keeper without a vineyard. I decided to leave, to find a place peaceful enough where, my soul would be rested and alone. But my senses (imagination, anger, and desire) would not leave me, though they heard what I said.

I looked up and there, in the meadow, a sage strolled by. He praised the Lord, exalted, and gave thanks. He was regal; like the angels, majestic, unaltered by days or years. His eyes were like doves, his temples like halves of a pomegranate. His back was not stooped, his strength undiminished. His sight was unimpaired and his vigor had not abated. As if annointed with oil, he had the fragrance of nard. His speech was most sweet and he was altogether desirable. "May you have peace in abundance," I said to him, "and

---

45. Schirmann, *Ha-Širah Ha-ʻIvrit*, 2: 71.

always speak with wisdom, and never err. Who are you? What is your name? What is your work? Where do you live?"

He replied in words like arranged pearls, in ordered phrases like the *Urim* and *Tummim*. "May God make your name famous," he said to me, "and may you prosper like an overflowing river; may the Lord be at your side and keep your feet clear of the snare! Hay ben Meqis is my name and the Holy City is my home. My tasks which you see me do, I perform tirelessly. I range over city and state, enter every nook and cranny. My father directed me in wisdom's way; he gave me knowledge and prudence. In the Holy City I was the darling at his side; sitting in his shade delighted me; I did not budge; His fruit was sweet and delicious to my taste. [46]

שִׁמְעוּ, חֲכָמִים, מִלַּי,/ וְיוֹדְעִים, הַאֲזִינוּ אֵלַי!/ בִּינוּ, אִישִׁים, וִישִׁישִׁים,/ וְהַקְשִׁיבוּ, בּוֹעֲרִים, וּנְעָרִים,/ כִּי אֱמֶת יֶהְגֶּה חִכִּי וּמִפְתַּח שְׂפָתַי--מֵישָׁרִים./ אֲזַי עָזַבְתִּי אֶת בֵּיתִי/ וְנָטַשְׁתִּי אֶת נַחֲלָתִי,/ הִנַּחְתִּי מְקוֹמִי/ וּמוֹלַדְתִּי וְעַמִּי,/ כִּי נֶחֱרוּ בִי בְּנֵי אִמִּי,/ שָׁמוּנִי נוֹטֵר לְלֹא כַרְמִי./ קַמְתִּי לִנְסֹעַ/ וּלְבַקֵּשׁ מַרְגּוֹעַ,/ כְּדֵי שֶׁתָּנוּחַ נִשְׁמָתִי/ וְתִנָּפֵשׁ נַפְשִׁי וְתִתְיַחֵד יְחִידָתִי,/ וְעַמִּי רֵעִים/ לִדְבָרַי שׁוֹמְעִים.

וָאֵרֶא--וְהִנֵּה אִישׁ זָקֵן הוֹלֵךְ בַּשָּׂדֶה/ מְשַׁבֵּחַ לָאֵל יִתְעַלֶּה וּמוֹדֶה./ דְּמוּתוֹ כִּדְמוּת הַמְּלָכִים/ וְהוֹדוֹ כְּהוֹד הַמַּלְאָכִים,/ לֹא הֶחֱלִיפוּהוּ הַזְּמַנִּים/ וְלֹא שִׁנּוּהוּ הַשָּׁנִים./ עֵינָיו כְּיוֹנִים/ וְרַקָּתוֹ כְּפֶלַח הָרִמּוֹנִים,/ לֹא עָוְתָה קוֹמָתוֹ וְלֹא כָשַׁל כֹּחוֹ,/ לֹא כָהֲתָה עֵינוֹ וְלֹא נָס לֵחֹה,/ שְׁמָנָיו טוֹבִים כְּרֵיחַ נְרָדִים,/ חִכּוֹ מַמְתַקִּים וְכֻלּוֹ מַחֲמַדִּים./ וָאֹמַר לוֹ, "שְׁלוֹמְךָ יִשְׂגֶּה/ וּבְחָכְמָה תָּמִיד תֶּהְגֶּה/ וְלַעַד לֹא תִשְׁגֶּה!/ בֶּן מִי אַתָּה וּמַה שְׁמֶךָ/ וּמַה מְּלַאכְתְּךָ וְאֵי-זֶה מְקוֹמֶךָ?"

וַיַּעֲנֵנִי בְמִלִּים,/ מְמֻלָּאִים בְּאַבְנֵי מַרְגָּלִים/ וּבִדְבָרִים סְדוּרִים/ כִּתָמִים וְאוּרִים./ וַיֹּאמֶר לִי, "יֵיטֵב אֱלֹהִים אֶת שְׁמֶךָ/ וִיהִי כַנָּהָר שְׁלוֹמֶךָ,/ יְהִי תָמִיד בְּכִסְלֶךָ/ וְיִשְׁמֹר מִלֶּכֶד רַגְלֶךָ!/ חַי בֶּן-מֵקִיץ שְׁמִי/ וְעִיר הַקֹּדֶשׁ מְקוֹמִי,/ וּמְלַאכְתִּי אֲשֶׁר אַתָּה רוֹאֶה/ אֶעֱשֶׂנָּה וְלֹא אֶלְאֶה--/ אֲשׁוֹטֵט בְּכָל עִיר וּמְדִינָה/ וּבְכָל צַד וּפִנָּה,/ וְאָבִי הִדְרִיכַנִי דֶּרֶךְ חָכְמָה/ וְלִמְּדַנִי דַעַת וּמְזִמָּה/ וָאֶהְיֶה אֶצְלוֹ אָמוֹן/ בְּבַעַל הָמוֹן/ בְּצִלּוֹ חִמַּדְתִּי וְיָשַׁבְתִּי וְלֹא אֶעְתָּק,/ כִּי פִרְיוֹ לַחֵךְ עָרֵב וְנִמְתָּק."

In his *Hay ben Meqis*, written in *maqāmah*-style rhymed prose, Ibn Ezra, the

46. Levin, *Yalqut Ibn Ezra*, p. 121; Schirmann, *Ha-Širah Ha-'Ivrit*, 1: 590–01.

restless vagabond, sets out on a tour of the heavenly spheres. The poem, which he presumably dedicated to Samuel Ibn Jāmi', is based on the Muslim philosopher Avicenna's *Hay ben Yoqẓān*. In his journey, Ibn Ezra is aided by a venerable sage from Jerusalem, who, it becomes apparent, is a personification of the poet's own intellect. The poet further reveals that the voyager is his own soul, now separated from his body: "I left home, I gave up my property." The reason for his departure is that "my mother's sons quarrelled with me," a phrase borrowed from Cant. 1: 6. The "mother's sons" are likely a reference to the limbs of the body who would lead the soul astray in the pursuit of worldly pleasures. Determined to free herself, the soul longs for the solitude needed to prepare for her mission. However, her senses will not depart and she is beset by "imagination," "anger," and "desire."

The soul now encounters Ḥay ben Meqiṣ, a venerable figure from Jerusalem whose father instructed him in "knowledge and prudence." He remembers the time spent with the father when he was the "darling at his side." In referring to himself with this conceit taken from Prov. 8: 30, Ḥay reveals that he is personified Wisdom, celebrated in the ode from chapter eight of that book. Characteristically, his speech is logical and orderly, the product of wise and reasonable thinking. Before setting out on the journey, the poet's soul is warned to "keep its feet clear of the snare." There is the continued fear that the senses, mentioned above, might interfere with the soul's progress.

B. JOURNEY'S BEGINNING

"Draw me after you, let us make haste," I said, "I exult and rejoice in you; I am made happy by your love, it delights me more than spiced wine and pomegranate drink." He cautioned me, "You will not be able to keep up with me and fly at my speed; your wings are broken and you have no pinions." "O that I had wings like a dove! I would fly away and be at rest!" I exclaimed. "My Lord, forgive my impudence; I have comitted my cause to you, entrusted you with my fortune. You are my hope and my confidence; bind up my wound and heal my hurt."

He took me to a path nearby which led to a broad and wide terrain divided into thirds, each dim and distant. One originated in the waters and ended in the heavens. Of the two remaining (and of primary value), the first extended to the east and the second to the west. Each cast its light upon the other and reciprocated its splendor. From time's beginning the world's estate was divided among them. Only he who is privy to God's secrets can ascend these lofty heights.

A fountain flows by the border of this terrain, its warble can be heard from a distance. From a river stream its waters become a mighty torrent. It heals every bruise and ache, it cures and brings relief. As we approached standing on its shore, he removed my clothes, threw them to the ground, and hastened me, naked, into the waters.

"Drink the waters from the fountain," he ordered me, "and sip the flow from its well. Then will your break be healed, your pinions repaired, and you will have wings to fly heavenward." I drank from the life-giving waters reviving the soul, and every hurt and infection disappeared, even grievous and lasting maladies. The waters were a balm to me, repairing the breach in my wing and pinion. [47]

אָמַרְתִּי, "מָשְׁכֵנִי אַחֲרֶיךָ נָרוּצָה,/ אָגִילָה בָךְ וְאֶעֱלֹצָה,/ בִּדְרָכֶיךָ אֶשְׂמַח וְאָשִׂישׂ/ מִיֵּין הָרֶקַח וּמֵעֲסִיס."/ וַיֹּאמֶר לִי, "לֹא תוּכַל לָרוּץ נֶגְדִּי/ וְלָעוּף עִמָּדִי--/ וּכְנָפֶיךָ נִשְׁבָּרִים/ וְאֵין לָךְ אֲבָרִים."/ וָאֹמַר, "מִי יִתֶּן-לִי אֵבֶר כַּיּוֹנָה,/ אָעוּפָה וְאֶשְׁכֹּנָה!/ בִּי אֲדֹנִי,/ אַל תֶּפֶן אֶל זְדוֹנִי,/ כִּי אֵלֶיךָ גִּלִּיתִי אֶת רִיבִי,/ וְעָלֶיךָ הִשְׁלַכְתִּי יְהָבִי/ וּלְךָ תוֹחַלְתִּי וְשִׂבְרִי--/ רְפָא חָלְיִי וַחֲבֹשׁ שִׁבְרִי!"/ וַיּוֹלִיכֵנִי דֶרֶךְ קְרוֹבָה/ אֶל אֶרֶץ אֲרֻכָּה וּרְחָבָה/ תֵּחָלֵק לִשְׁלֹשָׁה חֲלָקִים/ עֲמֻקִּים וּרְחוֹקִים:/ תְּחִלַּת הָאֶחָד מֵהֶם בַּמַּיִם/ וְסוֹפוֹ בַּשָּׁמַיִם,/ וּשְׁנַיִם הַנִּשְׁאָרִים/ אֲשֶׁר הֵמָּה הָעִקָּרִים--/ הָאֶחָד בַּמִּזְרָח קְצָתוֹ/ וְהַשֵּׁנִי בַּמַּעֲרָב רֵאשִׁיתוֹ,/ זֶה עַל זֶה יָהֵל אוֹרוֹ/ וְזֶה מִזֶּה יִלְבַּשׁ הֲדָרוֹ./ לָאֵלֶּה תֵּחָלֵק הָאָרֶץ בְּנַחֲלָה/ בָּרֹאשׁ וּבַתְּחִלָּה,/ וְלֹא יוּכַל לָלֶכֶת בְּאֵלֶּה הַמְּקוֹמוֹת הַגְּבֹהִים,/ כִּי אִם אִישׁ מָלֵא רוּחַ אֱלֹהִים.

וּבִקְצֵה הָאָרֶץ הַזֹּאת עַיִן תַּבִּיעַ,/ קוֹלָהּ מֵרָחוֹק תַּשְׁמִיעַ,/ פְּלָגֶיהָ--נְהָרִים/ וּמֵימֶיהָ--מַיִם אַדִּירִים,/ מְרַפִּים כָּל מַחַץ וּמַחֲלָה/ וּמַעֲלִים רְפוּאָה וּתְעָלָה./ וַאֲנַחְנוּ כַּאֲשֶׁר קָרַבְנוּ אֵלֶיהָ/ וְעָמַדְנוּ עָלֶיהָ,/ הִפְשִׁיטַנִי כְּתֻנְתִּי וְהִשְׁלִיכָהּ/ וַיּוֹרִידֵנִי עָרֹם לְתוֹכָהּ./ וַיֹּאמֶר לִי, "שְׁתֵה מַיִם מִמְּקוֹרָהּ/ וְנוֹזְלִים מִתּוֹךְ בְּאֵרָהּ,/ כִּי בָהּ יֵחָבְשׁוּ שְׁבָרֶיךָ/ וְיֵרָפְאוּ אֲבָרֶיךָ/ וְיִהְיוּ לְךָ כְנָפַיִם/ לָעוּף בַּשָּׁמַיִם."/ וָאֶשְׁתֶּה מִמֵּימֵי הַחַיִּים/ אֲשֶׁר לַנְּפָשׁוֹת מְחַיִּים,/ וַיָּסוּרוּ מִמֶּנִּי

47. Levin, *Yalqut Ibn Ezra*, pp. 124–25; Schirmann, *Ha-Širah Ha-'Ivrit* 1: 591–92.

מַכְאוֹבִים וּנְגָעִים/ וָחֳלָיִים נֶאֱמָנִים וְרָעִים,/ וַיִּהְיוּ לִי כַצָּרִי לַחֲבֹש אֶת שִׁבְרִי/ מִכְּנָפִי וְאֶבְרִי.

The poet's soul anxious to explore the heavenly spheres asks Ḥay, the intellect, to lead her. She is disappointed to learn that she will not be able to keep up with her guide since "her wings are broken" and without "pinions." She is not free to fly heavenward while carrying the baggage of her senses, "imagination," "anger" and "desire." Now pleading for relief, she is led by her compassionate Ḥay to view the three layers of the cosmos: the upper realm of incorporeal intelligible beings; the intermediate realm of the celestial spheres; and the lower sublunar earth. However, she must first be cleansed from the interference of her senses. To this end, she is directed to a purifying and healing fountain whose curative waters she drinks and finds that she is, at last, healed from her passions. In an extended metaphor, the soul, "naked," is "hastened" by the intellect into the flowing pool. The "naked" soul has resolved to shed her corrupting inclinations; only then can she be restored. It is likely that in this metaphor, Ibn Ezra had in mind the rabbinic comment [in *bT an* 16a], "One who has sinned and confesses his sin but does not repent may be compared to a man holding a dead reptile [which causes impurity] in his hand, for although he may immerse himself in all the waters of the world his immersion is of no avail to him."

In his account of the soul's cosmic journey guided by the intellect, Ibn Ezra acknowledges the influence of Avicenna's philosophical allegory, *Ḥay ben Yaqzān*. In several respects, however, Ibn Ezra's treatment of the theme differs from that of his Muslim predecessor. Characteristically, the Hebrew poet embellishes his story with a wide array of rhetorical figures, rich imagery and phonetic intensive phrasing, whereas Avicenna, the philosopher, is primarily concerned with presenting a rational argument supported by scholarly sources which he quotes at length. Moreover, Avicenna's voyager, unlike Ibn Ezra's, is merely informed (in abundant detail) of the cosmic realms, but does not venture to explore their sights and sounds. [48]

C. A TOUR OF THE EARTH

When I drank my fill and was healed from my hurt, he reached out his hand to take me and raise me from the fountain's depth. He led me to a land

---

48. Levin, *Avraham Ibn Ezra*, p. 183.

hoary with age that kills those who love it and devours its inhabitants. There we found tombs gloomy and dark, shunned by the sun and unfamiliar with the moon's glow. Behind them lay a boiling cauldron stoked by passion's heat; its flow did not cease, it churned on itself like sealed clay.

Those who live on the land are wretched and poor, their life, brutish and short. Yet, they build and plant even when they see their homes in ruin, their crops trampled under foot, their palaces in disarray, and their trees uprooted. All are destined to perish and no one will care or inquire.

Can they survive and not be scattered [to the winds]? Though joined by treaty and alliance against their many foes, they can find no peace or security, no contentment or joy. Every gaiety is modified by tragedy, every delight by lament, all mirth by disaster. Wisdom does not improve the lot of the wise, nor is the race won by the swift; the brave are not saved by their valor, and death's time overtakes them all. [49]

אֲנִי כַּאֲשֶׁר שָׁתִיתִי דַיִּי/ וְנִתְרַפֵּאתִי מֵחֳלָיִי,/ שָׁלַח יָדוֹ וּלְקָחַנִי/ וּמִמְּצוּלוֹת הָעַיִן הֶעֱלַנִי/
וַיְבִיאֵנִי אֶל מְדִינָה/ קְדוּמָה וִישָׁנָה/ הוֹרֶגֶת אוֹהֲבֶיהָ/ וְאוֹכֶלֶת יוֹשְׁבֶיהָ./ בְּתוֹכָהּ אֹהָלִים/
חֲשֵׁכִים וַאֲפֵלִים,/ הַשֶּׁמֶשׁ רְחוֹקָה מֵהֶם/ וְהַיָּרֵחַ לֹא יִזְרַח עֲלֵיהֶם./ וְאַחֲרֵיהֶם עֵין חַמָּה/
בְּתוֹכָהּ תָּבוֹא הַחַמָּה/ מְקוֹרָהּ אֵינֶנּוּ נִסְתָּם/ תִּתְהַפֵּךְ כְּחֹמֶר חוֹתָם.

וּבַמְּדִינָה אֲנָשִׁים/ דַּלִּים וְרָשִׁים,/ יְמֵיהֶם מְעַט וְרָעִים/ וְהֵמָּה בּוֹנִים וְנוֹטְעִים/ וְרוֹאִים
הַבִּנְיָנִים יֵהָרְסוּ/ וְהַזְּרָעִים יֵרָמְסוּ/ וְהָאַרְמוֹנִים יִסָּתְרוּ/ וְהָאִילָנִים יֵעָקְרוּ/ וְהַכֹּל נוֹפְלִים
בְּמוֹקֵשׁ/ אֵין דּוֹרֵשׁ וְאֵין מְבַקֵּשׁ./ וְאֵיךְ יַעֲמֹדוּ/ וְלֹא יִתְפָּרְדוּ?/ וְהֵמָּה מְקֻבָּצִים
וּמְחֻבָּרִים/ מֵאוֹיְבִים וְצָרִים!/ אֵין לָהֶם שֶׁקֶט וְשַׁלְוָה/ וְנַחַת וְחֶדְוָה,/ כִּי הַדְּבָרִים הַטּוֹבִים/
בְּרָעִים מְעֹרָבִים:/ הַחֶדְוָה/ בְּמַדְוֶה,/ וְהַשִּׂמְחָה/ בַּאֲנָחָה,/ וְהַשָּׂשׂוֹן/ בְּאָסוֹן./ הַיּוֹדְעִים לֹא
יִמְצְאוּ חֵן בְּדַעְתָּם/ וְהַקַּלִּים לֹא יָרוּצוּ בְּקַלּוּתָם,/ וְאַנְשֵׁי חַיִל לֹא יִנָּצְלוּ בְחֵילָם,/ כִּי עֵת
וָפֶגַע יִקְרֶה אֶת כֻּלָּם!

Now that the soul has been purged from her corrupting senses, she begins her cosmic tour guided by divine wisdom. Their first destination is the sublunar earth that "devours its dwellers." The language is borrowed from the reconnaissance report of the land of Canaan by the Israelite spies [in Num. 13: 32]. In this inhospitable

49. Levin, *Yalqut Ibn Ezra*, p. 128; Schirmann, *Ha-Širah Ha-'Ivrit*, pp. 593–94.

realm, man is destined for the sunless grave and often worse; beyond the grave is hell's churning cauldron. Despite their wretched existence and indifference to each other, they persevere and thereby earn the poet's admiration. Will the human race survive? The poet is not optimistic.

For Ibn Ezra, the redeeming element in man's earthly career is his ability to be guided by wisdom and reason. This talent enables the soul to focus on its higher destiny in the celestial realm where "death's time" is powerless. This theme would be echoed by Italy's preeminent poet, Dante Alighieri (1265–1321) in his *Divina Commedia*. Like Ibn Ezra's protagonist, Dante makes the visionary cosmic journey beyond the grave and records his impressions from memory. His Ḥay ben Meqiṣ is the Latin poet Virgil, master of classical reason. In his quest to ascend the mountain of spiritual fulfillment, Dante also encounters impediments in the form of "avarice," "gluttony," and "lust." However, unlike Ibn Ezra's voyager who must be reminded of his failings ("Keep your feet clear of the snare"), Dante is fully aware of being unworthy. When he and Virgil set out on their epic travels from the dark wood (a symbol of man's sinful nature), Dante is hesitant:

> But why should I come here? or who permits it?
> I am not Aeneas, I am not Paul;
> Neither I myself nor others think me worthy. (*Prologue: Inferno II, line 31*).

In confessing his inadequacy, Dante, the Christian, reflects the Thomistic tension between grace and human effort, a problem that Ibn Ezra did not have. [50]

D. THE RIM OF FIRE

On the borders of this terrain, a fire raged reaching up into the heavens. In soaring flames and smoldering embers its lustre flashed like swords and sparkled like stars. Unquenched by rain, unaltered by flood. Rocks melted in its pyre; stones oozed from its blaze.

When I saw it and took note of its size, my hands went weak and my knees buckled; grief dimmed my eyes, my face fell from fear. I faltered on my

---

50. F. Fergusson, *Dante*, pp. 89, 99.

feet; my soul trembled. The sage came to my side, stood me on my feet, and said, "Do not faint from fear! When you walk through fire you shall not be burned, and the flames shall not consume you." He went before me, saying, "Come, God has blessed you." Promptly, he took my hand and led me through the pyre. I saw the flames licking at us, their sparks firing at our side. Surrounded by the blaze, we came through unharmed. [51]

וְאַחֲרֵי הַגְּבוּל הַזֶּה אֵשׁ אוֹכֵלָה,/ אֶל הַשָּׁמַיִם עוֹלָה,/ גֶּחָלֶיהָ בּוֹעֲרִים,/ וּרְשָׁפֶיהָ סוֹעֲרִים/
לְהָבֶיהָ כַּחֲרָבִים,/ וּשְׁבִיבֶיהָ כַּכּוֹכָבִים,/ לֹא יְכַבֶּהָ הַגְּשָׁמִים/ וְלֹא יִשְׁטְפוּהָ הַיַּמִּים./
הַסְּלָעִים יִמַּסּוּ מִמְּדוּרוֹתֶיהָ/ וְהַצּוּרִים יָזוּבוּ מִשַּׁלְהֲבוֹתֶיהָ.

אָנֹכִי כַּאֲשֶׁר רָאִיתִי אוֹתָהּ/ וְחָזִיתִי דְמוּתָהּ,/ רָפוּ יָדַי וְכָשְׁלוּ בִרְכַּי/ וְעָשְׁשׁוּ מִכַּעַס עֵינַי/
וְנָפְלוּ מִפַּחַד פָּנַי,/ וְלֹא יָכֹלְתִּי לַעֲמֹד,/ כִּי נַפְשִׁי נִבְהֲלָה מְאֹד./ וַיִּגַּשׁ הָאִישׁ אֵלַי/
וַיַּעֲמִידֵנִי עַל רַגְלַי/ וַיֹּאמֶר אֵלַי,/ "אַל תִּירָא וְאַל יֵרַךְ לְבָבָךְ,/ כִּי תֵלֵךְ בְּמוֹ אֵשׁ לֹא
תִכָּוֶה וְלֶהָבָה לֹא תִבְעַר בָּךְ!"/ וַיַּעֲבֹר עַל פָּנַי/ וַיֹּאמֶר, "בּוֹא, בְּרוּךְ יְיָ!"/ וַיִּקָּחֵנִי מְהֵרָה/
וַיַּעֲבִירֵנִי בַּמְּדוּרָה./ וָאֵרֶא הַלְּהָבִים לְפָנֵינוּ מְשַׁקִּים/ וְהַשְּׁבִיבִים סְבִיבוֹתֵינוּ דּוֹלְקִים/
וְהָרְשָׁפִים אוֹתָנוּ מַקִּיפִים--/ וַאֲנַחְנוּ שְׁלֵמִים וְאֵין אָנוּ נִשְׂרָפִים.

In his tour of the earth, Ibn Ezra relies on Aristotle's physics and Ptolemy's geocentric astronomy. In the view of Ibn Ezra's younger contemporary, the Jewish Aristotelian, Abraham Ibn Daud (1110–1180), the natural arrangement of the four elements, earth, water, air, and fire is considered to be circular. Earth, characterized by dryness and cold, is in the center; then water, moisture and cold; air, moisture and heat; fire, dryness, and heat. [52] In order for Ibn Ezra's protagonist to travel beyond earth's borders, he must first penetrate its outer fiery layer. Overwhelmed with fear of the massive flames and the roaring inferno, he is reluctant to proceed. Reassured by his sagacious guide (using God's language in comforting Israel, in Is. 43: 2), he successfully negotiates the menacing wall of fire.

In the previous episode, the poet conveys the lesson that wisdom [= Hay ben Meqis] can help the soul see its earthly career in perspective and direct its attention to a higher purpose beyond the grave. In the present encounter with fiery nature, the soul learns that wisdom can also enable it to overcome fear.

---

51. Levin, *Yalqut Ibn Ezra*, p. 127; Schirmann, *Ha-Širah Ha-'Ivrit*, 1: 593–94.
52. See C. Sirat, *A History of Jewish Philosophy*, p. 145.

E. THE PLANETS

As we left the terrain and escaped its heat, I observed that near the earth were eight (spheric) kingdoms with large mansions, fortified and sturdy like mirrors of cast metal. Their towers are pressed close to each other so that no air can pass between them. They are held together in an intimate embrace and cannot be separated; their habits are constant and unchanging. They command a host of stars too numerous to count.

Musicians all, they sing together God's praises and are always prepared to serve their Maker. Faithful to their charge, they honor their contract. No evil befalls them, no scourge comes near their tent. They are animated by a yearning; their labor is borne out of love (for God). Resolve is written on their features, their souls brim with desire. From the clear heavens--there resides the fountain of gardens and the well of life-giving waters--light beams down upon them. [53]

וַיְהִי כַּאֲשֶׁר יָצָאנוּ מִתְּחוּמָם/ וְנִצַּלְנוּ מֵחֻמָּם,/ וָאֵרֶא אֵצֶל הַמְּדִינָה/ מַמְלְכוֹת שְׁמֹנָה,/
לָהֶם זְבוּלִים/ עֲצוּמִים וּגְדוֹלִים,/ אַמִּיצִים וַחֲזָקִים/ וְכִרְאִי מוּצָקִים,/ אֶחָד בְּאֶחָד יִגָּשׁוּ
גַּגֵּיהֶם/ וְרוּחַ לֹא יָבוֹא בֵינֵיהֶם,/ אִישׁ בְּאָחִיהוּ יְדֻבָּקוּ/ יִתְלַכְּדוּ וְלֹא יִתְפָּרָקוּ,/ מִנְהֲגוּתָם
לֹא תַחֲלֹף וְלֹא תִשְׁתַּנֶּה/ וְצִבְאוֹתָם לֹא תִסָּפֵר וְלֹא תִמָּנֶה.

וְכֻלָּם מְנַצְּחִים/ וּבְרָן יַחַד מְשַׁבְּחִים,/ לְעוֹלָם עוֹמְדִים/ וּלְצוּרָם עוֹבְדִים,/ שׁוֹמְרִים
חֻקּוֹתָם/ וּמַחֲזִיקִים בִּבְרִיתָם,/ רָעָה לֹא תְאֻנֶּה/ וְנֶגַע לֹא יִקְרַב בְּאָהֳלֵיהֶם./ לְכִתָּם--לֶכֶת
שׁוֹאֲפִים,/ וַעֲבוֹדָתָם --עֲבוֹדַת נִכְסָפִים,/ צוּרוֹתָם שׁוֹקְדוֹת/ וְנַפְשׁוֹתָם סוֹלְדוֹת,/ כִּי עֲלֵיהֶם
יִזְרַח הָאוֹר/ מִמְּעוֹן טָהוֹר וְנָאוֹר,/ שָׁמָּה מַעְיַן גַּנִּים/ בְּאֵר מַיִם חַיִּים.

Upon leaving the earth, the voyagers encounter the realm of the eight spheres, including the Moon, Mercury, Venus, the Sun, Mars, Jupiter, Saturn and the sphere of the twelve constellations of the zodiac. In medieval astronomy the spheres are placed one above the other "like layers of onions" and between them no vacuum

---

53. Levin, *Yalqut Ibn Ezra*, pp. 127-28; Schirmann, *Ha-Širah Ha-'Ivrit*, 1: 594.

intervenes. [54] The spheres as music makers is a conceit which Jewish scholars derive from Job 38: 7, "When the morning stars sang." In his biblical commentary on this verse, Ibn Ezra suggests that the musical sounds are made by the rapid motion of the spheres circling the earth, a view proposed earlier by the Pythagoreans. [55]

Unlike the modern astronomer who, thanks to Isaac Newton, proposes that the motion of the planets is self-explanatory and hence, self-sufficient, Ibn Ezra and his medieval contemporaries considered the cosmos to be under God's direct control. The spheres and stars were believed by Jewish Aristotelians to be living beings endowed with a soul and with knowledge and intelligence. Their movement was explained by Maimonides as being motivated by a "desire for the thing imagined...the object of which an idea has been formed." Hence, he argues, "the heavenly sphere must have a desire for the ideal which it has comprehended, and that ideal, for which it has a desire, is God...When we say that God moves the spheres, we mean it in the following sense: the spheres have a desire to become similar to the ideal comprehended by them." [56]

Ibn Ezra's view that light from the heavens beams down upon the spheres is elaborated by Maimonides, who, after noting that Creation is divided into (1) "the pure Intelligences," (2) "the bodies of the spheres" and (3) "the transient earthly beings," concludes that "the ruling power emanated from the Creator, and is received by the Intelligences according to their order; from the Intelligences part of the good and the light bestowed upon them is communicated to the spheres, and the latter...transmit forces and properties unto the beings of this transient world." [57]

F. VENUS

The ladies in the third kingdom are carefree. With lyres held in hand, they play and celebrate with pipes and nightingales. With drum and timbrel, cymbal and harp, they whirl and leap, dance and sing.

---

54. See Maimonides, *Mišneh Torah, Sefer Ha-Madda'*, 3. 3.
55. Maimonides, *Moreh Ha-Nevukhim*, 2. 8.
56. Maimonides, *Moreh Ha-Nevukhim*, 2. 4.
57. Ibid., 2. 11.

They are ruled by a queen, soft–skinned and delicate, with a face like the rising sun and the full moon. Her eyes are piercing swords, her teeth, a flock of shorn ewes all alike and flawless. Her lips are a crimson thread, her locks are wavy, black as a raven. Her cheeks are halves of a pomegranate behind her veil. Her navel is a rounded bowl and her demeanor resembles the sun. She radiates light and all who look upon her are awed and aroused. [58]

וּבַמַּמְלָכָה הַשְּׁלִישִׁית נָשִׁים שַׁאֲנַוּוֹת,/ מְנַגְּנוֹת וּמְעַנּוֹת,/ תּוֹפְשׂוֹת כִּנּוֹרִים/ וְעוּגָבִים
וּזְמִירִים/ וְתֻפִּים וּמְחוֹלִים/ צְלָצְלִים וּנְבָלִים/ מְפַזְּזוֹת וּמְכַרְכְּרוֹת/ וּמְרַקְּדוֹת וּמְשׁוֹרְרוֹת./
עֲלֵיהֶן מַלְכָּה/ עֶנְגָּה וְרַכָּה,/ פָּנֶיהָ כַשֶּׁמֶשׁ בְּצֵאתוֹ/ וְכַיָּרֵחַ בְּתֻמָּתוֹ./ עֵינֶיהָ כַּחֲרָבוֹת/
וְשִׁנֶּיהָ כְּעֵדֶר הַקְּצוּבוֹת/ שֶׁכֻּלָּם מַתְאִימוֹת/ וּמִשְׁכוֹל שְׁלֵמוֹת/ כְּחוּט הַשָּׁנִי שְׂפָתוֹתֶיהָ/
וּכְעֵצֵין הָעוֹרֵב קְוֻצּוֹתֶיהָ,/ כְּפֶלַח הָרִמּוֹן רַקָּתָהּ/ מִבַּעַד לְצַמָּתָהּ/ אַגַּן הַסַּהַר שָׁרְרָהּ/ וְתֹאַר
הַחַמָּה תָּאֲרָהּ./ אוֹרָהּ יִגַּהּ וְיָהֵל--/ וְכָל רֹאָהּ יִתְמַהּ וְיִבָּהֵל.

The moon is the first kingdom in the itinerary of the voyagers. They find its inhabitant's "clean and wholesome," who with their young, energetic bodies are given to racing and are tireless. They are the officers of the sun whom they fear and whose radiance they reflect. The phases of the moon are determined by its distance from the sun. Departing the moon to visit Mercury, they are impressed with its noblemen and scholars, engineers and architects like Bezalel and Oholiab, builders of the desert sanctuary. Mercury's citizens are ruled by the sun's scribe who is privy to his master's movements, and while keeping a respectable distance from him is never far from his sight.

In Ibn Ezra's astrology the personified planets are empowered by God with the governance of the sublunar world. In his commentary on Ex. 33: 23, he writes, "Whatever the configuration of stars existing at his birth has decreed for an individual will surely befall him." The architects Bezalel and Oholiab were probably born on Mercury's day, Wednesday, or on its night which is "the one followed by

---

58. Levin, *Yalqut Ibn Ezra*, pp. 128–29; Schirmann, *Ha-Širah Ha-'Ivrit*, 1: 595.

Sunday." [59] This would account for their special gifts. In his characterization of Mercury, Ibn Ezra follows the view of the Hispanic–Hebrew philosopher and poet Solomon Ibn Gabirol who, in his epic poem, *Keter Malkhut*, 13, refers to Mercury as "the star of prudence and wisdom."

Likewise, the description of Venus owes much to Ibn Gabirol who pictures the planet as "a queen amid her hosts, her garments adorned like a bride's," and in her realm there is "peace and prosperity, dancing and delight." Ibn Ezra then embellishes the portrait of Venus with figures from Cant. 4: 2–3; 7: 3 ("Her teeth, a flock of shorn ewes...Her lips a crimson thread...Her navel is a rounded bowl") and from Arabic love poetry ("[Her] face [is] like the full moon. Her eyes are piercing swords). [60]

G. MARS

In Mars, the fifth kingdom, men were ruddy, spilling blood. Schemers resorting to flattery, they plunder at will. They make quarreling an art; war is their specialty. After taking bribes they murder their victims, leave the corpses lying on the ground and feed on their spoils. They love being wicked and deceitful and despise learning and prudence.

Their ruler is a contentious man given to fits of anger. With sword drawn he gnashes his teeth. His lancers are combat-ready, his spearmen prepared; his arrows are honed and his bows are bent and strung. His horses' hooves are flinty hard and his chariots ride like the whirlwind. The innocent are killed and the poor are robbed. He thrives on mischief; making trouble is his stock–in–trade. He is not embarrassed to tell a lie, nor ashamed of his lechery. [61]

וּבַמַּמְלָכָה הַחֲמִישִׁית אֲנָשִׁים אֲדֻמִּים/ שׁוֹפְכֵי דָמִים,/ סֵעֲפִים/ וַחֲנֵפִים/ וְשׁוֹדְדִים/
וּמְזִידִים./ הַקְּרָב אוּמְנוּתָם/ וְהַמִּלְחָמָה מְלַאכְתָּם,/ הַשֹּׁחַד לוֹקְחִים/ וְהַנְּפָשׁוֹת רוֹצְחִים,/
מַפִּילִים הַחֲלָלִים/ וְאוֹכְלִים הַשְּׁלָלִים,/ אוֹהֲבֵי אָוֶן וּמִרְמָה/ וְשׂוֹנְאֵי דַעַת וּמְזִמָּה./

59. See Abraham Ibn Ezra, *Reʾšit Hokhmah*, p. 201.

60. A. R. Nykl, *Hispano-Arabic Poetry*, p. 109; A. J. Arberry, *Arabic Poetry*, p. 20.

61. Levin, *Yalquṭ Ibn Ezra*, p. 129; Schirmann, *Ha-Širah Ha-ʿIvrit*, 1: 595–96.

שִׁלְטוֹנָם--אִישׁ מִלְחָמָה/ וּבַעַל חֵמָה,/ חֲרָבָיו מוֹרֵק/ וְשִׁנָּיו חוֹרֵק./ רְמָחָיו מוּכָנִים
וַחֲנִיתוֹתָיו עֲרוּכוֹת/ חִצָּיו שְׁנוּנִים וְקַשְׁתוֹתָיו דְּרוּכוֹת,/ פַּרְסוֹת סוּסָיו כַּצַּר נֶחְשָׁבוּ/
וְגַלְגִּלָּיו כַּסּוּפָה יִרְכָּבוּ./ הוֹרֵג נְקִיִּים/ וְגוֹזֵל עֲנִיִּים,/ הָאָוֶן פָּעֳלוֹ/ וְהֶעָמָל עֲמָלוֹ,/ לֹא
יִכָּלֵם מִדַּבֵּר מִרְמָה/ וְלֹא יֵבוֹשׁ מֵעֲשׂוֹת זִמָּה.

Before entering Mars, the voyagers visit the Sun, the fourth sphere, inhabited
by heroic men radiating light. Their monarch is like the flushed "bridegroom coming
out from his wedding canopy rejoicing as he bravely runs his course," a conceit
borrowed from Ps. 19: 6. "Like a shepherd [the Sun] feeds his flock," and "leads them
with wisdom." Its providential care for humankind is affirmed by Ibn Ezra in his
commentary on Ps. 19: 5 where he writes that "all living beings are dependent upon
the Sun."

Intelligence is one of the human qualities associated with the Sun, [62] and in
this capacity it serves as a buffer between the peace-loving ladies in Venus and the
warring men of Mars. The imagery of Martian "arrows honed,...bows bent and
strung,...horses' hoofs...flinty hard, and chariots...like the whirlwind," is adapted from a
description of Assyrian warriors in Is. 5: 28.

The red planet conjured up visions of blood-letting, violence and heat in the
medieval mind. However, the intelligent man, privy to astral behavior, may
anticipate that Mars, the hot planet, may cause him to be ill on Wednesday, its
particular day. In order to be protected from "the decrees of the stars" (diney
ha-mazzalot), he will dispense with all "hot" foods at that time. This is the power of
"wisdom" which in the form of the Sun mediates between Venus and Mars, even as
it enables a person to overcome the predictions of his horoscope. [63]

Throughout their journey "wisdom" has come to their aid, in suppressing the
demands of the senses and in overpowering fear. The pair continue on their tour of
the planets, visiting Jupiter with its "virtuous men" who disdain material wealth.
They are ruled by a just king who never resorts to violence. Their next stop is
Saturn, populated by cunning merchants, followed by the ninth sphere with the

---

62. Ibn Ezra, Re'šit Hokhmah, p. 198.
63. Ibn Ezra, Re'šit Hokhmah, p. 198; idem, Sefer Ha-Moladot, p. 66a; Langermann,
"Astrological Themes in Ibn Ezra," pp. 53-54.

twelve constellations of the zodiac. Beyond lies the Primum Mobile, a sphere built on formless void ('al tohu wa-vohu musad) whose movement sets in motion all that lies below it.

Standing at its edge, the cosmic tourists can see the realm of the angels and hear their hymns in praise of God.

"Is there anything else that I have not seen," asks the poet of his guide.

"Yes," is the response, "there is a 'place' unlike any other." That "place" is the seat of God, hidden from view and beyond time and space.

"How may I know it?" says the poet, "I have a strong desire to see it."

"If you will trust me, obey my instructions and follow me without fail. Being privy to your soul according to your talent and effort, you will be able to know and see Him," answered the wise Hay ben Meqis. With "the power of the soul, which is wisdom," man can transcend his limitations and ascend to God's "place." [64]

18.   A GAME OF CHESS

> I shall sing the praises of a staged battle, devised in early antiquity;
> Men of intellect conceived it in an arrangement of eight rows,
> Each divided into eight stations on a slate.
> Troops are deployed in the squared rows;
> Commanders with their regiments poised for combat face each other;
> They are ready for war whether advancing or encamping.
> Yet, no sword is drawn throughout the fray; theirs is a battle of wits.
> They are recognized by their emblems, the marks engraved
>   upon their bodies;
> Watching their movements, one could imagine them to be Moors
>   and Christians.
> The Moors begin the attack and the Christians fall back;
> First in the fracas are the foot-soldiers making their way to the front.

---

64. Ibn Ezra, *Sefer Ha-Moladot*, p. 65b ff.

Resisting them are the infantry, outflanking their foes;
Their forward march is not detoured; they do not retreat to the rear.
By choice they are the first to leap into action in three strides in
    any direction.
If they forage far from their barracks and reach the eight station,
They are free to range on all fronts like a governor; they are his
    equal in the struggle.
The governor is given wide latititude; his forays extend to four stations.
Now the elephant approaches primed for the contest; he stands to the side
    waiting to ambush;
He moves about like a governor, though he has the edge since
    [the elephant] is limited to three paces.
The steed races easily into combat, yet he chooses a winding path;
His movements are meandering and uneven confined to three stations.
Straight is the path of the rook down the length and breadth of the field;
He avoids the detours, his route is without curves and bends.
The king turns in all directions seeking to assist his subjects.
He is cautious in his forays whether at home or abroad in his camp.
When his enemy ascends upon him with malice, he is warned and tries
    to escape.
When the fearful rook is in pursuit driving him from chamber to chamber,
He will try to elude him, or find shelter with his soldiers.
All are bent on killing each other; with fury they destroy themselves.
The kings' champions are fallen, yet no blood was shed.
In one campaign the Moors prevail as Christians flee before them.
Now the Christians have the advantage; the Moors and their king are
    weakened from combat;
When the king is seized in an ambush, without mercy he is placed in
    a net;
Unable to save himself, there is no fortified city to which he can flee!
Condemned by the enemy, he submits; he is now without hope and is
    taken to his death;
His soldiers have perished fighting for his cause; their lives a ransom
    for his own;
Seeing their leader stricken, they leave the field, their glory vanished;

And yet, these mortally wounded will rise again
And once more they will do battle. [65]

אֲשׁוֹרֵר שִׁיר בְּמִלְחָמָה עֲרוּכָה/ קְדוּמָה מִן יְמֵי קֶדֶם נְסוּכָה.
עֲרַכְתִּיהָ מְתֵי שֵׂכֶל וּבִינָה,/ קְבַעְתִּיהָ עֲלֵי טוּרִים שְׁמֹנָה.
וְעַל כָּל טוּר וְטוּר בָּהֶם חֲקוּקוֹת/ עֲלֵי לוּחַ שְׁמֹנֶה מַחֲלָקוֹת,
וְהַטּוּרִים מְרֻבָּעִים רְצוּפִים/ וְשָׁם הַמַּחֲנוֹת עוֹמְדִים צְפוּפִים.
5   מְלָכִים נִצָּבוּ עִם מַחֲנֵיהֶם/ לְהִלָּחֵם, וְרֶוַח בֵּין שְׁנֵיהֶם.
פְּנֵי כֻלָּם לְהִלָּחֵם נְכוֹנִים,/ וְהֵמָּה נוֹסְעִים תָּמִיד וְחוֹנִים,
וְאֵין שׁוֹלְפִים בְּמִלְחַמְתָּם חֲרָבוֹת,/ וּמִלְחַמְתָּם--מְלֶאכֶת מַחֲשָׁבוֹת,
וְנִכָּרִים בְּסִימָנִים וְאוֹתוֹת,/ בְּפִגְרֵיהֶם רְשׁוּמוֹת וַחֲרוּתוֹת.
וְאָדָם יֶחֱזֶה אוֹתָם רְגוּשִׁים/ יְדַמֶּה כִּי אֲדוֹמִים הֵם וְכוּשִׁים.
10 וְכוּשִׁים בַּקְּרָב פּוֹשְׁטִים יְדֵיהֶם,/ אֲדוֹמִים יֵצְאוּ אֶל אַחֲרֵיהֶם,
וְהָרַגְלִים יְבוֹאוּן בַּתְּחִלָּה/ לַמִּלְחָמָה לְנֹכַח הַמְּסִלָּה.
וְהָרַגְלִי יְהִי הוֹלֵךְ לְנֶגְדּוֹ,/ וְאֶת אוֹיְבוֹ יְהִי נוֹטֶה לְלָכְדוֹ,
וְלֹא יַטֶּה בְּעֵת לֶכֶת אֲשׁוּרָיו,/ וְלֹא יָשִׂים פְּעָמָיו לַאֲחוֹרָיו,
וְאִם יִרְצֶה--יְדַלֵּג בַּתְּחִלָּה/ לְכָל עֵבֶר שְׁלֹשָׁה בַּמְּסִלָּה.
15 וְאִם יִרְחַק וְיָנוּד מִזְּבוּלוֹ/ וְעַד טוּר הַשְּׁמִינִי יַעֲלֶה לּוֹ--
כְּמוֹ פֶרֶז לְכָל פָּנִים יְהִי שָׁב/ וּמִלְחַמְתּוֹ כְּמִלְחַמְתּוֹ תַּחְשַׁב.
וְהַפֶּרֶז יְהִי מַטֶּה פְּסָעָיו/ וּמַסָּעָיו לְאַרְבַּעַת רְבָעָיו.
וְהַפִּיל בַּקְּרָב הוֹלֵךְ וְקָרֵב,/ וְהוּא נִצָּב עֲלֵי הַצַּד כְּאוֹרֵב,
כְּמוֹ פֶרֶז הֲלִכָתוֹ--אֲבָל יֵשׁ/ לְזֶה יִתְרוֹן לְמָה שֶׁהוּא מְשַׁלֵּשׁ.
20 וְהַסּוּס בַּקְּרָב רַגְלוֹ מְאֹד קַל,/ וְיִתְהַלֵּךְ עֲלֵי דֶרֶךְ מְעַקָּל,
עֲקַלְקַלּוֹת דְּרָכָיו לֹא סְלוּלוֹת,/ בְּתוֹךְ בָּתִּים שְׁלֹשָׁה לוֹ גְבוּלוֹת
וְהָרוּךְ יַהֲלֹךְ מִישׁוֹר בְּדַרְכּוֹ,/ וּבַשָּׂדֶה עֲלֵי רָחְבּוֹ וְאָרְכּוֹ,
וְדַרְכֵי עִקְּשִׁים הוּא לֹא יְבַקֵּשׁ,/ נְתִיבוֹ מִבְּלִי נִפְתָּל וְעִקֵּשׁ.
וְהַמֶּלֶךְ מְהַלֵּךְ עַל צְדָדָיו,/ לְכָל רוּחוֹת וְיַעֲזֹר אֶת עֲבָדָיו,
25 וְיִזָּהֵר בְּעֵת שִׁבְתּוֹ וְצֵאתוֹ/ לְהִלָּחֵם וּבִמְקוֹם תַּחֲנוֹתוֹ,
וְאִם אוֹיְבוֹ בְּאֵיכָה יַעֲלֶה לוֹ/ וְיִנָּעֵר בּוֹ--וְיִבְרַח מִגְּבוּלוֹ.
וְאִם הָרוּךְ בְּאֵימָה יֶהְדְּפֵהוּ/ וּמֵחֶדֶר לְחֶדֶר יִרְדְּפֵהוּ--
וְיֵשׁ עִתִּים אֲשֶׁר יִבְרַח לְפָנָיו,/ וְעִתִּים יֵשׁ לְסַתְרוֹ לוֹ הֲמוֹנָיו.
וְכֻלָּם הוֹרְגִים אֵלֶּה לְאֵלֶּה,/ וְזֶה אֶת זֶה בְּרֹב חֵמָה מְכַלֶּה,
30 וְגִבּוֹרֵי שְׁנֵים הַמְּלָכִים/ חֲלָלִים מִבְּלִי דָמִים שְׁפוּכִים.
וְעִתִּים יִגְבְּרוּ כוּשִׁים עֲלֵיהֶם--/ וְיָנוּסוּ אֲדוֹמִים מִפְּנֵיהֶם,

65. Schirmann, *Ha-Širah Ha-'Ivrit*, 1: 585–87.

וְעָתִים כִּי אֱדוֹם יִגְבַּר--וְכוּשִׁים / וּמַלְכָּם בַּקֶּרֶב הֵם נֶחֱלָשִׁים.
וְהַמֶּלֶךְ יְהִי נִתְפָּשׂ בְּשַׁחְתָּם/ בְּלִי חֶמְלָה וְיִלָּכֵד בְּרִשְׁתָּם,
וְאֵין מָנוֹס לְהִנָּצֵל וּמִפְלָט/ וְאֵין מִבְרָח לְעִיר מִבְצָר וּמִקְלָט!
35 וְעַל יַד צַר יְהִי נִשְׁפָּט וְנִשְׁמָט/ וְאֵין מַצִּיל--וְלַהֲרֹג יְהִי מָט.
וְחֵילוֹ בַּעֲדוֹ כֻלָּם יְמוּתוּן/ וְאֶת נַפְשָׁם פְּדוּת נַפְשׁוֹ יְשִׁיתוּן,
וְתִפְאַרְתָּם כְּבָר נָסְעָה וְאֵינָם/ בְּשׁוּרָם שֶׁכְּבָר נִגַּף אֲדוֹנָם,
וְיוֹסִיפוּ לְהִלָּחֵם שְׁנִיָּה--/ וְיֵשׁ עוֹד לַהֲרוּגֵיהֶם תְּחִיָּה!

Ibn Ezra's playful commentary on the game of chess--one of three he wrote
on the subject--is in marked contrast to the serious tone of the previous cosmic tour
in the company of personified "wisdom." The poet and polymath whose range of
interests encompassed all the known sciences of his day, could find time for leisure
hours diversion in a game that was not without its redeeming features. This was "a
battle of wits" that required sustained intelligence. Ibn Ezra's poems on the
subject--probably the oldest of their kind by a European author--were designed to
teach the uninitiated the rules of the game. The poet's colorful method of instruction
envisions chess as a contest between the Moors, the black pieces, and the Christians,
the red. Unlike current practice, the black, in Ibn Ezra's day, had the opening move
(line 10) in which the pawn could go to the third square (line 14).

The chess warriors had Hebrew names. The foot-soldier [= pawn] was *ragli*;
the queen, *paraz* [= governor, after Hab. 3: 14], and the knight, *sus* (Hebrew: horse).
Pil [= elephant, from the Arabic *Al-fil*] was the counterpart to the bishop. The name
of the rook-castle, *rokh* is preserved in the modern English. The game was a popular
pastime for Jews in the Middle Ages. R. Solomon b. Isaac (RaŠI, 1040-1105) mentions
it in his commentary on *bKet* 61b, as does Ibn Ezra's contemporary, Judah Halevi in
Sefer Ha-Kuzari 5. 20. 61]. Maimonides, in his comments on *mSan* 3. 3, forbids its
play for money. Despite the mock-serious tone of this poem, Ibn Ezra may be
advocating this harmless sport as a moral equivalent of war. In the excitement of
play the combatants are enabled to vent a full range of emotions. They can "ascend
upon" the enemy "with malice," and "with fury...destroy." "Bent on killing" they seize
their opponents in an ambush, and without mercy lead them to their death. Now
leaving the field, the players are purged through the recognition that despite their
passions in the heat of battle "no blood was shed" and their "mortally wounded"
soldiers will rise again.

GOD

19.   LIFE'S PARADOX

When I yearn to praise You, I am satisfied;
When I desire to adore You, I am refreshed;
I rest secure in my fear of You;
I wear terror like a garment.
I am exalted when I bow before You;
When I am humbled You are there to lift me up.
Though I am in bondage to the sons of my brother and of my maidservant;
I am free whenever I worship You.
The pain You bring me is sweetness
To the spirit, the heart and the soul. [1]

--/-ס--/-ס--//--/-ס--/-ס--

אֶשְׂבַּע--בְּעֵת אֶרְעַב לְהַלְלָךְ,/ אֶרְוֶה--בְּיוֹם לַעֲבֹד לָךְ אֶצְמָא.
בֶּטַח אֲנִי אֶשְׁכֹּן בְּפַחְדָּתִי/ מִמָּךְ, וְאֶלְבַּשׁ כַּמְעִיל אֵימָה.
רַמְתִּי--בְּיוֹם שַׁחְתִּי לְפָנֶיךָ,/ אֶשְׁפַּל--אֲבָל קַרְנִי בְּךָ רָמָה.
הַרְבֵּה פְדוּת עִמִּי--בְּיוֹם עָבְדִי/ לְשִׁמְךָ בְּנֵי אָח גַּם בְּנֵי אָמָה.
5   מֶה עָרְבוּ כָּל עַצְבוֹתֶיךָ/ לַלֵּב וְלָרוּחַ וְלַנְּשָׁמָה.

Ibn Ezra's paradox is sustained throughout this "permission" (*rešut*) hymn. In the use of this rhetorical figure, the poet seeks to separate appearance from reality. What at first seems impossible is actually entirely plausible to the man of faith, exiled from his native land and in bondage to Christians [= "sons of my brother (Esau)"] and Muslims [= "(sons) of my maidservant (Hagar)"].

There is an additional shock value in Ibn Ezra's paradox. Its pointed contrast is calculated to arouse the Jewish worshipper and help him overcome the fear of being abandoned in Israel's long exile. The poet's figures of radical devotion to the

---

1. Levin, *Širey Ha-Qodeš...Ibn Ezra*, 1: 55–56.

beloved are borrowed from the Bible ("Though He slay me, yet will I trust in Him," Job 13: 15) and from Arabic love poetry. One of the basic modes of 'Abbasid verse is paradox; that the lover prefers pain over indifference is best expressed by an anonymous Arab poet, "A wounded heart is dearer to me than a calm mind without you." [2]

20.   GOD'S PROVIDENCE

O God, You have searched me and know my mind;
You discern my thoughts from afar; You are privy to my every move.
You anticipate my plans; my walking and reclining.
You observe and are familiar with my ways.
You see the word forming in my heart before it reaches
My tongue; You know when my days will end;
You hem me in behind and in front and from above;
You guide me with your right hand, while your left supports me.
You fill the high heavens and distant sea;
Where can I go from your presence when You confront me everywhere?
Darkness does not conceal me; nothing obscures your view.
It is You who reveals my secrets.
In the beginning You formed me; You knit me together in the womb;
In its depth You crafted my delicate frame.
Your eyes beheld my bare limbs; they were all recorded
In your book; in due time they took their separate shapes.
How vast are the sum of your thoughts, they are most
Difficult to comprehend; my "knowledge" and "wisdom" is foolishness.
I thank You for your wonders; I am grateful for your mercies.
By your power I am sustained; to You belong my breath and my soul. [3]

$$---\text{ס}/--[\text{ס}]-/---\text{ס}/--[\text{ס}]-$$

אֱלֹהַי, חֲקַרְתַּנִי וַתֵּדַע מִזְמָתִי
וְרֵעִי לְמֵרָחוֹק וְשִׁבְתִּי וְקִימָתִי.

---

2. See Hamori, "Love Poetry (*Ghazal*), pp. 212–13.

3. Cf. Levin, *Širey Ha-Qodeš...Ibn Ezra*, 1: 32.

בָּנַתָ כָּל תְּכוּנָתִי וְאָרְחִי וְרִבְעִי אַתָּ

זֵרִיתָ, וְהִסְכַּנְתָ דְּרָכַי לֹא בְעָצְמָתִי.

5 רָאִיתָ דְבַר לִבִּי בְּטֶרֶם קָצֶה מִלָּה

בִּלְשׁוֹנִי, וְיָדַעְתָ אַחֲרִיתִי וְחָמָּתִי.

הֵן קֶדֶם וְהֵן אָחוֹר צַרְתַּנִי וְעַל רֹאשִׁי

שַׁתָּ כַּף יְמִינָךְ, וְיָדְךָ בְּאַדְמָתִי.

מָלֵאתָ שְׁמֵי שַׁחַק וְאַחֲרִית יָם,

10 אָן מֵרוּחֲךָ אֵלֵךְ - וְשָׁם אַתָּה לְעֻמָּתִי?

חֹשֶׁךְ לֹא יְשׁוּפֵנִי, כִּי אֵין מִמְּךָ יַחְשִׁיךְ,

וְאַתָּה אֲשֶׁר תּוֹצִיא לָאוֹר תַּעֲלָמָתִי

הֵן קֶדֶם קְנִיתַנִי וּבַבֶּטֶן תִּסְכְּנִי

וְתַעַשׂ בְּתַחְתִּיּוֹת אֶת עָצְמִי וְרִקְמָתִי.

15 גָּלְמִי רָאֲתָה עֵינָךְ וְעַל סִפְרָךְ כֻּלָּם

יִכָּתֵבוּ, וְלֹא אֶחָד מֵהֶם אָז בְּקַדְמָתִי.

וְלִי יָקְרוּ לִמְאֹד רֵעֶיךָ וּמֶה עָצְמוּ

רָאשֵׁיהֶם, וּמֶה נִּבְעַר כָּל דַּעְתִּי וְחָכְמָתִי.

אוֹדְךָ עַל פְּלָאֶיךָ, אוֹדְךָ עַל חֲסָדֶיךָ,

20 בָּךְ מַעֲמַד גּוּיָתִי, לָךְ רוּחִי וְנִשְׁמָתִי!

This "permission" (rešut) hymn to the Sabbath and festival morning service prayer, "The breath of all that lives praises You" (Nišmat kol ḥay tevarekh 'et šimkha) is a liturgical setting of Psalms 139. In his Bible commentary Ibn Ezra writes that this psalm is "distinguished for its insight into the nature of God and that...there is no psalm like it." He recommends it to all humans who, "according to their abilities in understanding the ways of God (u-k-fi binat 'adam be-darkhey ha-šem) and the nature of the soul, are advised to meditate on its meaning."

Characteristic of Hispano-Hebrew universalism, in which the intellectual, whether Jewish, Muslim or Christian, was held in highest esteem, Ibn Ezra, in his Bible commentary, recommends Psalm 139 to all intelligent beings. [4] This cosmopolitan tendency is reflected in Ibn Ezra's introduction to his philosophical work, Yesod Mora':

"Humans have no advantage over the animals" (Eccles 3: 19) except the

---

4. See Scheindlin, The Gazelle, pp. 10–12.

soul...She will return to God...who gave her. All wisdom [with which the soul is formed [5]] gives life to the one who possesses it. There are many sciences to be studied; they are like the steps of a ladder leading to the ultimate knowledge [of God]. [6]

While writing for intellectuals in his Bible commentaries and philosophical works, Ibn Ezra puts forth these views. However, in many of his liturgical writings he is primarily concerned with communicating to the lay public. In this "permission" request, the poet hews closely to the plain meaning of the scriptural text. His purpose is to reaffirm the traditional value concept of "Divine Providence" (hašgahah peratit) in which God knows all individuals in their particularity. In his Bible commentary [on Gen. 18: 21] he qualifies this view in saying, "The Whole (God) knows every part through the genera but not through the individual."

Ibn Ezra, the philosopher, faced with the problem of explaining the relationship between God "the whole" of the world in its entirety and the sublunar individual uses the taxonomic rankings of genus and species. The characteristics of the species "mammal" can be seen in each of its "genera." God, like the "genera," encompasses the taxon in its totality, not in its particularity; the latter is defined by the lower rankings. [7] In writing this hymn for the synagogue, however, the poet has another priority.

21.   GOD'S PRESENCE

God has apportioned my lot in life; He is my tower and strength;
He makes me His friend; He makes me His friend.

He is One and no unit precedes or follows Him;
All is contained in the One alone; He brought it out of nothing completed;
Planets and stars speak of His eternal presence;

5. Eccles. 7: 12 and Ibn Ezra' s comment.
6. Levin, *Yalqut Ibn Ezra*, p. 315; see also Ibn Ezra's comment on Hos. 7: 3, "'Let us press on to know the Lord:' For this [knowledge of God] is the [profound] basis of the sciences; and it is for this purpose alone that man was created."
7. Sirat, *History of Jewish Philosophy*, p. 107.

He labors in secret healing the sick;

He works concealed without tools that can be seen.

Within me I can see God's wonders; there is nothing beside Him;

He is with me, and I am amazed at His never-failing mercies.

I kneel before Him and boast that He takes pleasure in His servant.

 He is the banner at my right hand; on the left He stands protecting me.

 He is my mountain when I am depressed; He is my help when I fall.

His spirit lifts me up; I fear Him with all my heart.

I call upon Him by the [Ineffable] Name which I learned from the

  prophet He sent me.

My thought cannot conceive the heavens;

But He is near to be found:

 My help and my fate, my portion and my lot.

 He is my refuge in distress, the light in my darkness.

What can I say when He knows all before I speak?

Yet, I will never stop calling upon His name, for He is my hope.

He will save my soul from hell and give me strength.

 In Him I delight, He is the fullness of my joy; all my praise is His.

 My voice swells with excitement for Him; my flute

  sings of His presence. [8]

--ס/---//--/---ס/---

שֵׁם אֵלִי מְנָת גּוֹרָלִי,/ מִגְדָּלִי וְחֵילִי,
כִּי הוּא יַעֲשֶׂה שָׁלוֹם לִי,/ שָׁלוֹם יַעֲשֶׂה לִי.

אֶחָד אֵין לְפָנָיו אֶחָד,/ גַּם כֵּן אַחֲרָיו לֹא
וּבְאֶחָד לְבַד הִתְאַחָד / כָּל הֵפִיק וְכֻלּוֹ,
5   יָעִיד עַל אֲשֶׁר לֹא נִכְחַד/ מַעְגְּלוֹ וְדִגְלוֹ,
וּבְכָל מַעֲשָׂיו הוּא פֶלִיא,/ הוּא מַרְפֵּא לְחָלִי,
הוּא יִפְעַל בְּאֶפֶס כְּלִי/ בֶּאֱמֶת, לֹא בְּשֶׁלִי.

_____

8. Levin,, Širey Ha-Qodeš...Ibn Ezra, 1: 77–78.

בִּי אוֹתוֹת אֱלֹהֵי אֶרְאֶה,/ אֵין עוֹד מִלְּבַדּוֹ,

הוּא עִמִּי וְאִם אֶשְׁתָּאֶה/ כָּל רֶגַע לְחַסְדּוֹ,

10 לוֹ אֶכְרַע וּבוֹ אֶתְגָּאֶה,/ כִּי רוֹצֶה בְעָבְדּוֹ;

הוּא עַל יַד יְמִינִי דְגְלִי,/ הוּא גַּם עַל שְׂמֹאלִי,

הוּא הָרִי בְעֵתוֹת שִׁפְלִי,/ הוּא מִסְעָד בְּנָפְלִי.

רוּחוֹ נוֹסָה בִלְבָבִי/ וּבְכָל לֵב יְרֵאתָיו,

וּבְשֵׁם לִמְּדַנִי נָבִיא/ לִי שָׁלַח--קְרָאתָיו,

15 רָחוֹק מִזְּבוּל מַחְשָׁבִי/ אַךְ קָרוֹב מְצָאתָיו;

הוּא עֶזְרִי וְהוּא גוֹרָלִי,/ הוּא חֶלְקִי וְחֶבְלִי,

הוּא מָנוֹס בְּיוֹם צָרָה לִי,/ הוּא נֵרִי בְאָפְלִי.

מָה אֹמַר וְהַכֹּל יָדַע/ טֶרֶם שֶׁאֲדַבֵּר?

אַךְ מִפִּי שְׁמוֹ לֹא אֶגְדַּע,/ כִּי אֵלָיו אֲשַׂבֵּר,

20 נַפְשִׁי מִשְּׁאוֹל הוּא יִפְדַּע/ וַחֲיָלִים אֲגַבֵּר;

בּוֹ אָגִיל וְאֶשְׂמַח כֻּלִּי,/ בּוֹ כָל מַהֲלָלִי,

בּוֹ יִגְבַּהּ לְמַעְלָה קוֹלִי,/ בּוֹ יָרֹן חֲלִילִי.

In this *muwashshah* hymn, Ibn Ezra expounds on the relationship between God and man in traditional terms drawn primarily from the Bible. The opening "belt" is adapted from verses in Ps. 16: 5 and 61: 4; Prov. 18: 10 and Is. 27: 5. However, in the first strophe, the poet presents arguments drawn from contemporary philosophy. "He is One and no unit precedes or follows him" is probably borrowed from Ibn Gabirol's *Keter Malkhut*, 2: "You are One, but not like a unit to be grasped or counted, for number and change cannot reach You." In this practice, the Spanish poets are following a precedent set by Sa'adyah Gaon (882–942), head of the Babylonia academy at Sura who first introduced themes from religious philosophy into the synagogue liturgy. [9]

Added to these is a theme from contemporary Jewish mysticism: "I call upon Him by the [Ineffable] Name which I learned from the prophet [Moses] He sent me." A fuller exposition of this conceit is given in Ibn Ezra's comments on Ex. 6: 2-3, "God also spoke to Moses...'I am the Lord. I appeared to Abraham, Isaac and Jacob as 'El Shaddai, but by my name YHWH, I did not make myself known to them.'"

---

9. See M. Zulay, *Ha-'Askolah Ha-Payṭanit Šel R. Sa'adyah Gaon*, pp. 99ff.

From this it is suggested that God revealed to Moses some of the hitherto undisclosed features of the Divine Name. Sa'adyah Gaon in a liturgical work writes, "The ancients knew the Ineffable Name...They would call upon it when facing a crisis." The knowledge of the Name and its power was undoubtedly handed down through the generations to those who were considered worthy. Ibn Nagrela, commander of the Granadan armies, invoked it during the battle with Isma'il Ibn 'Abbad of Seville, and here, Ibn Ezra reveals that he too is privy to its secret. [10]

22.   I HAVE BUT ONE REQUEST

Would that my ways were steadfast in keeping your laws!
I have found no rest except in my desire for You.
I am ready to serve You; lead me in your just path.
   I have but one request: I want to earn your favor.
   I seek nothing from You except your presence.

Truth knows that no one is your equal; how then can You be compared?
To what can I liken your labor when all is made by You?
Since I am your creature what can I say [that You know not]?
   Even my thoughts and talents belong to You.
   All your efforts witness to You, not me.

Boundless is your compassion, and who is not in your debt?
There is no truth but You and the work of your hands.
Even those who deny You testify to your presence!
   Wherever I turn, I find You;
   I am connected to You, for nothing separates us.

No sooner than I leave your presence do I hasten after You;
Your beauty is all that my eyes can see;
My ears hear only your command!
   My heart's secrets are revealed to You;
   Whatever I say is within your hearing.

---

10. Ibid., p. 224; Weinberger, *Jewish Prince in Moslem Spain*, pp. 140–41.

Send help to the tempter's captive;

Put your Name upon his lips and make your home in his heart;

Pity him when he lifts his eyes to your place in heaven.

  Reach out your hand and let it rest upon the faithful.

  Let your face shed light upon us in our darkness. [11]

6/6

אַחֲלַי יִכֹּנוּ דְרָכַי/ לִשְׁמֹר חֻקֶּיךָ,

כִּי מְנוּחָה לֹא מָצָאתִי/ כִּי אִם בְּחָשְׁקֶךָ,

עַבְדְּךָ אֲנִי--הַדְרִיכֵנִי/ בְּדֶרֶךְ צִדְקֶךָ.

הֵן שָׁאַלְתִּי אַחַת הִיא--/ לְהָפִיק רְצוֹנֶךָ,

לֹא אֲבַקֵּשׁ מִלְּפָנֶיךָ/ כִּי אִם פָּנֶיךָ.   5

בֶּאֱמֶת אֵין עֵרֶךְ אֵלֶיךָ--/ וְאֵיךְ אַמְשִׁילֶךָ?

אוֹ לְמִי אֲדַמֶּה פָּעֳלֶיךָ?/ וְהַכֹּל פָּעֳלֶךָ!

אַתְּ בְּרָאתַנִי --וּמָה אוֹסִיף לְדַבֵּר אֵלֶיךָ?

מַחְשְׁבוֹת רוּחִי וְקִנְיָנִי/ הֵם קִנְיָנֶיךָ,

לֹא לְמַעֲנִי אַתָּה עוֹשֶׂה/ כִּי אִם לְמַעֲנֶךָ.   10

רֹאשׁ וְסוֹף אֵין לַחֲסָדֶיךָ--/ וּמִי לֹא יוֹדֶךָ?

וֶאֱמֶת, אֵין בִּלְעָדֶיךָ/ וּמַעֲשֵׂה יָדֶיךָ,

וַאֲשֶׁר בְּשִׁמְךָ כִחֵשׁוּ--/ הֵם הֵם עֵדֶיךָ!

יַחֲשֹׁב לִבִּי כֹּה וָכֹה--/ הִנֵּה הִנֶּךָ!

אֶפְגָּעֲךָ בָךְ, כִּי אֵין מַבְדִּיל/ בֵּינִי וּבֵינֶךָ.   15

מִלְּפָנֶיךָ אֲנִי יוֹצֵא/ וְרוּצֵי אַחֲרֶיךָ--

מַחֲזֶה בַּל רָאוּ עֵינַי--/ לְבַד מֵהֲדָרֶךָ,

מַאֲמָר לֹא שָׁמְעוּ אָזְנַי--/ רַק מַאֲמָרֶיךָ!

אוֹת חָתְמוּ לִבִּי--הִנֶּךָ/ רוֹאֶה בְעֵינֶיךָ,

וַאֲשֶׁר סֵפֶר פִּי--הִנֵּה עוֹלֶה בְאָזְנֶיךָ!   20

עַל אֲסִיר יֵצֶר רַע--צַוֵּה יְשׁוּעוֹת פָּנֶיךָ,

זִכְרְךָ בְּפִיו שִׂים, וּבְלִבּוֹ/ בְּנֵה בֵית מְכוֹנֶךָ.

11. Levin, Širey Ha-Qodeš...Ibn Ezra, 1: 107–09; Schirmann, Ha-Širah Ha-'Ivrit, 1: 604–05; Scheindlin, The Gazelle, pp. 219–25.

רַחֲמֵהוּ בְּשְׂאֵתוֹ עֵינָיו/ לְכִסֵּא מְעוֹנֶךָ.
הַט זְרוֹעֲךָ וּתְהִי יָדְךָ/ עַל אִישׁ יְמִינֶךָ,
25   וּבְמַחֲשַׁכִּים עָלֵינוּ/ נְסָה אוֹר פָּנֶיךָ.

The hymn, named *me'orah* (from the Hebrew *'or*, light) is part of the *yoṣer* cycle of benedictions recited before the *šema'* during the Sabbath and festival morning service. "Would that my ways were steadfast" built in the form of a *muwashshah* was chanted prior to the recitation of the second to the last benediction before the *šema'*: Praised are You O Lord, creator of lights (*yoṣer ha-me'orot*). Its closing line, "Let your face shed light upon us (*nesah 'or panekha*) in our darkness," links readily with the benediction that follows.

In this hymn Ibn Ezra revisits the theme of the divine-human relationship with conceits that verge on pantheism. The figure, "I am connected to You, for nothing separates us" (line 15) is in line with his commentary on Gen. 1: 26, "God is the One; He made all; He is all," and in Ex. 23: 21, "He is all and from him comes all." In this Ibn Ezra appears to stray from the traditional transcendent Creator-God of the Bible.

A related image from contemporary philosophy (line 12), "There is no truth but You," is echoed in Ibn Ezra's *Yesod Mora'*, 10. 2, "God is the One, and there is no being, but by cleaving to him." Another conceit on divine pervasiveness, "No sooner than I leave your presence do I hasten after You" (line 16) is suggested in Gabirol's *Keter Malkhut*, 38: "If You pursue my iniquity, I will flee from You to Yourself; I will shelter myself from your wrath in your shadow." Combined with the figures drawn from contemporary Neoplatonism are the familiar impressions of the beloved adapted from Canticles and the Arabic *ghazal*. Among these is the elegant, "Your beauty is all that my eyes can see" (line 17).

The hymn closes with a traditional appeal for divine guidance in helping the poet overcome his base temptation (*yeṣer ra'*). Ibn Ezra's plea that God make his home in the poet's heart recalls Jer. 32: 40, "And I will put into their hearts reverence for Me, so that they may not turn from Me." The Muslim mystic, Manṣūr b. Husayn al-Hallāj (d. 922) wrote, "Within my heart Thou dwellest; therein, of Thee, are secrets./ Good be that house for Thee, nay, good Whom there Thou findest!" The Whom that the Thou (=God) finds in the poet's heart is Itself. [12]

23.   GOD, MY DESIRE

I delight in the love of my God more than in the love of life itself;
I desire him—despising every other attraction.

I wondered why some chose another, like rubbish by comparison!
Would a wise man chase after wealth or the vigor of youth?
Lovers are bound to part; or the beloved is wroth and the lover perishes;
  But I lust after the Beloved who made me; there I will find
     every treasure;
  I rest content that He will not depart; He repairs the broken spirit.

Passion's lovers are plagued by jealousy; but the One I love can be trusted;
If, like me, others are enamoured of Him, I rejoice in their company.
When I am deprived of His presence all good sense leaves me;
  I come closer to behold His beauty; His majesty exalts me.
  I inscribe His name on my heart; His honeyed memory
     my mouth proclaims.

When I consider why the goods of the world are esteemed,
I find that their lustre fades with time and I yearn for God's riches;
The longer I know Him the more I am in awe and in love.
  I tremble for my wayward soul distracted from its fearful passion
     for Him.
  I am content when I hunger for Him, satisfied when I thirst.

Passion for Him brings contentment, while other lovers suffer.
His bidding is hidden in my heart; would that He could live there.
I am vindicated because of Him; what do you now say, my soul?
  The soul, hewn from the living Rock, is filled with treasure from
     God's throne.

---

12. Levin, *Avraham Ibn Ezra*, pp. 100–05; Lings, "Mystical Poetry," p. 247.

The Rock confronts her with the reminder that she was made to
honor His name. [13]

-ס-/--/---//-ס-/--/---

אַהֲבַת אֵלִי לִי עָרְבָה--/מֵאַהֲבַת נַפְשִׁי נִפְלָאָה,
בּוֹ אֶחְשֹׁק, עַד כָּל אַהֲבָה/--בִּלְתִּי אַהֲבָתוֹ--אֶשְׂנָאָה!

בִּינוֹתִי בִּדְבַר בּוֹחֲרֵי/ בִּלְתּוֹ, כִּי הוּא שָׁמָם סֳחִי.
אֵיךְ יִרְדֹּף אִישׁ לֵב אַחֲרֵי/ הוֹן יָקָר, אוֹ לֶחַ לְחִי?
5   וּנְדוֹד יָקָר, אוֹ יֶחֱרֶה/ בּוֹ אַף הַחֲשׁוּק--לֹא יֶחִי!
עַל דּוֹד קַנַּי אֶעְגְּבָה,/ בּוֹ כָל הוֹן יָקָר אֶמְצָאָה,
מְנוּדוֹ בֶּטַח אֶשְׁכְּבָה,/ הוּא חַיֵּי רוּחַ נִכְאָה.

רֹב קִנְאָה עַל כָּל דּוֹד, וְזֶה/ דּוֹדִי אֶחָד בּוֹ אֶבְטָחָה,
אִם יִרְבּוּ אוֹהֲבָיו אוֹחֲזֵי/ דַרְכּוֹ עִמִּי--בָּם אֶשְׂמָחָה.
10   אִם בִּלְתִּי פָנָיו אֶחֱזֶה--/ תּוּשִׁיָּה מֶנִּי נִדְּחָה.
לִרְאוֹת הֲדָרָתוֹ אֶקְרְבָה,/ וּבְגַאֲוָתוֹ אֶתְנַשָּׂאָה,
וּשְׁמוֹ עַל לִבִּי אֶכְתְּבָה/ וּבְפִי צוּף זִכְרוֹ אֶקְרָאָה.

הֵן כָּל דָּבָר נִכְבָּד, כְּמוֹ/ נַפְשִׁי בִּיסוֹדוֹ חָשְׁבָה,
יֵקַל--אִם יִתַּם נָעֲמוֹ;/ אָכֵן, לְכָבוֹד אֵל אֶתְאַבָּה,
15   כִּי כָל אוֹסִיף דַּעַת שְׁמוֹ--/ אוֹסִיף יִרְאָה גַּם אַהֲבָה.
יְרֵאתִי רוּחִי שׁוֹבֵבָה,/ אַהֲבָתוֹ עַל כֹּל נוֹרָאָה,
שָׂבַעְתִּי עַד לֹא אֶרְעֵבָה,/ רָוִיתִי עַד לֹא אֶצְמָאָה.

מָנוֹחַ יַנְחִיל חִשְׁקֵךְ--/ אַךְ כָּל חוֹשֵׁק הוּא נַעֲנֶה,
בִּלְבָבִי אֶצְפֹּן חִקֵּךְ/ וַאֲקַו, אוּלַי שָׁם תַּחֲנֶה,
20   יוֹם צָדַקְתִּי--מִצִּדְקֵךְ,/ וִיחִידָתִי מַה תַּעֲנֶה?
מְצוּר הַחַיִּים חֻצָּבָה,/ וּכְבוֹד כֵּס כָּבוֹד נִמְלָאָה,
עָלַיִךְ צוּר הִתְיַצָּבָה,/ כִּי לִכְבוֹד שְׁמָךְ נִבְרָאָה.

The *muwashshaḥ* hymn, an *'ahavah* from the Sabbath and festival morning
service *yoṣer* cycle, was chanted prior to the last benediction before the *šema'*,

---

13. Levin, *Širey Ha-Qodeš…Ibn Ezra*, 1: 167–69.

"Praised are You, O Lord who loves His people Israel" (*ha-boher be-'amo yisra'el be-'ahavah*). In the obligatory liturgy, this benediction celebrates God's gift of the Torah, which is taken as a sign of His love for Israel. In Ibn Ezra's poetic addition to the benediction, the focus is on man's love for God in figures drawn from the Arabic *ghazal* and contemporary Neoplatonism. There is no mention of Israel in the hymn.

In his rhetorical argument, the poet trumpets the benefits of divine love over its carnal opposite. The seductive "fawn" or "gazelle," pet names for the beloved, is flirtatious and not dependable ("Lovers are bound to part"). She (or he) is subject to mood swings and brings grief to the heartsick lover ("the beloved is wroth and the lover perishes"). Not so the divine Beloved who "will not depart" and who "can be trusted." Among the other advantages is that there is no trace of jealousy among God's lovers ("Passion's lovers are plagued by jealousy...[and] / If, like me, others are enamoured of Him, I rejoice in their company").

In the *ghazal* the hopelessly infatuated lover is rebuked for his folly by the "reproacher," a tedious moralist. [14] Although at first the poet proclaims his exclusive devotion to God "despising every other attraction," at the close he rejoices at being vindicated adding, "What do you now say, my soul?" In the struggle with his "wayward soul," his "reproacher," the poet admits that he was "distracted from [his] passion for [God]." It is likely that he was attracted to "the goods of the world" only to learn that "their lustre fades with time." In the relationship with divinity, the "reproacher" reflects the inner debate whether to embrace God or the world. The poet is vindicated and the debate is resolved when the soul "hewn from the living Rock" (*mi-sur ha-hayyim husevah*) [15] is made aware of her mission on earth "to honor His name."

24.   ONE FATHER

The stars above and the mortals below

---

14. See Pagis, *Hebrew Poetry*, p. 49.

15. Ibn Gabirol, *Keter Malkhut*, 29: "O Lord, who can comprehend Your power? You have created for the splendor of Your glory a pure radiance, hewn from the Rock of rocks (*mi-sur ha-sur nigzarah...*)."

All come from one Father whose name is a blessing forever.

"God awesome in splendor; all greatness is His due!"
An army proclaims it making haste on its rounds.
They camp in circles connected like curtains;
  Appearing to veer to the left or the right,
  God steadies them and they hang suspended while He remains
      concealed above.

God turned their circular shapes into homes for seven rulers.
They proceed in a straight path, but if they stray
He supports them with his right arm and they are drawn by His love.
  Their movements make music, their way of saying thanks;
  They do it willingly and permit no one to interfere.

The breath of God holds them aloft, it renews their strength.
They rotate themselves in the pursuit of God who guides them.
Wreathed by His glory crown, they are embraced by His love.
  He raises and sets them, reveals and conceals.
  Their phases, high and low, witness to the living God their maker.

Dear are the cherubs, cherished like God's sons;
Designated by His fingers, they approach His throne;
Sometimes, they spawn thunder or bring down rain.
  They emanate from His light and appear in varied shapes.
  They bear the chariot throne while His Name supports them. [16]

$$--\textrm{ס}/--//--\textrm{ס}/--$$

שָׁמַיִם וְחֵילָם/ וּבְנֵי אֲדָמָה לְמוּלָם,
אָב אֶחָד לְכֻלָּם/ וּשְׁמוֹ מְבֹרָךְ לְעוֹלָם.

"אֵל נוֹרָא תְהִלּוֹת/ לוֹ יָאֲתוּ כָּל גְּדוֹלוֹת!"

---

16. Levin, *Širey Ha-Qodeš…Ibn Ezra*, 1: 72–74; Schirmann, *Ha-Širah Ha-'Ivrit*, 1: 613–14.

תְּבַעֶנָה הַמַּלּוֹת/ מִתְרוֹצְצוֹת עַל מְסִלּוֹת,

5 רָאשֵׁיהֶן בִּגְלּוֹת/ עַל מַחְבְּרוֹת הָעֲגֻלּוֹת,

פַּעַם עַל שְׂמֹאלָם/ גַּם עַל יְמִינָם שְׁבִילָם,

אֶל הַשּׁוֹם וְתָלָם/ בְּתֶלִי, וְהוּא רָם וְנֶעְלָם.

בָּרָא אֶל פְּלָכִים/ בָּתִּים לְשִׁבְעָה מְלָכִים,

הוֹלְכִים עַל דְּרָכִים/ יָשָׁרוּ--וְאִם הֵם הֲפוּכִים

10 בִּימִינוֹ תְמוּכִים/ וּבְאַהֲבָתוֹ מְשׁוּכִים,

כִּי פִיהֶם וְקוֹלָם--/ רוּצָם, וְהוּא מַהֲלָלָם,

זֶה חֶפְצָם וְאוּלָם/ אֵין זָר לְהַשִּׂיג גְּבוּלָם.

רוּחַ אֶל הֱנִיפָם,/ כֹּחַ וְעֹז הֶחֱלִיפָם,

רָאשֵׁיהֶם בְּסוֹפָם,/ טוֹב יִרְדְּפוּ, טוֹב רְדָפָם;

15 הַחֶסֶד אֲסָפָם/ וּצְנִיף כְּבוֹדוֹ צְנָפָם,

הוֹרִידָם וְהֶעֱלָם,/ גַּם הֶעֱלִימָם וְגִלָּם,

גִּבְהוּתָם וְשִׁפְלָם--/ עֵדוּת לְאֵל חַי פְּעָלָם.

מַה יָּקְרוּ כְּרוּבִים/ כִּבְנֵי אֱלֹהִים חֲשׁוּבִים,

אֵל כִּסְאוֹ קְרוֹבִים/ וּבְאֶרֶץ בְּעוֹתָיו כְּתוּבִים,

20 מוֹלִידִים שְׁבִיבִים/ פַּעַם--וּפַעַם רְבִיבִים,

מְאוֹרוֹ אֲצָלָם/ וּלְרֹב תְּמוּנוֹת פְּעָלָם,

נוֹשְׂאִים כֵּס זְבוּלָם--/ אַךְ שֵׁם אֲדֹנָי סְבָלָם.

The poem, a *muwashshah*, is an introduction (*muharrak*) to the *barekhu* (Praise the Lord, Source of blessing), the first of the *šema'* benedictions. It is based on Psalm 19. Ibn Ezra, in his Bible commentary, praises this psalm as a valuable introduction to astronomy. In the liturgical treatment, the poet combines biblical conceits in which God is manifested in the phenomena of the heavens with Ptolemaic astronomy. The "seven rulers" are the seven planets which combine with the constellation of stars in the zodiac and the Primum Mobile to form the cosmos. The Primum Mobile was an invisible sphere whose movement set in motion all that lay below it.

From a literal reading of Psalm 19, Ibn Ezra's contemporaries concluded that the heavens provide a track along which the personified sun runs its course. In due time all the seven planets were perceived to have their separate courses on which they ran their divinely appointed rounds. With characteristic paradox, Ibn Ezra observes, "They rotate themselves in the pursuit of God who guides them." Their hope is to find the divine "place" in the Empyrean, which is beyond space and time. Earlier rabbis [in *bHag* 13b] speculated about this "place," which is mentioned in Ez. 3: 12 and concluded that "no one knows His place."

The "army" of stars and planets "emanate" from His light (*me-'oro 'aṣalam*). True to contemporary Neoplatonism, Ibn Ezra perceived the individual soul emerging from the Universal Soul. In this process all comes from God in a descending order. First is the intelligible being which the Torah calls "Glory" (*kavod*); from it emanates the Universal Soul, known as *the Glory of the God of Israel*; the third emanation is the world of the angels and the spheres. These initial emanations are spiritual and luminous. [17] On its separate ways the "army" makes music singing God's praises, as told in Job 38: 7, "When the morning stars [= seven planets, see Ibn Ezra commentary] sang together, and all the sons of God (*bene 'elohim*) shouted for joy."

Stationed above the seven planets are the angels called "the sons of God" (see Job, above) and are identified with the eighth sphere of fixed stars divided into the twelve signs of the zodiac. They are entrusted with the governance of the sublunar world sending "thunder or...rain," even as they shoulder the "Chariot Throne" of God who supports them. Again, the playful poet closes with a provocative paradox, hopeful--as he would write in his Bible commentaries--that a word to the wise is sufficient.

25.   GOD'S IDENTITY

We sing to the living God while we have the breath of life.

His teaching reveals His faithfulness,
But who is familiar with His identity?
The key to understanding is in the heavens.
    His armies of stars race before our eyes pointing: Here is our God.

---

17. See Sirat, *A History of Jewish Philosophy*, p. 84.

In the high clouds it is clearly inscribed:
"Behold the living God, master of prevailing winds."
There in the lightning we see His conversations;
   The earth confirms it and the hills agree.

Behold the work of God in the flowering tree,
The swarm in the seas tells it truthfully;
The winged bird calls out to its Maker;
   Every reptile is grateful and companies of beasts sing His praises.

O Source of Life, our sustainer,
You invite us to call You by name;
In the image of angels You made us;
   And when Adam's sin brought us to death, You restored us to life. [18]

ס---/--/ס---

בְּשֵׁם אֵל חַי הֶגְיוֹן לְשׁוֹנֵנוּ,/ בְּעוֹד רוּחַ בְּאַפֵּינוּ.

אֱמוּנָתוֹ תַרְאֶה אֱמוּנָתוֹ
וּמִי יוּכַל בּוֹא עַד תְּכוּנָתוֹ?
בְּשָׁמַיִם אוֹתוֹת תְּבוּנָתוֹ,
5   צְבָאֵימוֹ רָצִים לְעֵינֵינוּ,/ וְיוֹרוּנוּ, הִנֵּה אֱלֹהֵינוּ!

בְּעָבֵי רוֹם נִכְתָּב דְּבַר צָחוֹת:
'רְאוּ אֵל חַי מוֹשֵׁל בְּכָל רוּחוֹת,'
וּבִבְרָקִים שָׁם נֶחֱזֶה שִׂיחוֹת,
וְהָאָרֶץ תִּקְרָא וְתַעֲנֵנוּ/ וְהֶהָרִים יַעֲנוּ בְּפָנֵינוּ.

10   רְאוּ מַעֲשֵׂה הַצּוּר בְּעֵץ פּוֹרֶה,
עֲדֵי שֶׁרֶץ מַיִם אֱמֶת יוֹרֶה
וְעוֹף כָּנָף אֶל פּוֹעֲלוֹ קוֹרֵא,
וְכָל רֶמֶשׂ קוֹלָם יְחַנֵּנוּ/ וְסוֹד חַיּוֹת בִּשְׁמוֹ יְרַנֵּנוּ.

---

18. Levin, Širey Ha-Qodeš...Ibn Ezra, 1: 61-62.

מְקוֹר חַיִּים, אַתָּ הֶחֱיִיתָנוּ

15   וְלִקְרֹא אֶת שִׁמְךָ קְרָאתָנוּ,

לְזֹאת בִּדְמוּת מַלְאָךְ בְּרָאתָנוּ;

וְאִם חַטַּאת אָדָם תְּמִיתֵנוּ--/ הֲלֹא אַתָּה תָשׁוּב תְּחַיֵּינוּ.

This introduction (muḥarrak) in the form of a muwashshaḥ is based on Psalms 19 and 104. Its basic thesis is that God's identity is demonstated most clearly in the stellar configurations of His creation and in the natural phenomena of the sub-lunar world. "In the lightning we see His conversations (siḥot)" is a conceit adapted from the verse in Ex. 20: 15, "And all the people *saw* the thunder (ro'im 'et ha-qolot)"--with their mind's eye.

"You invite us to call You by name" is related to the rabbinic comment [in *Gen. Rabbah* 17. 5] on Gen. 2: 2, "'And the man gave names to all cattle.' Said He to him, 'And what is your name?' It is fitting that I be called Adam, because I was created from the ground ('adamah),' he replied. 'And what is My name?' 'It is fitting for You to be called *'Adonay* (Lord), since You are Lord over all Your creatures,' he replied." God creating man in the image of the angels is understood in light of Ibn Ezra's comment on Gen. 1: 26, "'Let us make man in our image, after our likeness'...An angel is made in God's image," and his note on Ex. 3: 15, "Man's soul is in their (the angels') *genus.*"

The closing two strophes suggest that this hymn was to be chanted during the Pentecost service. This may be inferred from the phrase, "in the lightning we see His conversations," and its source in the Revelation at Sinai account in Exodus 20, and the note of gratitude to God "our sustainer"--literally, "who grants us life" (he-ḥeyitanu). Combined with this is the closing, "You restored us to life," which is probably based on the rabbinic comment [in *Pirqey de Rabbi Eliezer*, 41], "The voice of the first [commandment] went forth...[and] the Israelites who were alive [then] fell upon their faces and died. The voice of the second [commandment] went forth, and they were quickened, and they...said to Moses, 'You speak to us and we will obey; but let not God speak to us lest we die' (Ex. 20: 19)."

26.   NO ONE SHARES HIS POWER

He alone is God, no one shares His power; His marvels I find in me.

Why would I seek another to guide me in life, when He is
    my heart's strength?

To bring Him honor He fashioned me in the womb until my birth;
He breathed the breath of life into my nostrils until I revived;
He put wisdom into my heart and gave me the choice between
      life and death;
  I will make ready my heart's weapons, I am poised for my war.
  Can I prevail, my plan succeed, when the enemy is within me?

God, distant in His highest heavens, is nearer than my inward parts;
All who seek to find Him are washed pure from falsehood
With my [mind's] eye I see Him; love wells up in my vision;
  I am wearied from searching to know His mind;
  No one is privy to His inner life, not sage or prophet.

Remembrance of Him overcomes me; I yearn at the mention of His name.
I rehearse His words with my soul and delight in His presence;
I am drawn to the light from His fountain and hope for its reward;
  I ask only for His free gift, I pray that my Father not be angry;
  What can I plead in my behalf? He knows I have no merit to offer. [19]

--ס-/--//--/--ס-/--

אֵל אֶחָד וְאֵין זָר אִתּוֹ,/ מוֹפְתָיו אֶמְצָאָה בִי;
אֵיךְ אֶדְרוֹשׁ בְּחַיַּי בִּלְתּוֹ--/ וּשְׁמוֹ צוּר לְבָבִי?

בָּרָא עַל כְּבוֹדוֹ רִקְמַת/ גָּלְמִי עַד הֱיוֹתִי,
וַיִּפַּח בְּאַפִּי נִשְׁמַת/ חַיִּים עַד חֲיוֹתִי.
5 וַיִּתֵּן בְּיַד לֵב חָכְמַת/ סוֹד חַיַּי וּמוֹתִי--
אֶעֱרֹךְ אֶת כְּלֵי מִלְחַמְתּוֹ,/ אֶקְרַב אֶל קְרָבִי,
מָה אָדָם וּמַה מַּחְשַׁבְתּוֹ,/ אַךְ עִמִּי יְרִיבִי?

19. Levin, *Širey Ha-Qodeš...Ibn Ezra*, 1: 272–73; Schirmann, *Ha-Širah Ha-'Ivrit*, 1: 601–12. Schirmann's אֶעֱרֹךְ (line 6) is preferable to Levin's אֶעֱרֹךְ since it conforms to the meter.

רָחוֹק מִשְּׁמֵי שָׁמָיו--רַק/ קָרוֹב מִקְרָבִים,
כָּל חוֹפֵשׁ דְּרָכָיו מֹרַק,/ שֶׁטַּף מִכְּזָבִים.
10 אֶרְאֶנּוּ בְעַיִן, זֹרַק/ עָלָיו מֵי אֲהָבִים--
אַךְ דַּעַת יְקַר מַחְשַׁבְתּוֹ/ הֶלְאָה מַחְשָׁבִי,
לֹא עָמַד בְּסוֹד מַתְכֻּנְתּוֹ/ כָּל חָכָם וְנָבִיא.

מָלֵא פִי וְלִבִּי זִכְרוֹ,/ כִּי לִשְׁמוֹ אֲאַוֶּה;
בּוֹ אֶשְׁתַּעְשְׁעָה וּדְבָרוֹ/ עִם נַפְשִׁי אֲחַוֶּה.
15 אֲמַשֵּׁךְ לְנַחַל אוֹרוֹ/ וּלְטוּבוֹ אֲקַוֶּה.
טוֹב חִנָּם בְּדָרְשִׁי תִּתּוֹ--/ אַל יִחַר לְאָבִי!
מָה אַעַן? וְהֵן עַל דַּעְתּוֹ,/ אֵין לִי שַׁי לְהָבִיא.

The poet's closing lines asking for God's forgiveness suggest that this
muwashshah was part of the synagogue liturgy for the Ten Days of Repentance. In
his opening "belt" Ibn Ezra affirms God's exclusive sovereignty--a polemic against
Christian trinitarianism. It is likely that in his travels in Italy, France, and England,
the poet was obliged to defend his view on the absolute unity of God. "Why would
I seek another," may reflect the proselytizing attempts of Christian missionaries in
Ibn Ezra's day.

Man's purpose in life is to bring honor to his Creator by enlisting "wisdom"
in the struggle against his base inclination [= "the enemy"]. Wisdom will aid him to
discover the divine in his "inward parts," and will cleanse him from falsehood.
Presumably, the "falsehood" is the trinitarianism referred to above. Driven by desire
to see the pervasive Beloved, he catches a glimpse of Him with the mind's eye.
However, the elusive Deity will not reveal His thoughts even to the prophet.
Moreover, human intellect, as opposed to the intuition of the mind's eye, is incapable
of conceiving God's purpose. This conceit is shared by Judah Halevi, Ibn Ezra's
contemporary:

"My heart and my inward parts have found You;

But my intellect cannot comprehend You." [20]

Characteristically, Ibn Ezra highlights Deity's pervasiveness with a rhetorical paradox, "God, distant in His highest heavens, is nearer than my inward parts."

In his search for God's presence the poet rehearses with his soul the instructions that will draw him to the supernal "light...fountain" and its rewards. In this conceit, Ibn Ezra reflects the view of contemporary Neoplatonism that the soul, imprisoned in the body, can liberate itself by acquiring Wisdom and return to its source in the heavens. [21]

27.   HE SUSTAINS THE WORLD WITH HIS CARE

God, mighty in action, His wonders are too numerous to count;
Praise Him in the heavens; praise Him, all His host!

Indeed, there is no limit to His grandeur; it baffles every one;
He sustains the world with His care;
Men are confused by His motives.
By His honor He protects the earth with His mantle;
  With unseen winds He reveals His hidden arsenal
  Where He stores the thunder and lightning, rains and mists.

Unbounded in power, He is exalted above acclaim;
To whom shall we liken Him since He is the maker of all?
He endowed the stars with strength; He alone can count them;
  He makes notes in His ledgers listing the fate of His creatures;
  But His books are sealed; only His prophets are privy to their secrets.

His radiance kindles the lights in heaven; His galaxies sing to Him;
Armed by His might, they are faithful in doing His will;
Their course is steady as they race carrying His chariot throne;
  Awe and terror follow the throne, and God's seat bears its bearers!

---

20. Halevi, *Širey Ha-Qodeš*, 2: 331.
21. See Sirat, *A History of Jewish Philosophy*, p. 84.

On it were engraved the faces of honest men, eagles, and lions. [22]

-ס--//-ס--//-ס-/-ס--.

אֵל אֲשֶׁר מַעֲשָׂיו עֲצוּמִים,/ מִסְפֹּר עָצְמוּ פְלָאָיו;
הַלְלוּהוּ בַּמְּרוֹמִים,/ הַלְלוּהוּ כָּל צְבָאָיו!

בֶּאֱמֶת אֵין קֵץ לְהוֹדוֹ,/ נִבְעֲרָה כָּל הַנְּשָׁמָה,
מַעֲמִיד עוֹלָם בְּחַסְדּוֹ,/ לַחֲקֹר עַל מֶה וְלָמָּה;
5 כִּי לְמַעַן שֵׁם כְּבוֹדוֹ/ שָׁת רְקִיעוֹ עַל אֲדָמָה;
כִּי בְרוּחוֹת נַעֲלָמִים/ שָׁם יְגַלֶּה מַחֲבוֹאָיו--
שָׁם בְּרָקִים, שָׁם רְעָמִים,/ שָׁם גְּשָׁמָיו, שָׁם נְשִׂיאָיו.

רֹאשׁ וְתַכְלִית אֵין לְגָדְלוֹ,/ וַעֲלֵי כָּל מַהֲלָל רָם.
מַה תְּמוּנָה נַעֲרֹךְ לוֹ,/ כָּל תְּמוּנוֹת הוּא יְצָרָם?
10 וֶאֱיָלוּת שָׁם לְחֵילוֹ,/ כִּי לְבַדּוֹ הוּא סְפָרָם.
עַל סְפָרִים שָׁת רְשׁוּמִים/ כָּל אֲשֶׁר יְקַר בְּרוּאָיו--
אַךְ סְפָרָיו הֵם חֲתוּמִים,/ לֹא יְבִינֵם רַק נְבִיאָיו.

מִמְּאוֹרוֹ כָּל מְאוֹרִים,/ יַעֲרִיצוּהוּ הֲמוֹנוֹ,
כִּי בְכֹחוֹ נֶעֱזָרִים/ לַעֲשׂוֹת תָּמִיד רְצוֹנוֹ.
15 מַעְגְּלֵיהֶם הֵם יְשָׁרִים/ עִם מְרוּצַת כֵּס גְּאוֹנוֹ--
כֵּס פְּחָדִים הוּא וְאֵימִים,/ כֵּס חֲסִין נוֹשֵׂא לְנוֹשְׂאָיו--
שָׁם דְּמוּת אָדָם תְּמִימִים,/ שָׁם נְשָׁרָיו שָׁם לְבִיאָיו.

This *'ofan*, a *muwashshaḥ*-style hymn in the *yoṣer* cycle, was chanted on the Sabbath and festival morning service immediately before "Soaring celestial creatures roar, responding with a chorus of adoration" (*we-ha-'ofannim we-ḥayyot ha-qodeš mitnasse'im le'ummat serafim*). Its general theme in the liturgy is based on the angelic choir singing the *trishagion* in Is. 6: 3. While in his opening Ibn Ezra follows the traditional practice, he later turns to God's inscrutability, "Men are confused by His motives."

---

22. Levin, *Širey Ha-Qodeš...Ibn Ezra*, 1: 279-80; Schirmann, *Ha-Širah Ha-'Ivrit*, 1: 612; The alliteration *'al meh we-lamah* (line 4) in Schirmann's text is preferable to Levin's *mah zeh we-lamah*.

Echoing God's response to Job (chapter 40), likewise perplexed, the poet catalogues Deity's governance of nature in a sequence of word repetitions, "*šam yegalleh maḥavo'aw*--/ *šam beraqim, šam re'amim,* / *šam gešamaw, šam nesi'aw*" (lines 6-7, and again in line 17). God also delegates His authority to the stars: "He makes notes in His ledgers (*sefarim*) listing the fate of His creatures." The astral constellations and their movements--the "ledgers" in the heavens"--are empowered with determining human destiny. Only the prophet whose "individual soul is illumined by the universal soul" is privy to the secrets of stellar control. [23]

In the closing strophe the poet adapts the four "faces" in Ezekiel's vision of the throne chariot (chapter one). In Ibn Ezra's treatment the "faces" of the "eagle" and "lion" refer to the astral configurations in these forms. These personified constellations of the Primum Mobile, the ninth sphere, are perceived as the bearers of God's "chariot throne" which is identified as the tenth sphere Empyrean. [24] The poet closes with a characteristic paradox, "God's seat bears its bearers!" To Ezekiel's poetic vision of God enthroned above His creatures and borne by them, Ibn Ezra adds the philosophic caveat that He is not dependent upon His bearers.

28.   IN GOD'S HANDS

God, exalted in grandeur; praised be His glorious name.

He fashioned every form,
Both hidden and revealed;
Even reason's rule
By himself He established! Who is privy to His council?

They who see His bounty
In the course He takes,
How can they deny him?
All are His creatures; they are His witness, vouching for Him.

---

23. See Ibn Ezra's comment on Ps. 139: 18; J. Guttmann, *Philosophies of Judaism*, p. 119.

24. See Ibn Ezra's commentary on Ps. 8: 4.

Whoever considers His wonders
With his heart and his eyes,
And with the guidance of His prophets,
He will be grateful throughout life that his breath is in God's hands. [25]

--ס-/--/--ס-/--
--ס-/--

אֵל נִשְׂגָּב בְּהוֹדוֹ--/ בָּרוּךְ שֵׁם כְּבוֹדוֹ.

בָּרָא כָּל תְּמוּנָה,
נִרְאָה אוֹ צְפוּנָה,
וִיסוֹד הַתְּבוּנָה
5   בִּשְׁמוֹ הֶעֱמִידוֹ--/ מִי עָמַד בְּסוֹדוֹ?

רוֹאֵי רַב בְּטוּבוֹ
בַּהֲלִיכוֹת נְתִיבוֹ--
אֵיכָה כְּחֲשׁוּ בוֹ?
כָּל נוֹלָד יְלָדוֹ/ הוּא שַׂהֲדוֹ וְעֵדוֹ.

10   מִתְבּוֹנֵן פְּלָאָיו
בְּלִבָּבוֹ, וּמַרְאָיו,
וּבְדִבְרֵי נְבִיאָיו--
יוֹדְנּוּ בְעוֹדוֹ/ כִּי רוּחוֹ בְיָדוֹ.

It is likely that this hymn was an introduction to the Sabbath and festival
barekhu (Praise the Lord, Source of blessing) which the poet repeats in the first
"belt" of his *muwashshaḥ*: "Praised (*barukh*) be His glorious name." The opening
strophe celebrates God's transcendence: He creates all forms revealed in stellar bodies
and in the sublunar world, and concealed as angels. Although He founded the earth
by "wisdom" and established the heavens by "understanding" (Prov. 3: 19), they too
are His creatures.

In emphasizing God's control over "reason's rule," Ibn Ezra, champion of

---

25. Levin, *Širey Ha-Qodeš...Ibn Ezra*, 1: 156-57; Schirmann, *Ha-Širah Ha-ʿIvrit*, 1: 600.

scientific inquiry, is suggesting that intellectual effort alone is insufficient. This point
is made clearer in his commentary on Deut. 18: 11, "[The way of] truth is that man's
heart be always wholly (*tamim*) with His Creator. When he relies upon his own
wisdom in the pursuit of truth and of that which shall be [by some means] other
than God, his heart is wanting (*ḥaser*, here used as the antonym of *tamim*)." [26]

In the closing strophe Ibn Ezra lists three agents which help verify God's
presence. These include the individual soul which resides in the heart. Having been
"hewn from Deity's rock" [27] and being immortal like the angels, the soul has a
privileged access to divinity with which it hopes ultimately to be reunited. Man's
"eyes," the windows of his perceptive ability, can witness to God's work revealed in
the order and design of nature. Likewise "the prophets," endowed with the talent to
decode Deity's message, urge man to be grateful for his dependence on the Creator
("that his breath is in God's hands").

29.   YOU ASK FOR NO REWARD

O Source of all that breathes,
In your judgment You have given wisdom to the heart,
And the gift of eloquence to the tongue;
It is true that by your mere command You made all things effortlessly!

My fate is in your hands; I am speechless [in your presence],
My lips fail me; each moment
I am reminded of You within me; wherever I turn
You confront me with the rules You taught me—this is a
    blessing You gave me.

You are most generous in your kindness to me,
When my mind is feeble and I fail to understand myself;
Whether asleep or awake, I draw my strength from You;
You show me mercy and shower me with favors, and ask for no reward!

---

26. See Langermann, "Astrological Themes," p. 53.
27. Ibn Gabirol, *Keter Malkhut*, 29.

How good You are to me when I have failed You!

You hide my flaws and hear my cry;

When You put me to the test, I succeed with your help;

You redeemed my soul and saved my life, your aid has never failed.

While dwelling in the heights, You provide for the lowly;

You are gracious to all and work wonders for them;

Secure is your throne with your majesty displayed;

Creator of all and sovereign, You are exalted over everything. [28]

ס--/---/ס--/---/ס---
ס--/---/ס--/ס--/---

אֱלֹהֵי הָרוּחוֹת/ לְכָל בָּשָׂר אַתָּה,

וְחָכְמָה בַּטוּחוֹת/ בְּחָכְמָתְךָ שַׁתָּה,

וְגַם דַּבֵּר צָחוֹת/ בְּיַד לָשׁוֹן תִּתָּה--

אֱמֶת כָּל חוֹלַלְתָּ/ וּבוֹ לֹא עָמַלְתָּ,/ רַק בְּפִיךָ מִלַּלְתָּ!

בְּיָדְךָ עִתּוֹתַי/ וּמַה זֶּה פִּי יַעֲנֶה--   5

וְקָצְרוּ שְׂפָתוֹתַי;/ וְכָל רֶגַע הִנֵּה

בְּקִרְבִּי אוֹתוֹתַי,/ וְאָן לִבִּי יִפְנֶה--

וְאוֹתוֹ הִגְבַּלְתָּ/ בְּדָת שֶׁהִנְחַלְתָּ,/ לִי בְרָכָה אָצַלְתָּ!

רְחָבִים וַאֲרֻכִּים/ חֲסָדֶיךָ עִמִּי,

וְרַעְיוֹנַי רַכִּים/ וְלֹא אָבִין גָּלְמִי,   10

וְעֵת נוּם וּבְהַשְׁכִּים/ בְּךָ עֶצֶם עַצְמִי,

וְעָלַי חָמַלְתָּ/ וְטוֹבוֹת גָּמַלְתָּ/ לִי גְמוּל לֹא שָׁאַלְתָּ!

הֲכִי טוֹב עָשִׂיתָ/ וְאָנֹכִי אֶרְשָׁע,

וְחוֹבִי כִסִּיתָ/ וְאֶל שַׁוְעִי תֵּשַׁע,

וְאַחַר נִסִּיתָ/ לְבָבִי בָּךְ נוֹשַׁע,   15

וְנַפְשִׁי הִצַּלְתָּ/ וְחַיַּי גָּאַלְתָּ,/ מֵעֶזֶר לֹא חָדַלְתָּ!

---

28. Levin, *Širey Ha-Qodeš...Ibn Ezra*, 1: 294–95; Schirmann, *Ha-Širah Ha-'Ivrit*, 1: 606–07.

מְרוֹמִים שָׁכַנְתָּ/ וּשְׁחִים מָלֵאתָ,

וְכָל יֵשׁ חוֹנַנְתָּ/ וְלַעֲשׂוֹת הִפְלֵאתָ,

וְכִסֵּא כּוֹנַנְתָּ/ וְעָלָיו נַעֲלֵיתָ,

20 וְהַכֹּל פָּעַלְתָּ/ וּבַכֹּל מָשַׁלְתָּ/ וַעֲלֵי כֹל גָּדַלְתָּ!

This permission request (*rešut*) before the recitation of the *qaddiš* was chanted in Franco–German and North African congregations during the Sabbath and festival morning service. In a variation of the *muwashshaḥ*, the closing "belt" is formed in rhyming tercets instead of the standard couplet. The longer endings give balance to the shorter strophes which are divided by internal rhyme.

In the opening strophe, the poet affirms man's preeminence. Among the creatures in the sublunar world, he alone is given the gift of eloquence and the wisdom to make choices. However, God transcends human preeminence in His ability to act independently, without effort or eloquence ("By your mere command You made all things"). In the second strophe the poet acknowledges that his fate is in God's hands. Yet, he retains the freedom to choose God's commands ("You confront me with the rules You taught me"). This is in line with rabbinic teaching [in *Avot* 3. 19], "Everything is foreseen, yet freedom of choice is granted."

In the second and third strophes Ibn Ezra, characteristically, describes his intimate personal relationship with God. [29] The tone is a mixture of awe ("I am speechless...My lips fail me") and gratitude for God's unfailing generosity and understanding. Even the occasional insecurity in the relationship ("When You put me to the test") is overcome by the confidence that he has not been abandoned ("I succeed with your help"). The closing strophe ("You are exalted {*gadalta*} over everything") leads in to the *qaddiš* ("Exalted {*yitgaddal*} and hallowed may He be throughout the world of His own creation").

30.   ERE I KNEW YOU

Although I have not seen You with my eyes, it is true that You are God;
I have envisioned You through Your gracious gifts each moment.

---

29. Levin, *Avraham Ibn Ezra*, p. 90.

Your kindness sustained me ere I knew You;
Even now You remember me, though I have often forgotten You.

You wish to do me good without repayment;
You are highly exalted, but I find You near at hand.

I delight in your teaching, like a bridegroom with his bride;
I call upon the God of my life when I cry out to You. [30]

ס--/ס---ס/--ס//ס--/ס---/ס--/ס---.

אֱמֶת אֵל אֱמֶת אַתָּה--וְאִם לֹא רְאִיתִיךָ,
וְאוּלָם בְּרֹב טוּבְךָ בְּכָל עֵת חֲזִיתִיךָ.

בְּטֶרֶם יְדַעְתִּיךָ חֲסָדִים גְּמַלְתָּנִי,
וְעַד כֹּה זְכַרְתַּנִי--וְכַמָּה נְשִׁיתִיךָ.

5   רְצוֹנְךָ לְהֵיטִיב לִי בְּלִי קַחְתְּךָ שָׂכָר,
וְנִשְׂגָּב מְאֹד שִׁמְךָ--וְקָרוֹב מְצָאתִיךָ.

מְשׂוֹשִׂי בְדָתֶיךָ כְּחָתָן עֲלֵי כַלָּה,
וְאֶקְרָא לְאֵל חַי בְּעִתּוֹת קְרָאתִיךָ.

This "petition" (baqqašah) was part of a "Forgiveness Rite" (seder ha-seliḥot) observed by Jewish congregations during the month of Elul and the Ten Days of Repentance, and on fast-days. Early forms of the baqqašah, like Sa'adyah Gaon's, "You alone are God" ('Attah hu' 'adonay levaddekha) and, "O Lord open my lips" ('Adonay sefatay tiftaḥ) and Ibn Gabirol's Keter Malkhut were lengthy prayers in rhymed prose. A variation of the extended baqqašah first appeared in the work of the Hispanic poet, Isaac Ibn Mar Saul, an older contemporary of Ibn Gabirol. To balance and enhance the prose prayers in the "Rite of Forgiveness" service, Mar Saul,

---

30. Levin, Širey Ha-Qodeš...Ibn Ezra, 1: 53; Schirmann, Ha-Širah Ha-'Ivrit, 1: 599–600.

aware of his congregation's fascination with Arabic poetic forms, composed his "petitions" in *qaṣīdah* style with quantitative meter. [31]

In this hymn, Ibn Ezra follows the new practice, albeit with his own variation. Instead of the standard *ha-merubbeh* meter: --v/---v/---v, there are rhyming couplets with *ha-'arokh* meter: ---v/--v/---v/--v. [32] Unlike earlier treatments of the genre which focused on judgment and repentance, Ibn Ezra's *baqqašah* is a hymn of adoration to a caring God. "Your kindness sustained me ere I knew You," is an echo of Ibn Gabirol's, "Before I was You preceded me with your mercies" (*Keter Malkhut*, 35). Both hark back to God's assurance to Jer. (1: 5), "Before I formed you in the womb I knew you, and before you were born I consecrated you."

In his "petition" Ibn Ezra effectively employs a contrast of ideas. "I have not seen You...[but] I have envisioned You through Your gracious gifts...You remember me, though I have...forgotten You...You are highly exalted, but I find You near at hand." The rhetoric of antithesis is often found in Prov. ("It is better to live in a desert land than with a contentious and fretful wife," 21: 19), and was recommended by Aristotle, "because contraries are easily understood" (*Rhetoric* 3. 9. 8).

31.   THE ALL COMES FROM HIM

> I call upon Him who delights in song and psalm;
> Exalted be His awesome name.
>
> When I consider [the universe] and see its beauty everywhere,
> I celebrate the Lord who records it all.
> He built man from earth
>   And placed in his heart a soul that was pure;
>   There she lives like a sovereign in a citadel.
>
> God resides in all that is; the All comes from Him;
> No being like Him is possible;

---

31. *Siddur R. Saʿadyah Gaon*, pp. 47ff, 64ff; Schirmann, *Ha-Širah Ha-'Ivrit*, 1: 257ff.
32. See Fleischer, *Širat Ha-Qodeš Ha-'Ivrit*, p. 410; Schirmann, *Ha-Širah Ha-'Ivrit*, 1: 50–52.

Compared to Him all is nothingness!
   Despite the effort, all creatures are deficient;
   God's wisdom is from man withheld.

His marvels are in the heights; there his angels assemble
Around His throne, ready to serve;
Constellations of stars are in fear of Him;
   He sets the beams of His chambers upon the waters;
   He orders the heavens to be calmed by His winds.

Terrifying displays of power are His creation,
The visible world bears witness to His majesty;
He reveals secrets to His prophets;
   The soul, precious in His sight,
   He will guide in a straight path. [33]

$$\text{--/--ס/---//--//--/--ס/---}$$
$$\text{--/--ס/---}$$

הַבּוֹחֵר בְּשִׁירֵי זִמְרָה/ אֶקְרָא,/ יִתְגַּדַּל שְׁמוֹ הַנּוֹרָא!

אֶתְבּוֹנֵן--וּבְכֹל שָׁפַר,
וַאֲרַנֵּן/ לְאֵל כֹּל סָפַר,
וִיכוֹנֵן/ אֱנוֹשׁ מֵעָפָר
5 וּבְלִבּוֹ נְשָׁמָה בָרָה/ בָּרָא,/ כַּמֶּלֶךְ בְּתוֹךְ הַבִּירָה.

בַּכֹּל הוּא/ וּמִיָּדוֹ כֹל,
כָּמֹהוּ/ הֱיוֹת לֹא יָכֹל,
כַּתְּהוּ/ לְנֶגְדּוֹ הוּא כֹל!
מָה אָמַר--וְיַד כָּל נִבְרָא/ קָצְרָה,/ דַּעְתּוֹ מֵאֱנוֹשׁ נִבְצָרָה!

10   רָם פִּלְאוֹ/ וְסוֹד עֶלְיוֹנָיו,
עִם כִּסְאוֹ/ מְשָׁרְתֵי פָנָיו,

33. Levin, Širey Ha-Qodeš...Ibn Ezra, 1: 344-45; Schirmann, Ha-Širah Ha-'Ivrit, 1: 608-09.

מוֹרָאוֹ/ עֲלֵי אוֹפַנָּיו,
בַּמַּיִם עֲלִיּוֹת קָרָה,/ קָרָא--/ שָׁמַיִם בְּרוּחוֹ שִׁפְרָה.

מוֹרָאִים/ בְּכָל מַעֲבָּדוֹ,
15   כִּי נִרְאִים/ מְעִידֵי הוֹדוֹ;
לִנְבִיאִים/ יְגַלֶּה סוֹדוֹ,
כִּי נֶפֶשׁ בְּפָנָיו יָקָרָה/ הוֹרָה/ לָלֶכֶת בְּדֶרֶךְ יְשָׁרָה.

This is a request for permission (*rešut*) before reciting the *qaddiš* ("Exalted
{*yitgaddal*} and hallowed may He be etc."), as indicated in the opening "belt:" Exalted
(*yitgaddal*) be His awesome name. As in his *rešut*, "O Source of all that breathes"
(Poem #29), Ibn Ezra employs a variation of the *muwashshaḥ* by constructing the
"belt" in tercets instead of the conventional couplets. Added to this is the uncommon
practice of limiting the middle colon in the tercet to one unit: "*Ha-boḥer be-širey
zimrah/ 'eqra'/ yitgaddal šemo nora'*" (line 1).

Reflecting the theme of the *qaddiš*, the poet, in the first strophe, celebrates
the glory of the universe and its Creator who "records (*safar*) it all." This conceit is
adapted from the *Sefer Yeṣirah* where God enacts the work of creation through the
combinations of the Hebrew letters that were inscribed on heavens' spheres. [34] The
creation of man results from a combination of opposites: grimy dirt and pure
spirit--an antithesis that defines a life-long struggle in the human condition.

In the strophe following the poet hints at the relationship between God, the
world of the pure forms ("the All:" *kol*), and the creatures of the sublunar world
made in the likeness of the forms above it. A fuller exposition of this relationship is
found in Ibn Ezra's philosophic work, *Yesod Mora'* 12. 3, "In this way the intelligent
will be able to know the One insofar as the All (*kol*) is attached to it, whereas to
know it insofar as its total good is concerned is beyond the power of a created
being." [35] Man's inability to "know...[the] total good" of "the One" is echoed in the
closing "belt:" "Despite the effort, all creatures are deficient; God's wisdom is from
man withheld."

---

34. See G. Scholem, "Kabbalah," in *JE*, 10: 507.
35. Sirat, *A History of Jewish Philosophy*, p. 107.

32.   HE LEAVES HIS MARK ON THE STARS

Armies in the heights unanimously acclaim your holiness.

God the mighty, exalted above a circle of wonders,
Is the Lord who leaves His mark [36] on the stars.
Encompassing the throne, they sing in a chorus;
Numbering in the thousands, they are the last survivors and first created.

He appointed officers with seven ranks;
Day and night they hasten on their rounds
To the north and south surrounding the fixed stars;
Some complete their course in a day, others in months and years.

The planets race fueled by His large power;
They may range far from earth's borders or turn and draw near;
These to the east, others to the west;
On their mission they are guided by God's command to march
              forward or make camp.

The sphere suspended above the earth
Resonates with life; music echoes there;
The moon's mystery is revealed for all to see;
In their separate ways, all witness to the faithful God. [37]

--/--ס-/-ס--/---/-ס-
---/-ס-/-ס--

מַחֲנוֹת עֶלְיוֹנִים--/כֻּלָּם כְּאֶחָד קְדֻשָּׁה עוֹנִים.

אַדִּיר, אֲשֶׁר נַעֲלָה סוֹד פִּלְאוֹ,

---

36. This reading *'ot bi-ṣeva'o* is based on A. Mirsky's text of this poem. See his
"Ha–Ziqah Še–Bayn Širat Sefarad Li–Drašot Ha–Za–L," pp. 248–53.
37. Levin, *Širey Ha–Qodeš...Ibn Ezra,* 1: 158–59; Schirmann, *Ha–Širah Ha–'Ivrit,* 1:
610–11.

הוּא הָאֱלֹהִים אוֹת בִּצְבָאוֹ,
כָּל אִישׁ יְזַמֵּר סְבִיבוֹת כִּסְאוֹ--
5 הֵם לְאַלְפֵי מוֹנִים,/ הֵם אַחֲרוֹנִים וְהֵם רִאשׁוֹנִים.

בָּרָא מְשָׁרְתִים בְּשִׁבְעָה מַעֲלוֹת,
יִתְרוֹצְצוּ יוֹם וְלֵיל בִּמְסִלּוֹת
צָפוֹן וְיָמִין סָבִיב מַזָּלוֹת--
זֶה לְיָמִים נִמְנִים,/ זֶה לֶחֳדָשִׁים וְזֶה לַשָּׁנִים.

10 רוּץ הַגְּלִילִים בְּעֻזּוֹ הָרַב,
יִרְחַק גְּבוּל עֵת וּפַעַם יִקְרַב,
אֵלֶּה לְמִזְרָח וְאֵלֶּה לְמַעֲרָב--
אִישׁ לְדַרְכּוֹ פוֹנִים,/ נוֹסְעִים עֲלֵי פִּיו וְעַל פִּיו חוֹנִים.

מָעוֹן אֲשֶׁר עַל אֲדָמָה נַעֲלָה--
15 שָׁמָּה הַמֶּלָה וְשָׁם קוֹל נִפְלָא,
סוֹד הַלְּבָנָה לְעֵין כֹּל נִגְלָה
עַל מְכוֹנוֹת שׁוֹנִים,/ לִהְיוֹת לְעֵדִים לְאֵל נֶאֱמָנִים.

This 'ofan in the form of a muwashshah was chanted in North African congregations on Sabbaths and festivals. While its primary theme is the adoration of Deity by an angelic assembly--based on Is. 6: 1-3--Ibn Ezra broadens its focus to include the newer Ptolemaic astronomy. The astral chorus around the divine "chariot throne" is identified with the constellation of stars in the eighth sphere. They are hailed as "the last survivors and first created"--although as God's creatures they cannot be co-eternal with Him. "He leaves His mark on the stars" ('ot bi-ṣvao') is based on the comment of Reš Laqiš [in bHag 16a], "By what Biblical exposition was he [Rabbi Aqiva] able to learn this [= to distinguish God's Presence so as to avoid Elišah ben Avuyah's error of dualism, or (according to another interpretation) so as not to look in the direction of the Divine Presence (šekhinah)]?...[By remembering the verse from Is. 48: 2:] 'The Lord of hosts is His name,' He sets his mark among His host [of stars] (*'ot hu' ba-ṣava' šelo*)." [38]

The seven planets on separate levels are God's "officers" active in the region of the eighth sphere of fixed stars. Their maneuvers are determined by divine command ordering them "to march forward or make camp." This image of astral space as a military service is seen in the opening "belt:" "Armies in the heights etc." The Hebrew *maḥanot* (= armies, sing. *maḥaneh*) is often used to designate soldiery (in Deut. 23: 10; Josh. 10: 5; Jud. 4: 15–6).

The "armies" are heard singing on their trail. The music of the spheres is suggested to Ibn Ezra by Ezekiel's vision of God's throne chariot, "When they (the creatures bearing the 'chariot') moved I heard the sound of their wings...a sound of tumult like the sound of an army." [39] The poet singles out the moon for clues to unraveling the mystery of the stellar world. He expands on this in his *Re'šit Hokhmah* (chap. 8, p. 215): "Because the moon is near the earth and accelerated in its course, it increases the conjuction of planets by communicating its force to them without ever receiving any force from them...That is why the ancients said that it influences every deliberation and the beginning of any task."

33.   GOD'S THOUGHTS

> Though God's thoughts cannot be fathomed, His wonders are
> > plain to see;
> He sows righteousness and reaps victory.
>
> God, awesome in splendor, arrayed on his throne,
> Has charted highways for the planets who do His bidding;
> For each He fixed a time for every task;
> > He attracts the straying and repels the colliding;
> > He weakens the arrogant and heals the afflicted.

---

38. Reš Laqiš's comment is based on the reading of *bHag* in the *'Eyn Ya'aqov*. The latter was the accepted text of the Talmud in Spain. See A. Mirsky, "Ha-Ziqah Še-Bayn Širat Sefarad Li-Drašot Ha-Za-L," p. 249.

39. Ez. 1: 24 and Ibn Ezra's commentary; see also his comment on Job 38: 7.

His mighty hand is displayed in the heights,
His signet ring seals the heavens;
The two luminaries He made to rule the earth;
He unleashes the rains that give drink and remembers the weeks
Of harvest when the hungry are satisfied.

His stars hasten before him. Sitting in circles, they
Are his loyal witness, even man among them.
Though He is exalted, His eyes peer into human hearts;
He hears their cry, He gathers up their tears;
He relieves their distress on judgment day.

Who made the vault arching over the earth?
Who held it firm with lighting bolts cast in the waters?
Who stationed His spheres encompassed in stately display?
Hard as mirrors of cast metal, they are God's arms;
They engrave the starry hosts; they sow supernal lights. [40]

$$\text{--(ס)/-ס--//--(ס)/-ס--.}$$

מַחְשְׁבוֹת אֵל עֲמֻקּוֹת,/ מִפְעֲלוֹתָיו יְדוּעוֹת;
זוֹרֵעַ צְדָקוֹת,/ מַצְמִיחַ יְשׁוּעוֹת.
אֵל נוֹרָא תְהִלּוֹת,/ עַל כִּסְאוֹ בְשִׁבְתּוֹ
לִמְשָׁרְתָיו מְסִלּוֹת/ שָׁם לַעֲשׂוֹת מְלַאכְתּוֹ,
5   חֹק נָתַן לְמַלֹּאת/ כָּל דָּבָר בְּעִתּוֹ--
הוּא יַקְרִיב רְחוֹקוֹת,/ הוּא יַרְחִיק נְגוּעוֹת,
הוּא יַרְפֶּה חֲזָקוֹת,/ הוּא יְרַפֵּא נְגוּעוֹת.

בַּשַּׁחַק גְּבוּרוֹת/ יָדוֹ הָעֲצוּמָה,
מֶרְכַּבְתּוֹ בְצוּרוֹת/ טַבַּעְתּוֹ חֲתוּמָה
10   וּשְׁנֵי הַמְּאוֹרוֹת/ הִמְשִׁיל עַל אֲדָמָה--
הוּא יָעִיר לְהַשְׁקוֹת,/ הוּא יִשְׁמוֹר שְׁבוּעוֹת

---

40. Levin, *Sirey Ha-Qodeš...Ibn Ezra*, 1: 357-59; Schirmann, *Ha-Širah Ha-'Ivrit*, 1: 609-10. Schirmann's reading יַרְפֶּה (line 7) is preferable to Levin's יְרַפֶּה since it conforms to the meter.

הַקָּצִיר, וְרַקּוֹת/ תָּשׁבְנָה שְׁבֵעוֹת.

רָץ חֵילוֹ לְפָנָיו,/ חוּגִים הֶעֱמִיד--בָּם
עֵדָיו נֶאֱמָנָיו,/ הָאָדָם בְּקִרְבָּם.
15 הוּא נִשְׂגָּב, וְעֵינָיו/ צוֹפוֹת מַה בְּלִבָּם--
הוּא יִשְׁמַע צְעָקוֹת,/ הוּא יֶאֱסֹף דְּמָעוֹת
הוּא יַרְחִיק מְצוּקוֹת/ בִּפְרוֹעַ פְּרָעוֹת.

מִי בָרָא אֲגֻדּוֹת,/ עַל אֶרֶץ יְסָדָם?
שָׁת זִיקוֹת לְיַדּוֹת/ בַּמַּיִם יְסוֹדָם
20 וַעֲגֻלּוֹת כְּבַדּוֹת/ סָבִיב הֶעֱמִידָם?
הֵם כְּרָאֵי חֲזָקוֹת,/ הֵם הֵם הַזְּרוֹעוֹת,
בָּם חַיּוֹת חֲקוּקוֹת/ בָּם אוֹרוֹת זְרוּעוֹת.

This *me'orah* hymn was chanted before the benediction "Praised are You, O Lord, Creator of lights" (*yoṣer ha-me'orot*) during the Sabbath and festival morning service. The closing line in the final strophe, "they sow supernal lights (*'orot*)" was designed to lead into the benediction. The *me'orah* is in the *muwashshaḥ* style, although its meter does not consistently follow the classic quantitative principle in which two elements forming a Hebrew syllable, the *tenu'a* (movement = {-}) and *yated* (peg = {v})--designated by the mobile *šewa'* and its *ḥataf* derivatives--are used in combination. [41]

Ibn Ezra's *me'orah* builds on the benediction theme by detailing the genesis of supernal light and its relation to God. Starting with the verse from Gen. 1: 16–18, "God made the two great lights etc," the poet expands on the theme with references from contemporary science and from sources in Jewish mysticism, notably the *Sefer Yeṣirah*. Beginning with a rhetorical antithesis ("Though God's thoughts cannot be fathomed, His wonders are plain to see") the poet elaborates on the nature of the planets and their movements visible to the eye. God, their guide keeps them on a steady course ("He attracts the straying and repels the colliding"). Like an earthly monarch who signs on a document to make it official, God "seals" the heavens with "His signet ring." The conceit is adapted from the *Sefer Yeṣirah* 3. 6 where the Hebrew letters are the instruments with which God seals the work of creation.

41. See Habermann, *Toledot Ha-Piyyuṭ We-Ha-Širah*, 1: 265ff.

Although the planets are endowed with the power to govern the sublunar world, God may intervene in special circumstances ("He weakens the arrogant and heals the afflicted"). From his Bible commentaries and writings on astrology, we learn that Ibn Ezra assigns the Jews to the influence of the planet Saturn, the most elevated of all by virtue of its being in the seventh sphere viewed from the earth. To the planet Mars are assigned "the soldiers, their commanders, the thieves...those who shed blood...and those who are like them." [42] The special circumstances that call for divine intervention in astral governance occur when the fate of the Jews is involved. This is in line with Ibn Ezra's comment on Deut. 4: 19, "God has appointed the various heavenly bodies to govern the other nations, reserving Israel for His special guardianship." [43]

34.   GOD'S TORAH

> I live by adhering to God's Torah,
> And am hopeful that the Master will pay my wages.
> In her (Torah's) garden paradise I want to be,
> Her river will satisfy my thirst.
> I have found You (God) with my mind's eye and again
> With Your Torah's help, O Glorious In Power.
> Give me wisdom to do the right;
> When I exalt You, I gain esteem with Your help.
> Neither heaven nor earth can contain
> Your majesty, much less my feeble effort.
> All her life my soul longs for Your shelter,
> And when I fall, the mention of your name lifts me up. [44]

$$--ס/---ס/---ס//--ס/---ס/---ס$$

בְּדָת אֵל אֶדְבְּקָה חַיֵּי בְשָׂרִי,
אֲקַוֶּה מֵאֲדוֹנָה תֵּת שְׂכָרִי.

---

42. Ibn Ezra, Re'šit Ḥokhmah, p. 197.
43. See Langermann, "Astrological Themes in Ibn Ezra," p. 59.
44. Levin, Širey Ha-Qodeš...Ibn Ezra, 1: 26.

בְּגַן עֶדְנָה לְהִתְעַדֵּן רְצוֹנִי
וְעִתּוֹת צְמָאוֹנִי הוּא נְהָרִי.
5 רְאִיתִיךָ בְּעֵין הַלֵּב וְאֹחַר
בְּתוֹרָתָךְ, בְּכֹחַ נֶאֱדָרִי.
הֲבִינֵנִי עֲשׂוֹת דֶּרֶךְ נְכוֹחָה,
אֲגַדֶּלְךָ--וְאַף תַּגְדִּיל הֲדָרִי.
מְרוֹמִים וַהֲדוֹמִים לֹא יְכִילוּן
10 כְּבוֹדֶךָ--וְאַף כִּי מַאֲמָרִי.
חֲסוֹת בָּךְ אוּתָה נַפְשִׁי בְּעוֹדָהּ
וּבְשָׁחוֹתִי שְׁמָךְ שָׂמְתִּי פְאֵרִי.

The *qaṣīdah*-style hymn is a "permission request" (*rešut*) in the liturgy for
Simḥat Torah (Festival of Rejoicing with the Torah). The poet leaves no doubt that
this hymn was intended for the festival in his reference to the Torah by name, "With
Your Torah's help" and by metaphor, "I live by adhering to God's Torah." In the
latter citation, the Hebrew *be-dat 'el*--based on Deut. 33: 2, "At His right hand was a
fiery law ('*eš dat*)"--refers to the Torah. [45]

The hope that "the Master will pay my wages" is adapted from the rabbinic
comment [in *'Avot* 2. 21], "Your Employer [= God] can be relied upon to reward you
for your labors." The "reward" that the poet hopes for is entrance into Torah's
"garden paradise." This conceit is drawn from Ps. 36: 9, "They feast on the abundance
of Your house, and You give them drink from the river of Your delights." In his
commentary on this verse from Psalms, Ibn Ezra notes that "house" refers to those
"who serve God in the seclusion of their homes; their service refreshes their spirit
and the knowledge of God's presence delights them."

This "knowledge" enables the poet to find God with his intellect ("mind's
eye") and the help of the Torah. The need for the latter in attaining the desired goal
demonstrates in this instance Ibn Ezra's commitment to Jewish distinctiveness,

---

45. See *bBer* 62a, "The Torah was given with the right hand, as it says [in Deut. 33:
2], 'At His right hand was a fiery law unto them'."

comparable to that of his contemporary Judah Halevi. [46] *'Eyn ha-lev*, literally, "the heart's eye" is best translated as "mind's eye" since the soul, the seat of the intellect is located in the heart.

---

46. For another view of Jewish distinctiveness in Ibn Ezra's philosophy, see Langermann, "Astrological Themes in Ibn Ezra," p. 70, "When his (Ibn Ezra's) philosophy *cum* natural astrology is laid bare, it is clear that there are no organic essential differences between Jew and non-Jew, certainly nothing of the order demanded by Judah Halevi."

THE SOUL

35.   THE SOUL'S PASSION

Can my soul ever cool its passion
To adhere to the life-giving Rock?
With Him Wisdom's fountain abides
Watering her grain and displaying her fruit.
The stately shape of the soul in her glory
Resembles a bride bedecked with jewels.
Every age retells God's praises,
And the reborn nation will thank Him. [1]

--/-ס--/-ס--//--/-ס--/-ס--

אֵיךְ תֶּחֱשֶׁה נַפְשִׁי--וּמַאֲוַיֶּהָ
לִחְיוֹת עֲדֵי תִדְבַּק בְּצוּר הֶחָיֶהָ?
בָּהּ מַעְיְנֵי חָכְמָה וּמִמֶּנָּה
תֻּשְׁקֶה קְצִירֶיהָ וְזֶה פִרְיָהּ.
רִקְמַת גְּוִיָּתָהּ מְהֻדָּרָה,   5
תִּדְמֶה לְכַלָּה תַּעְדֶה כֶלְיָהּ.
מְהַלַּל אֱלֹהֶיהָ יְסַפֵּר דּוֹר
אֶל דּוֹר, וְעַם נִבְרָא יְהַלֶּל-יָהּ.

The hymn is a permission request (*rešut*) presumably before the recitation of the Sabbath and festival morning service prayer, "The breath of all that lives praises You, Lord God" (*Nišmat kol ḥay*). Built in the style of a *qaṣidah*, its elegant hemistichs are metrically balanced. The soul's odyssey is the main theme of the hymn.

In line with contemporary Jewish Neoplatonism, Ibn Ezra laments the fate of his soul now separated from her celestial home. She longs once again to "adhere" (*tidbaq*) to her divine source. The poet elaborates on this conceit in his commentary on Ps. 1: 3, "'They [who delight in God's Torah] yield their fruit in its season…In all that they do, they prosper.' The [ripened] fruit is a metaphor for the intelligent soul

---

1. Levin, *Širey Ha-Qodeš…Ibn Ezra*, 1: 25; Schirmann, *Ha-Širah Ha-'Ivrit*, 1: 598–99.

sufficiently endowed with the knowledge of God's Torah that it is able to acknowledge its Creator...and adhere (*tidbaq*) to her celestial world. She is like the ripened fruit which separates from the tree because it is no longer needed."

However, knowledge alone will not enable the soul to reach her goal. She must also engage in the practice of pious deeds ("...here is her fruit"). Here Ibn Ezra echoes the view of Ibn Gabirol in his *Meqor Ḥayyim*, 1. 2. [2] The soul that is free of her bodily confinement is likened to the bride leaving her father's house to be united in marriage with her beloved. Likewise, will Israel now in exile be reborn and return to its native land. The term "reborn nation" (*'am nivra'*), taken from Ps. 102: 12, elicits from Ibn Ezra the comment, "[Israel] will be reborn when God will return the exiled to Zion."

36.   CHASING AFTER TIME'S MISTAKES

> O my soul, return to God and be saved
> From Time's snare. How long must you crave foolishness?
> Having considered the mystery of your birth, why do you rebel?
> Your behavior should disappoint you and make you ashamed.
> Enough of chasing after Time's mistakes.
> Do not weaken in your war against temptation;
> Take hold of Wisdom and turn to the Intellect;
> Pray night and morning and know Who [confronts you].
> Put on Reason's valued garment; wrap it around you,
> Never fail to keep the promise to your Master.
> Fortify yourself with His love—and you will find peace
> Forever in His holy heights, there rejoicing. [3]

8-10

אֶל אֵל שׁוּבִי, יְחִידָה וְהִמָּלְטִי
מִפַּח זְמַן, עַד אָנָה הֶבֶל תֶּהֱמִי?
בִּינִי אֶל סוֹד יְסוֹדֵךְ, לָמָה תִבְעָטִי?

---

2. Sirat, *A History of Jewish Philosophy*, p. 72.
3. Levin, *Širey Ha-Qodeš...Ibn Ezra*, 1: 49.

מִמַּעֲשֶׂיךָ בֹּשִׁי וְהִכָּלְמִי!

5 רַב לָךְ רְדֹף זְמַנֵּךְ הַמַּחְטִיא,
רִיבִי תָמִיד בְּיִצְרֵךְ וְהִלָּחֲמִי.
הֵאָחֲזִי בַּחָכְמָה וְלַשֵׂכֶל נְטִי,
לַיִל וָיוֹם הִתְפַּלְּלִי וְתֵדְעִי לְמִי.
מַדֵּי יְקַר תְּבוּנָה לְבָשִׁי וַעֲטִי,

10 כָּל עֵת לְבֹעֲלַיִךְ נִדְרֵךְ שַׁלְּמִי.
חִזְקִי בְּאַהֲבָתוֹ--וְאָז תִּשְׁקְטִי
בִּמְרוֹם קָדְשׁוֹ לְעוֹלָם, וּבוֹ תִנְעָמִי.

In this "permission request" (resut), the poet admonishes his soul—which he calls "my only one" (yehidah) after Ps. 22: 21—to beware of the blandishments of Time. The personification of "Time" and the "World" was a commonplace conceit in medieval Hispano-Hebrew literature. [4] Both were condemned for their fickleness and deceit. Time lulls the soul into a false sense of security urging her to seize the day and give no thought for the morrow. To counter this *carpe diem* mentality, the poet bids the soul to remember its divine pedigree. The battlefield imagery ("Do not weaken in your war against temptation") adds urgency to the soul's predicament. She is advised to defend herself with wisdom and intelligence against the enemy.

However, human effort alone will not be enough for the soul "to find peace...in His holy heights." God's help is required: "Pray night and morning..." Unlike the humanism of Ibn Gabirol who holds the soul can purify itself from the pollutions of Time and the World "by knowledge and pious deeds" (be-'ezrat ha-yedi'ah we-ha-pe'ulah), Ibn Ezra recommends divine aid as well. [5] "Pray...and know Who [confronts You]" is adapted from the rabbinic comment [in *bBer* 28b], "When you pray, know before whom you are standing."

---

4. See Levin, "'Zeman' We-'Tevel' Be-Širat Ha-Hol Ha-'Ivrit," pp 68–79.
5. Ibn Gabirol, *Meqor Hayyim*, 1. 2; Sirat, *A History of Jewish Philosophy*, p. 72, "It seems indeed that the 'practice' suggested by our author [Ibn Gabirol, in *Meqor Hayyim* 1. 2] corresponds to a somewhat vague notion of moral conduct rather than to the precisely defined acts required by the rabbinic commandments".

37.   PUT AWAY TIME'S DELICACIES

O soul, emanated from the luminous fount of life,

You are hewn from the pure and holy place,

A unique creation without form,

Your worth surpasses wisdom and honor.

Do you not know why you were sent down to earth,

And why you are confined in the body's dark recess?

Why do you persist in childish play

And chase the folly of the accursed earth?

Your sleep may be sweet at the outset,

Awakened, you will be bitter with regret.

Put away Time's delicacies. Why

Would you be a vagabond and outcast when you leave the body?

Consider well the honor that is yours; it is the source of your [pride];

You are blessed to be a fearful servant of the living God.

Be well-advised in this World, so that

In the World-To-Come you may be bound up with the Lord. [6]

ס/---ס/---ס//--ס/---ס/---ס--

אֲצוּלָה מִמְּקוֹר חַיִּים מְאִירָה,
גְּזוּרָה מִמְּקוֹם קֹדֶשׁ טְהוֹרָה,
בְּרוּאָה מִבְּלִי תַּבְנִית יְחִידָה
וּמֵחָכְמָה וּמִכָּבוֹד יְקָרָה--
רְאִי עַל מָה שְׁלוּחָה אַתְּ בְּתֵבֵל   5
וְלָמָּה זֶה בְּגוּף אֹפֶל עֲצוּרָה?
הֲלָעַד תִּרְדְּפִי יַלְדוּת וְשַׁחֲרוּת
וְהַבְלֵי הָאֲדָמָה הָאֲרוּרָה?
מְתוּקָה לָךְ בְּרֵאשִׁיתָךְ שְׁנָתָה--
וְהִיא קָשָׁה בְּאַחֲרוֹנָה וּמָרָה.   10
חֲמוּדוֹת הַזְּמַן עָזְבִי--וְלָמָּה
בְּצֵאתֵךְ תִּהְיִי גֹלָה וְסוּרָה?
זְכֹר לַחְקֹר כְּבוֹדֵךְ--זֶה יְסוֹדֵךְ,

---

6. Levin, Širey Ha-Qodeš...Ibn Ezra, 1: 55.

וְטוּבֵךְ--לַעֲבֹד אֵל חַי בְּמוֹרָא.

15 קְחִי עֵצָה לְעוֹלָם זֶה, לְמַעַן

בְּעוֹלָם בָּא תְּהִי עִם אֵל צְרוּרָה.

In this introduction (petiḥah) in the style of a qaṣīdah, the poet reminds his soul of her mission on earth. She is emanated from the Universal Soul, termed "God's Glory" (kevod 'adonay) and "the Source of Life" (meqor ḥayyim). In Jewish Neoplatonism the Universal Soul is identified with the tenth sphere, the sphere of the Intellect which is the divine "Chariot Throne." [7]

Although Ibn Ezra does not answer his rhetorical question, "Do you know why you were sent down to earth?" his oftentimes mentor, Ibn Gabirol provides a clue in his Keter Malkhut 31: "You have placed the soul in the body...to teach and show it the path of life." Echoing Arabic ascetic poetry (zuhdiyyāt), the soul is warned against being distracted from its focus on the Eternal by the wiles of illusory "Time" and the "World." "Your sleep may be sweet at the outset, / Awakened, you will be bitter with regret" is a conceit consistent with the Platonic distinction between appearance--the sweet dreams of sleep--and harsh reality upon awakening.

When failing in her mission, the soul cannot be reunited with her supernal source. Being weighed down by the burden of her dishonor she is unable to traverse the several spheres leading to her native home. Ibn Ezra's rhetorical question to the soul, "Why would you be a vagabond and outcast (golah we-surah) when you leave the body?" is modelled after Ibn Gabirol's comment [in Keter Malkhut, 30], "If she [the soul] has been defiled...All the days of her impurity she shall be a vagabond and outcast (golah we-surah)." The distinction between this World and the World-to-Come is based on rabbinic teaching. In the Ethics of the Fathers 4.21, "Rabbi Jacob taught, "This world is compared to a foyer which leads to the world-to-come. Prepare yourself in the foyer, that you may be worthy to enter the main hall."

38.   THE BEARER OF HIS WONDERS

Emanated from the glory of God your maker

---

7. See Ibn Ezra's comment on Ps. 8: 4.

You were borne on the shoulders of four beasts,

And you are the bearer of His embracing wonders—

Where can you hide from His pervading presence?

Think what you will do when He comes to search

Your hiding places; surely He will see and hear you!

Be honest with Him who understands perfectly

And do not question His methods.

You have nothing to your credit except a prayer;

Who were you before coming to life by His mercy?

Know that all that is in heaven and on earth

Comes but to praise the honorable name of your Maker. [8]

ס‎---/ס--//ס‎---/ס--//ס‎---/ס--

אֲצוּלָה מִכְּבוֹדוֹ אֵל בְּרָאָךְ

וְעַל אַרְבַּע דְּמוּת חַיּוֹת נְשָׂאָךְ,

בְּקִרְבֵּךְ גַּם סְבִיבֵךְ מִפְעֲלוֹתָיו--

וְאָן תִּסָּתְרִי, כִּי הוּא מְלָאָךְ?

5   רְאִי מַה תַּעֲשִׂי, כִּי הוּא יְחַפֵּשׂ

חֲדָרַיִךְ וְיִשְׁמָעֵךְ וְיִרְאָךְ.

הֱיִי נָא עִם תְּמִים דֵּעוֹת תְּמִימָה

וְאַל נָא תִשְׁאֲלִי עַל מַעֲשָׂיו אֵיךְ.

מְאוּמָה אֵין בְּיָדֵךְ, רַק דְּבָרֵךְ,

10   וּמִי אַתְּ עַד אֲשֶׁר חַסְדּוֹ הֱבִיאָךְ?

דְּעִי כִּי כֹל בְּשָׁמַיִם וָאֶרֶץ--

לְבָרֵךְ שֵׁם כְּבוֹד יוֹצְרֵךְ וּבוֹרְאָךְ.

This is an admonition to the soul in the form of a *qaṣidah*-style "permission request" before the recitation of the *qaddiš* ("Exalted and hallowed may He be etc."). The tone, as in the previous hymn, is personal and intimate. The poet represents the Intellect reminding the soul of its ancestor, the divine "chariot throne" borne by the "four beasts" in Ezekiel's vision (1: 5).

There is no place for the soul to hide since God's presence is pervasive. This

---

8. Levin, *Širey Ha-Qodeš…Ibn Ezra*, 1: 54; Schirmann, *Ha-Širah Ha-ʿIvrit*, 1: 598.

conceit bordering on pantheism is characteristic of Ibn Ezra for whom God "is the One; He made all; He is all." [9] The soul will not outwit God ("Be honest with Him who understands perfectly"), nor should it question His methods. The latter warning is based on Ps. 73: 11, "Then they say, 'How could God know? Is there knowledge with the Most High?'"

"You have nothing to your credit except a prayer" is an admission of complete helplessness and dependence. This is the ideal condition in Ibn Ezra's perception of the divine–human relationship in which absolute merit and value reside only in God. Moreover, existence itself is a gift that He endows ("Who were you before coming to life by His mercy?").

39.   IN THE DARK OF MY FOLLY

Before I was born You sealed my fate,
How can I serve another when all Your creatures be?
I want to serve You, but my ill-fortune prevents me;
I look for Your light in the dark of my folly.
In You I rejoice wherever I may be;
In my vagabond life Your word is a candle in the road. [10]

ס/--ס/---ס/--ס//---ס/--ס/---ס/--ס---

בְּטֶרֶם הֱיוֹת נַפְשִׁי חֲתוּמִים סְפָרֶיךָ
וְאֵיךְ אֶדְרְשָׁה בִּלְתָּךְ--וְהַכֹּל יְצוּרֶיךָ?
רְצוֹנִי לְעָבְדָךְ, אַךְ זְמַנִּי מְנָעַנִי,
וְעִם מַחְשָׁךְ יִצְרִי אֲקַוֶּה לְאוֹרֶךָ.
5   בְּךָ יַעֲלֹז לִבִּי בְּשִׁבְתִּי וְקוּמִי, גַּם
בְּהִתְהַלְּכִי, כִּי נֵר לְרַגְלִי דְּבָרֶךָ.

It is likely that this "permission request" (rešut) has been preserved only in part. Of its three surviving qaṣidah-style strophes the first two begin with the letters bet and reš respectively. Presumably the first strophe began with alef and a missing

---

9. See Ibn Ezra's comment on Gen. 1: 26.

10. Levin, Širey Ha-Qodeš...Ibn Ezra, 1: 28; Schirmann, Ha-Širah Ha-'Ivrit, 1: 599.

fourth strophe opened with the letter *mem*, spelling the poet's name "Abram." Name signature in liturgical works was a common practice of Ibn Ezra and his contemporaries.

"Before I was born You sealed my fate" translates literally "Your books were sealed" (*ḥatumim sefarekha*). In Ibn Ezra's comment on Ps. 69: 29, "'Let them be blotted out from the book of the living,' I have explained elsewhere that the *book of the living* refers to the heavens where the destinies of all who are to be born are inscribed."

"I want to serve You, but my ill-fortune prevents me," would seem to imply that since God empowers the stars with the governance of the sublunar world, man cannot save himself from astral decrees. However, in his comment on Ex. 33: 23, Ibn Ezra writes, "Whatever the configuration of stars existing at his birth has decreed for such an individual will surely befall him, unless he be protected by a power superior to the power of the stars." That superior power is man's mind as Ibn Ezra notes in his *Sefer Ha-Mivḥarim* ("B" version, f. 131a): "He who has it in his configuration to be poor...cannot become rich, except for this: because man's soul comes from a place higher than all the stars, man can by means of his mind (*da'ato*) mitigate his misfortune somewhat." [11] The poet's prayer, "I look for Your light" in line four is that appeal to a power higher than the stars.

40.   A SUMMONS

I am summoned to appear before the King in His palace;
I am stricken with fear because I have not been obedient.
O Lord, I have heard of Your judgment and I tremble.

O my soul, what excuses will you make
When you are weighed on a just scale?
Why complain? Did not God give you the means
To do right, but you were misled by foolishness;
You never gave it any thought; you did not listen to reason
    Asking you: What are you doing and why are you here?

---

11. Langermann, "Astrological Themes in Ibn Ezra," pp. 51-52.

You willfully followed your passions' lead;
You have indulged yourself now and have forgotten about the morrow
When God will expel you from the body's shell
And recompense you for the sins you committed;
They are inscribed in the written record.
   The choice is yours today; I urge you to be honest.

In the carcass of a lion you found a honeycomb;
You feasted and were corrupted, never thinking of the
Just God who, on a day, will call together the nations
Of the world to judgment and revive the dead.
Instead you imagined: the day would never come—
   The world's splendor is before me, I want it for my own!

Your roving gaze leads you to the grave;
Your passion for deceit betrays you;
They will not help you, but they will lead you to hell,
A place of fiery sparks and glowing embers inflaming you.
The worldly glitter you cherish will fade on judgment day.
   Moved by regret you will cry: I hurt because I am a rebel! [12]

5/5

אֶל בֵּית הַמֶּלֶךְ/ לָבוֹא נִקְרֵאתִי;
רְעָדָה אֲחָזַתְנִי/ כִּי פִיו הִמְרֵיתִי,
אֲדֹנָי, שָׁמַעְתִּי/ שִׁמְעֲךָ, יָרֵאתִי!

בַּמֶּה, יְחִידָתִי,/ לְהִנָּצֵל תּוּכְלִי,
5   יוֹם עַל כַּף מֹאזְנֵי/ הַמִּשְׁפָּט תַּעֲלִי?
מַה תִּלּוֹנִי? וְאֶל/ בְּיָדַיִךְ שָׁם כְּלִי
לְהֵטִיב--וְאַתְּ תִּרְשָׁעִי,/ וּבַהֲבֵל תֶּהְבְּלִי,
בְּלִבֵּךְ לֹא תַחְשְׁבִי,/ בְּשִׂכְלֵךְ לֹא תִּשְׂכְּלִי

---

12. Levin, *Širey Ha-Qodeš...Ibn Ezra*, 1: 508–10; Schirmann, *Ha-Širah Ha-'Ivrit*, 1: 602–03

לֵאמֹר: 'מַה זֶּה וְאֵיךְ/ וְלָמָּה נִבְרֵאתִי?

10 רָצִיתָ לָלֶכֶת/ אַחֲרֵי תַאֲוָתֶךָ,
תִּתְעַנְּגִי פֹּה--וְלֹא/ זָכַרְתְּ אַחֲרִיתֵךְ,
יוֹם אֵל יַפְרִידֵךְ/ מֵעַל גּוּיָתֵךְ
וְאֵל חֵיקֵךְ יָשִׁיב/ תַּגְמוּל פְּעֻלָּתֵךְ,
כִּי בְסֵפֶר רָשׁוּם/ חָקוּקָה אַשְׁמָתֵךְ.
15 הַיּוֹם לְעֻמָּתֵךְ/ נְתִיב תֹּם הוֹרֵיתִי.

הֵלֶךְ דְּבַשׁ מָצָאתָ/ בִּגְוִיַּת אַרְיֵה,
אָכַלְתָּ--וַתִּטְמָאִי,/ וְלֹא אָמַרְתְּ: 'אַיֵּה
אֱלֹהֵי הַמִּשְׁפָּט,/ יוֹם יֶאֱסֹף גּוֹיֵי
הָאָרֶץ לַדִּין/ וְהַמֵּתִים יְחַיֶּה?'
20 וְאָמַרְתְּ בִּלְבָבֵךְ:/ 'אוּלַי לֹא יִהְיֶה--
הוֹד עוֹמֵד לְנֶגְדִּי/ אֶתְאַוּ וּבְרֵאתִי!'

מַרְאוֹת עֵינַיִךְ/ בִּשְׁאוֹל יַשְׁלִיכוּךְ
וְתַאֲוֹתַיִךְ לְךָ-/רֶךְ רַע יַדְרִיכוּךְ;
לֹא יוֹעִילוּךְ--אֲבָל/ לְתֹפֶת יוֹלִיכוּךְ,
25 מְקוֹם גַּחֲלֵי כִידוֹ-/דֵי אֵשׁ יַתִּיכוּךְ,
וּמְאוֹרוֹת חֶלְדֵּךְ/ בְּמִשְׁפָּט יַחְשִׁיכוּךְ;
תִּנָּחֲמִי וְתֹאמְרִי:/ 'אוֹי כִּי מָרִיתִי.'

This prayer for forgiveness (selihah) was highly popular among Jewish worshippers and was included in the Franco–German, Spanish, Italian and Yemenite liturgies. The hymn, built in strophes resembling the muwashshah, opens with a "belt" in tercets which rhyme with the closing line in each strophe. The figure of the humble petitioner standing before the mighty monarch is drawn, in part, from the poet's own experience with his courtier patrons.

Presumably, the hymn was part of the "Rite of Forgiveness" (Seder Ha-Selihot) service as indicated in its several references to judgment and atonement. The soul "weighed" on a "just scale" is an image adapted from Job 31: 6, "Let me be weighed in a just balance, and let God know my integrity." Unlike Job, the poet fears that the soul's sins will incline the scales and bring God's punishment. The soul is given the choice to be guided by wisdom or to be "misled by foolishness." The "sins...inscribed in the written record" is a conceit based on the rabbinic image [in *Avot* 3. 16] of God with an "open ledger" and a "recording hand." Sin's metaphor is the misguided man feasting on a honeycomb "in the carcass of a lion." The figure, taken from the story of Samson [in Judg. 14: 8], telescopes the human predicament. Forgetting that an improperly slain animal is impure (Lev. 22: 8), Samson succumbs to its momentary delight. Adding to its lack of self-control is the soul's tendency to fall victim to illusion: "You imagined the day [of judgment] would never come."

The impure soul leading "to hell, / A place of fiery sparks" should be understood in line with Ibn Ezra's Neoplatonism. He, like Ibn Gabirol, considers the formless soul to be able to make the ascent to her divine home by her merits. If she fails in her mission she becomes "a vagabond and outcast" until "the days of her purification be fulfilled" (Ibn Gabirol, *Keter Malkhut*, 30). Elaborating on this, Ibn Ezra adds [in his comment on Is. 66: 24] that the impure soul unable to rise to heights remains imprisoned in the sublunar world in the charge of the "sphere of fire." [13]

41.   ADMONITION TO THE SOUL

> My soul, if you do not know what the future brings
> Look for the signs of your origin in the past!
> You are housed in vapor and built on emptiness.
> Your entrance is like your exit, your living is like your dying.
>   How can you be content herding a worthless wind?
>   Mend your ways; soon you will vanish like a shepherd's tent!
>   Efforts to find you will be in in vain--
>   How can you remain indifferent?
>
> Given to Passion and knowing her to be your enemy
> You have not noticed that your end is near.
> Her wine beguiles you, her bread entices you

---

13. In medieval astronomy, the "sphere of fire" is one of four encompassing the globe. The other spheres are air, water, and earth.

Until your defences are down
  And your [weakened] limbs will come back
  To witness against you. Now put away
  Your wine.
  How can you remain indifferent?

Long enough have you pursued what you must leave behind.
Choose instead to be attracted to God's delights.
How deceitful can you be:
Repenting once and sinning often?
  Will you acnowledge your Maker but one time and indulge yourself
          at will?
  How can your sin be forgiven when Temptation is at your right hand
  Accusing you?
  How can you remain indifferent?

Time has mocked you; it has driven you to mischief
You build and buy and are not satisfied.
When it all fades you will ask, "Have I trusted in vain?"
Your indulgence was your sole reward!
  Since your mission is to serve the living God, why
  Do you worship worldly goods? Repent and consider
  What you will say to your Master
  How can you remain indifferent?

O World, why have you enticed me with vapors?
I no longer care if you are gracious or cruel!
O Time, why should I rejoice at good fortune or mourn a tragedy?
I am but a transient here indifferent to your praise or blame,
  Your success or failure, tranquility or terror.
  Whether I be master or slave, death will ultimately

Separate us!

How can you remain indifferent? [14]

6/5

5/5

אִם לֹא תֵדְעִי, נַפְשִׁי, אַחֲרִיתֵךְ

קְחִי לָךְ מוֹפֵת וְאוֹת מֵרֵאשִׁיתֵךְ.

הֶבֶל יְסוֹדֵךְ וְעַל תֹּהוּ בְּנוֹתֵךְ,

בּוֹאֵךְ כְּצֵאתֵךְ וְחַיַּיךְ כְּמוֹתֵךְ.

5   וְלָמָּה תִרְגָּעִי/ וְרוּחַ שָׁוְא תִּרְעִי?

פְּנִי לָךְ, כִּי תִסְעִי/ כְּמוֹ אֹהֶל רֹעִי,

וּתְבַקְשִׁי וְאֵינֵךְ--

וְאֵיךְ עַל זֶה לֹא פָקַחְתְּ עֵינֵךְ?

בְּתַאֲוָה דָּבַקְתְּ אֲשֶׁר הִיא אוֹיַבְתֵּךְ

10   וְלֹא הִתְבּוֹנַנְתְּ כִּי תְקָרֵב עִתֵּךְ.

יֵינָהּ יוֹנֵךְ וְגַם פִּתָּהּ תְּפַתֵּךְ,

עַד יִיעֲפוּ אַנְשֵׁי מִלְחַמְתֵּךְ

וְנוֹשְׁאֵי כֵלַיִךְ--/ וְיָשׁוּב אֵלַיִךְ

גְּמוּל מַעֲלָלָיִךְ!/ לְזֹאת מֵעָלַיִךְ

15   הָסִירִי יֵינֵךְ!

וְאֵיךְ עַל זֶה לֹא פָקַחְתְּ עֵינֵךְ?

רַב לָךְ לִדְרֹשׁ אֵת אֲשֶׁר תַּעֲזֹבִי,

אֶל טוֹב אֲדֹנָי תִּנְהֲרִי אִם תֹּאבִי.

אֵיךְ תַּהְפּוּכוֹת בְּלִבֵּךְ תַּחְשֹׁבִי--

20   פְּעָמִים תְּשׁוֹבְבִי וּפַעַם תָּשׁוּבִי?

אִם אַחַת לְקוֹנֵךְ/ וְרִבּוֹת לִרְצוֹנֵךְ,

וְאֵיךְ יִתֹּם עֲוֹנֵךְ--/ וְהַיֵּצֶר לְשָׂטְנֵךְ

יַעֲמֹד עַל יְמִינֵךְ?

וְאֵיךְ עַל זֶה לֹא פָקַחְתְּ עֵינֵךְ?

25   הֵחֵל זְמָן בָּךְ; לְעָמָל נִדְדַחְתְּ,

---

14. Levin, *Širey Ha-Qodeš...Ibn Ezra*, 1: 387–88; Schirmann, *Ha-Širah Ha-'Ivrit*, 1: 596–99.

לִבְנוֹת וְלִקְנוֹת, וְעוֹדָךְ לֹא נָחַתְּ,
הַכֹּל יְכְלֶה--וְעַל מַה בָּטַחַתְּ?
הֲלֹא בְתַעֲנוּגֵךְ שְׂכָרֵךְ לָקָחַתְּ!
לְאֵל חַי אַתְּ אָמָה/ לְעָבְדֵהוּ, וְלָמָה
30   עָבַדְתְּ הָאֲדָמָה? שׁוּבִי וּדְעִי מַה
תֹּאמְרִי לַאֲדוֹנֵךְ!
וְאֵיךְ עַל זֶה לֹא פָקַחַתְּ עֵינֵךְ?

מַה לָּךְ, תֵּבֵל, תְּסִיתִינִי לְהָבֶל?
תְּנִי אוֹ לְקָחִי--אֲנִי עוֹד לֹא אֲקַבֵּל!
35   אֵיךְ אֶשְׂמַח עַל זְמָן, אוֹ אֶתְאַבֵּל?
מְעַט אֶשְׁכְּנָה בָךְ; יִנַּשֵּׂא אוֹ יִבֵּל,
יַעֲלֶה אוֹ יוֹרִיד/, יַשְׁקִיט אוֹ יַחֲרִיד,
וְאֶעֱבֹד אוֹ אָרִיד--/ הַמָּוֶת יַפְרִיד
בֵּינִי וּבֵינֵךְ!
40   וְאֵיךְ עַל זֶה לֹא פָקַחַתְּ עֵינֵךְ.

This self-rebuke (*tokhehah*) was part of the "vigil nights" (*leyley 'ashmurot*) service held at midnight or before dawn during the month of Elul and the Ten Days of Repentance. The poetic form of Ibn Ezra's *tokhehah* is modelled after Ibn Gabirol's "O restless soul, forsake your despair" (*shikhhi yegonekh, nefesh homiyyah*) [15] in this genre with its rhyming pattern: aaaa, bb, cc. The last line in each strophe is a repeated refrain.

In his rebuke the poet warns the soul not to be attracted to its transient home in this world ("You are housed in vapor and built on emptiness"). The poet's image of the soul as a wayward shepherd "herding a worthless wind" is adapted from Hos. 12: 2. The metaphor is extended in the judgment that follows, "Soon you will vanish like a shepherd's tent."

Unreasonable Passion designated by the feminine term *ta'awah* is hostile to the soul which in Ibn Ezra's Neoplatonism is identified with the Intellect. "Her (Passion's) wine beguiles you, her bread entices you" is smooth seductive speech hiding an ominous intent to weaken man's reasoning defences. "Choose instead to be

---

15. Schirmann, *Ha-Širah Ha-'Ivrit*, 1: 233-35.

attracted to God's delights" is a rhetorical argument that it is possible to enjoy a yet greater and more enduring pleasure.

Personified Time and the World and the ephemeral attractions that they offer are singled out for rebuke. The purified soul with its eye on the farther shore of its home in the heights is no longer affected by what transpires in the present world. This stoic indifference and withdrawal from the present is in line with contemporary Jewish Neoplatonism in its attempt to preserve the purity of the soul. In his commentary on Ps. 3: 5 Ibn Ezra seeks to connect this withdrawal with the rabbinic contrast [in *Avot* 4. 21] between the present world and the world-to-come, "God's servants forsake the passions of the present world, are content with their portion (*Avot* 4. 1) and consider their meager bread and water the equal of any feast (*Avot* 6. 4). Their thoughts and hearts are focused on the World-to-Come and they exchange the pleasures of the moment for delights that are eternal."

42.   IN THE CHOICEST PART OF MY BODY

I bow my face to the ground, lower I cannot go;
I prostrate myself before the Most High, exalted above every height.

With what shall I encounter Him if not my soul? Did it not come from
    Him held in His hand?
The most precious possession, He made it live in the choicest
    part of my body.

Since there is no limit to his greatness, how can my speech enhance it?
He is distant in the highest heavens and nearer than my flesh and bone;

I have come to You, my God, for no other can save me;
The throngs in heaven and earth, like me, are your handiwork;

Why would I seek their aid when human help is worthless!
There is no safety for the servant except with his Master;

What more is there to learn when I know that You made me from love;

Your mercies are infinite, but my sins outnumber the ocean sand;

Dare I lift my eyes to ask your help when they have offended You?
Shall my lips presume to speak when they have been perverse?

My pride has done me greater harm than an enemy assault;
I tremble with anguish; I hurt because I disobeyed!

My cruel impulse deceived me; I did not intend to anger You;
Only I have been hurt by my malice, while You were constant
     in your caring;

Show me how I can be helped; all I know is what You taught me;
I have heard my heart's plea hoping that You will hear it
     from the heavens. [16]

אֶשְׁתַּחֲוֶה אַפַּיִם אַרְצָה, כִּי אֵין לְמַטָּה מִמֶּנָּה,
אֶתְנַפֵּל לִפְנֵי עֶלְיוֹן, גָּבוֹהַ עַל כָּל גְּבוֹהִים

בַּמֶּה אֲקַדֵּם פָּנָיו כִּי אִם בְּרוּחִי? הֲלֹא הִיא מֵאִתּוֹ וּבְיָדוֹ,
בְּמִבְחַר גּוּפָתִי הוּא יְחַיֶּה, כִּי אֵין לְאִישׁ נִכְבָּד מִנַּפְשׁוֹ.

5   רֹאשׁ וָסוֹף אֵין לִגְדֻלָּתוֹ--וּלְשׁוֹנִי אֵיךְ תְּגַדְּלֶנּוּ?
רָחוֹק רָחוֹק מִשְּׁמֵי הַשָּׁמַיִם, וְקָרוֹב קָרוֹב מֵעַצְמִי וּבְשָׂרִי!

הִנֵּה בָאתִי לְךָ, אֱלֹהַי, כִּי אֵין מוֹעִיל זוּלָתֶךָ.
הֲלֹא צְבָא הַשָּׁמַיִם וְהָאָרֶץ כֻּלָּם נִבְרָאִים כָּמוֹנִי;

מֵהֶם אֵיךְ אֶדְרֹשׁ תְּשׁוּעָה--וּתְשׁוּעַת כָּל יָצוּר כָּזָב!
10   מָנוֹס אֵין לְעֶבֶד בִּלְתִּי לַאֲשֶׁר קָנָהוּ!

מָה אֲחַשֵּׁב לָדַעַת? וְיָדַעְתִּי כִּי לְהֵיטִיב לִי בְּרָאתַנִי,
מִסְפַּר עָצְמוּ חֲסָדֶיךָ--וּמֵחוֹל הַיָּם חַטֹּאתָי.

---

16. Levin, Širey Ha-Qodes...Ibn Ezra, 2: 148–49; Schirmann, Ha-Širah Ha-'Ivrit, 1:
605–06.

עַיִן אֵיךְ אֶשָּׂא אֵלֶיךָ? וְהִיא גַם הִיא חָטָאָה,
עוֹד מַה יַּעֲנוּ שְׂפָתָי? גַּם הֵמָּה הִרְשִׁיעוּ!

15   זְדוֹן לִבִּי עָשָׂה לְנַפְשִׁי אֲשֶׁר לֹא יוּכַל אוֹיֵב עֲשׂהוּ,
זַלְעָפָה אֲחָזַתְנִי מִמֶּנּוּ--אוֹי לִי כִּי מָרִיתִי!

רֹעַ יִצְרִי הִתְעָנִי, כִּי לֹא הָיָה רְצוֹנִי לְהַכְעִיסֶךָ,
רָעוֹתַי לִי לְבַדִּי הֵרֵעוּ--וְאַתָּה לְבַדְּךָ תַּעֲשֶׂה חֶסֶד!

הוֹדִיעֵנִי דֶּרֶךְ יוֹעִילֵנִי, כִּי כֹל יָדַעְתִּי אַתָּה הוֹדַעְתָּנִי;
20   הִשְׁמַעְתִּי דִּבְרֵי לִבִּי לְאָזְנִי--וְאַתָּה תִּשְׁמַע הַשָּׁמָיִם!

This *selihah*–type hymn, known as a *rehuta* [= beam] is distinguished by its
lack of rhyme or meter. This allowed for an unemcumbered and spontaneous
expression of prayer during the "Rite of Forgiveness" (*Seder Ha-Selihot*) service. The
rehuta, constructed with fragments, or "beams" of biblical words and verses, was a
popular form with early Italian and Franco–German poets. Pioneered in Spain by
Abraham Ibn Ezra, his *rehuta* model was widely imitated in later ages. [17]

Although the hymn is based largely on biblical conceits, some Neoplatonic
elements are included. In the second strophe the poet recontextualizes the verses in
Mic. 6: 6 ("With what shall I come before the Lord") and Zech. 4: 6 ("Not by might,
nor by power, but by my spirit {be-ruhi}, says the Lord of hosts") to read, "With
what shall I encounter Him if not my soul (be-ruhi)?" This leads into, "Did it not
come from Him," and refers to the emanation of the soul from the Universal Soul,
in line with contemporary Neoplatonism.

God's pervasive presence, which in Ibn Ezra's thinking borders on pantheism,
is suggested by the verse in Is. 66: 1, "Thus says the Lord, 'Heaven is my throne and
the earth is my footstool.'" In the poet's construction the conceit is turned into the
provocative paradox, "He is distant in the highest heaven and nearer than my flesh
and bone." Antithesis and paradox are common rhetorical figures in other parts of
the hymn. Most notable is the moving plea, "Dare I lift my eyes [in prayer] to ask

---

17. See Fleischer, *Širat Ha-Qodeš Ha-'Ivrit*, pp. 407, 440.

your help when they have offended You? Shall my lips presume to speak when they have been perverse?"

In closing, the poet resolves to heed the plea of the soul, lodged in the heart "the choicest part of my body" and prays that his repentance will reach God in the heavens.

ISRAEL

43. AWAITING THE REDEEMER

May it once more please the Lord to produce Israel's redeemer.

Chained, confined and imprisoned in a pit, they are unprotected;
Exiled, humbled, disdained, and poor, they cry out;
Beaten, doomed to perish and cursed, they are an everlasting waste,
While their attacker is firmly in power, willful, destructive and at
     peace with himself.
 He is aided by demons, invokes the stars, resorts to lies and deals
    with ghosts;
  But there is no divining in Israel.

Abused in their lifetime, scattered among islands, they are helpless.
Driven, dispersed, scorned and ostracised by all,
While the ignorant laugh and hiss and agitate against them in their torment;
They think that God has left them and their hope vanished, though
     He warned them.
 Yet every armed heathen and despot, encouraged to kill,
    rebels against God;
  But no one helps Israel.

Crushed and shattered, oppressed and wounded, their faces are somber.
Christians and Muslims devour and destroy them; exiled, their skin
     wastes away.
Trampled, befouled and restricted, God has walled them in.
Sold for nothing and persecuted, they are changed, their splendor is gone;
  Confused, their home demolished, their saints are seen as corrupt.
  This has come to pass in Israel.

Wretched and troubled, plundered and vagrant, they hope for You;
See their misery in prison and their cheek-filled tears, and bring them joy.
Be merciful and respond, rebuild them and buy back their freedom.
Jeshurun will sing your praises when they see revealed

Your glory and majesty in Your assembly and You returned to
  the Temple,
And Israel calling upon your name. [1]

--/-ס-(ס)/--(ס)

ס-/-ס-/--ס/--ס/--ס/--

יוֹאֵל עוֹד לְהָבִיא אֵל/ הַגּוֹאֵל לְיִשְׂרָאֵל.

אֲסוּרִים/ סְגוּרִים/ עֲצוּרִים/ בְּבוֹרִים,/ סָר עֲדֶן צֶלָם.
בְּגֻלוֹת/ וְשִׁפְלוּת, וְקַלּוּת/ וְדַלּוּת/ יִתְּנוּ קוֹלָם.
וְהוֹלְמָם/ הֲדָמָם,/ זְעָמָם,/ הֲשָׁמָּם/ שְׁמָמוֹת עוֹלָם--
5   וְהִנּוּ/ בְּכַנּוּ,/ רְצוֹנוֹ/ בְּאוֹנוֹ/ יַעֲשֶׂה--וְיִשְׁלָם;
וְחוֹבֵר/ חָבֵר/ וְהוֹבֵר/ וְדוֹבֵר/ שָׁוְא, וְאוֹב שׁוֹאֵל--
וְלֹא קֶסֶם בְּיִשְׂרָאֵל.

בְּזוּיִים/ בְּחַיִּים,/ זְרוּיִים/ בְּאִיִּים,/ אֵין לְאֵל יָדָם.
הֲרִיצוּם,/ הֱפִיצוּם,/ הֱלִיצוּם,/ הֱקִיצוּם/ כָּל בְּנֵי אָדָם.
10 וְרֵקִים מְשַׂחֲקִים/ וְשׁוֹרְקִים/ וְחוֹרְקִים/ שֵׁן בְּיוֹם אֵידָם,
בְּשׁוּרָם/ אֲבִירָם/ הֲסִירָם,/ וְשָׁבְרָם/ סָף--וְהוּא עֵדָם.
וְכָל זָר/ וְאַכְזָר/ מֵאָזָר/ וְנֶעֱזָר/ הוּא, וְרָד עִם אֵל--
וְאֵין עוֹזֵר לְיִשְׂרָאֵל.

רְעוּצִים,/ רְצוּצִים,/ לְחוּצִים,/ מְחוּצִים,/ תְּאָרָם קָדָר.
15 אֲכָלָם/ וְכִלָּם/ וְהִגְלָם/ וּבִלָּם/ נִין אֱדוֹם וְקֵדָר.
רְמָסָם,/ רְפָסָם/ וְעָשָׂם,/ וְעוֹשָׁם בַּעֲדָם גָּדָר,
וְחִנָּם/ נְתָנָם,/ וְעִנָּם/ וְשָׁנָּם/ מִבְּלִי הָדָר,
וְהֵמָּם/ וְשָׁמַם/ מְקוֹמָם,/ לְשׁוֹמָם/ זַךְ כְּמִתְגָּאֵל--
הָיְתָה זֹּאת בְּיִשְׂרָאֵל.

20 מְרוּדִים,/ טְרוּדִים,/ שְׁדוּדִים,/ נְדוּדִים,/ לָךְ יִיַחֲלוּ,
וְעָנִים/ בְּשִׁבְיָם/ וּבְכִיָם/ בְּלָחְיָם/ שׁוּר, וְיִצְהֲלוּ,
תְּחַנֵּם/ וְתַעֲנֵם/ וְתִבְנֵם/ וְתִקְנֵם/ לָךְ, וְנִגְאֲלוּ.
יְעִירוּן,/ יְשִׁירוּן,/ יְשׁוֹרוּן,/ יְשׁוּרוּן/ אַחֲרֵי גְלוּ

---

1. Levin, *Širey Ha-Qodeš…Ibn Ezra,* 1: 213–15.

כְּבוֹדָךְ/ וְהוֹדָךְ/ בְּסוֹדָךְ, יְסוֹדָךְ/ שָׁב לְהִדָּרְאֵל--
25   וְנִקְרָא שְׁמוֹ בְּיִשְׂרָאֵל.

This "redemption" (ge'ullah) hymn for the Sabbath and festival morning prayers was chanted before the benediction, "Praised are You, Lord, Redeemer (ga'al) of the people Israel." Built in the form of a *muwashshah*, this ge'ullah is distinctive for its assonance, alliteration and internal rhyme, as may be seen in the following from the first strophe:

> 'asuriml seguriml 'aṣuriml be–voriml sar 'aden ṣillam
> be–galutl we–šiflutl we–qallutl we–dallutl yittenu qolam;
> we–holemonl hedimmaml ze'amaml hešimmaml šimamot 'olam...

The phonetic intensive character of the poem augments the sense of urgency in the poet's plea for Israel's national restoration.

Ibn Ezra's lament that Jews are "unprotected" is likely a reference to the Almohade, 'Abd al–Mu'min who, in 1146, sought to convert the Jews to Islam by force. [2]   The enemies are aided by invoking demonic forces, ghosts and spirits, a practice forbidden to Israel (Deut. 18: 10–11) who trusts in God alone. Here, as in the following strophe, the poet points to the contrast between faithful Israel and the rebellious nations ("Yet every armed heathen and despot, encouraged to kill, rebels against God").

Having shown the contrast between Israel and the nations, the poet can effectively present the irony of their respective situations: "Beaten, doomed to perish and cursed...While their attacker is firmly in power...and at peace with himself." Their "attacker" is named the "sons of Edom and Qedar," a common reference to Christians and Muslims in the synagogue liturgy. [3]   As in most ge'ullah hymns, the closing strophe is a prayer for the ingathering of the exiles, the rebuilding of the Temple and Israel's national independence.

---

2. See notes to Poem #14 above, and see Baron, A Social and Religious History of the Jews, 3: 124–25.

3. Gen. 36: 1; 25: 13 and Zunz, Die synagogale Poesie des Mittelalters, p. 464.

44. THE WHISPER OF A FALLING LEAF

Am I as strong as a rock? Is my heart made of iron?
I do the work for my maidservant and my mother's sons are angry
  with me.

When I recall my happy days on earth,
When God's presence was in the Temple and I alone served Him.
Alas! Who will comfort me now that my beloved is gone?
  Alas! The home that once restored my soul is now a tent pitched
    by Arabs!
  Alas! The sheep are scattered and have become the prey of lions.

The day is spent and disaster is on the horizon; a fool would shut me
    off from light
Into darkness and I am lost. Would that God were my enemy!
I am terrified, the whisper of a falling leaf drives me away.
  I walk from stumble to stumble; pitfalls surround me.
  I fall down; every stone in the field is hostile.

Filled with endless reproach, I have no pleasure.
The wicked rejoice over me having their revenge:
My flesh has failed, only my bones remain.
  I pour out my life in my prayer; I plead with my Father,
  Perhaps He will look at me and bring my redeemer. [4]

--ס/---//---/-ס--

אִם כֹּחַ אֲבָנִים כֹּחִי?/ אִם בַּרְזֶל לְבָבִי?
אֶשָּׂא עֹל אֲמָתִי וּבְנֵי/ אִמִּי נִחֲרוּ בִי.

בַּעֲלוֹת עַל לְבָבִי יָמִים/ שָׂמַחְתִּי בְּחֶלְדִּי
וּכְבוֹד אֵל בְּבֵית עוֹלָמִים/ עָבַדְתִּי לְבַדִּי--
5   הָהּ, אֵיךְ אֲמַצְאָה תַּנְחוּמִים,/ כִּי סָר מַחֲמַדִּי?

---

4. Levin, Širey Ha-Qodeš...Ibn Ezra, 1: 182-83; Schirmann, Ha-Širah Ha-'Ivrit, 1: 620.

אֵיךְ אֹהֶל יְשׁוֹבֵב רוּחִי/ יַהֵל שָׁם עֲרָבִי!
הָה עַל שֶׂה פְזוּרָה, הִנֵּה/ הִיא טֶרֶף לְלָבִיא!

רַד יוֹמִי וְהֵן אֵיד עוֹלֶה,/ מְאוֹר יֶהְדְּפֵנִי
אֶל חֹשֶׁךְ אֱוִיל וָאֶכְלֶה--/ לוּ אֵל יִרְדְּפֵנִי!
10   נִבְעַתִּי, עֲדֵי קוֹל עָלֶה/ נִדָּף יִדְּפֵנִי.
אֵלֵךְ מִדְּחִי אֶל דְּחִי/ כִּי פַחִים סְבִיבִי;
נִכְשַׁלְתִּי--עֲדֵי כָל אַבְנֵי/ הַשָּׂדֶה יְרִיבִי.

מָלֵאתִי כְּלִמּוֹת עוֹלָם,/ חָסַרְתִּי נְעִימוֹת,
וּמְרֵעִים מְרִיעִים כֻּלָּם/ רָאוּ בִי נְקָמוֹת,
15   כִּי כָלָה שְׁאֵרִי אוּלָם,/ נוֹתְרוּ הָעֲצָמוֹת.
נַפְשִׁי אֶשְׁפְּכָה עִם שִׂיחִי,/ אֶתְחַנֵּן לְאָבִי--
אוּלַי אֶל לְבָבִי יִפְנֶה/ הַגּוֹאֵל לְהָבִיא.

In this "redemption" (ge'ullah) hymn in the form of a muwashshah, the poet refers to its theme by name in the closing strophe, "Perhaps...He will bring my redeemer (ha-go'el)." This eases the connection between the hymn and the benediction that follows it, "Praised are You, Lord, Redeemer (ga'al) of the people Israel."

Added to the ge'ullah's conventional pleas for Israel's national restoration are conceits drawn from Andalusian-Hebrew love poetry. The complaint (telunah) in the opening "belt," "Am I as strong as a rock? Is my heart made of iron?" could easily reflect the feelings of separated lovers longing to be reunited. "Alas! Who will comfort me now that my beloved is gone?" is identical to Ibn Ezra's complaint on being separated from his patron Samuel [Ibn Jāmi'?]:

> How will you comfort me, my friends
> Now that my darling 'fawn' has departed? [5]

The poet speaks for Israel who complains that she is in bondage to Muslims--the sons of Hagar, a maidservant to Sarah (Gen. 21: 10)--and Christians--

---

5. Schirmann, Širim Ḥadašim Min Ha-Geniza, p. 275.

the scion of Esau, Rebekah's son (Gen. 25: 23ff). Her national home is occupied by strangers and her children are scattered and defenseless.

In her despair, she is taunted by her masters who seek to persuade her to abandon her God ("a fool would shut me off from light/ Into darkness"). "Would that God were my enemy (lit. "pursue me")," is understood in light of David's comment to Gad [in II Sam. 24: 14], "Let me fall into the hands of the Lord, for His mercy is great; but let me not fall into human hands." Israel's cry, "[I am] filled with endless reproach," reflects an awareness of responsibility for her predicament in addition to the disgrace heaped upon her by the nations.

45.   MY ANOINTED KING IS DELAYED

My anointed king is delayed while I thread my way through the pitfalls;

The guardian angels of the nations are hostile to me; even to my
    angel I am
An enemy; this pains me and my people are desolate.
  For my fault the cherub flew away from my tent;
  Now that the assailants were without fear, their empire expanded.

Can he emerge unharmed going through fire and water? Captured by
    his foe
He is deprived of his dignity; men hide their faces from him.
All he does is wait for God, though the end is not in sight. [He
    says:], "His promises
  I will know, even when I fall and am near death;
  It is better for me to be imprisoned than [to lose hope] like the dead."

The attackers leaped with joy when they ambushed their prey;

They rejoiced on the day they saw my armies in full retreat;
They clapped their hands with delight when my saints tore
    their hair lamenting;
  Then my Levites' dancing turned to mourning and I became deathly ill;
  My cherished daughter is a vagrant, not seen again; Muslims hold
    her captive.

What do I say to them who taunt me except fearing to answer?
Though my enemy has prospered and I have lost, I can [still]
    pour out my heart to God;
Though generations may pass, my expectation will remain constant;
  My Redeemer lives; His regard for me retains its wonder;
  Yet sweeter than honey's taste is the marvel of His love. [6]

-ס-/-ס-//---ס/-ס-/-ס-

אָחֲרוּ פַעֲמֵי מְשִׁיחִי,/ אַךְ מוֹקְשַׁי קִדְּמוּ,
מַלְאֲכֵי גוֹי וְגוֹי עֲדֵי מַלְאָךְ/ הַבְּרִית נִלְחֲמוּ
בִּי כְצָרָי; לְזֹאת בְּכַפֵּי אָרְ,/ כִּי מְתֵי שָׁמֵמוּ.
נַעֲלָה הַכְּרוּב בְּרֹב מַעְלִי/ מֵעֲלֵי אָהֳלִי,
סָר מְגוֹרָהּ--וּמַמְלְכוּת אוֹיְבָה/ רָחֲבָה נָסַבָה.   5

בָּא בְמַיִם וְאֵשׁ--הֲיִמָּצֵא/ תָּם? בְּיַד צוֹרְרוֹ
סָר כְּבוֹדוֹ, וְאֵין אֱנוֹשׁ רוֹצֶה/ לַחֲזוֹת תָּאֳרוֹ,
רַק יְקַוֶּה לְאֵל; וְאִם קָצֶה/ אֵין--לְקֵץ דַּבְּרוֹ
שָׁאֶלְתִּי, וּמָעֲדָה רַגְלִי/ עַד לְשַׁחַת בְּלִי,
טוֹב לְנַפְשִׁי אֲשֶׁר בְּבוֹר יָשְׁבָה/ עַד כַּמֶּה נֶחְשָׁבָה.   10

רָקְדוּ לוֹחֲמִים אֲשֶׁר פַּחִים/ יָטְמְנוּ, יִלְכָּדוּ.
יוֹם רְאוֹת מַחֲנַי מְנָצָּחִים/ כֹּה וְכֹה--יִרְקֹדוּ,
יִמְחֲאוּ כַף לְכַף--וְהַקְּרֻחִים/ יִקְרְחוּ, יִסְפָּדוּ.
בְּהֵפָךְ אֶל נְהִי מְחוֹל מַחְלִי--/ רַב מְאֹד מַחְלִי,
נָדְדָה בַת יָקָר וְלֹא שָׁבָה/ עוֹד--וְשָׁבָה שָׁבָא.   15

---

6. Levin, Širey Ha-Qodeš…Ibn Ezra, 1: 377–78.

מָה אֲדַבֵּר לְלוֹעֲגִי--בִּלְתִּי/ מֵעֲנוֹת אֶחְשֹׁכָה
פִּי? וְאִם רָם עֶדֶן וְנָפַלְתִּי--/ לֵב לָצוּר אֶשְׁפְּכָה.
יַעֲבֹר דּוֹר וְדוֹר--וְתוֹחַלְתִּי/ עַד הֲלֹם נִמְשָׁכָה,
גּוֹאֲלִי חַי וְנִפְלָאתָה לִי/ אַהֲבַת גּוֹאֲלִי,
20   אַהֲבָה מִדְּבַשׁ לְפִי עָרְבָה,/ נִפְלְאָה אַהֲבָה.

The hymn known as *'ahavah* (love) was chanted during the Sabbath and
festival morning service before the benediction, "Praised are You, Lord, who in love
has chosen His people Israel (*ha-boher be-'amo yisra'el be-'ahavah*)." The poet,
speaking for his people, laments their prolonged exile even as their hope for
freedom and national restoration remains steadfast. Their promised redeemer
("anointed king") is late in coming, although they continue to search for clues
regarding the time of his arrival ("His [God's] promises [revealed to the Prophets] I
will know").

To the poet's complaint ("The guardian angels of the nations are hostile to
me"), there is an added element of pathos ("Even to my angel I am/ An enemy").
The reference is to a rabbinic legend [in *Yalqut Šim'oni*, Lam. #1009] that Israel's
guardian angels, Gabriel and Michael, set fire to the Temple with a torch given to
them by God. The view that each nation believed itself to have a guardian angel is
suggested in Dan. 10: 13.

Israel's isolation in exile is complete when the Divine Presence departs the
Temple after it is set ablaze: "...the cherub flew away from my tent." According to
legend [in *Lam. Rabbah*, Proem #24] the *šekhinah*, elevated above the cherubim on
the Ark of the Covenant, returned to the heavens after the Temple was destroyed.
Now that the assailants did not have God to fear they could conquer at will.

The sense of isolation by divine powers combined with willful human cruelty
leaves Israel with mere hope to which it must cling. And thereby is resolved the
tension between bitter disappointment ("My anointed king is delayed...the end is not
in sight") and the fierce trust that God has not forgotten them ("His regard for me
retains its wonder").

46.   MY HUSBAND HAS LEFT ME

She who is crushed like grain is heard to moan,
"My Husband has left me;
By my fault, my home is in ruins;
I was unfaithful and my pain is severe.
My singers are silent, they have no voice;
The pipes that made music, even their ornaments are captured.
Sadly, I have no adornment even as I regret being vain in excess;
    now foot-shackles are my cosmetics;
My prized possessions are in the pillagers' hostile hands; even my Husband
    returns to bar my freedom.

Would that my prayer intercede for me;
Poverty has made my voice faint like a ghost's.
The wretched ones have attacked, scattering my troops;
My soldiers are delivered to the enemy.
My foe rejoices over my distress;
I am like a ship mired in the ocean depths;
Sinking and exhausted, I wallow in the blood of corpses
    and the living God watches.
He is a witness to the deeds of the barbarians; why do they prosper
    and I am taken down to sit in the dust?

God, with Your right arm assert Yourself against my assailant
Who mocks my every word;
I speak kindly while he beats upon me
And relishes what was once my inheritance.
All joy perished when my name was blotted out;
I lost title [to my estate] and fell into ruin.
The hunter's son set a trap for me, seized my splendid
    daughter and tore her to shreds.
The kid must live with the lion who has nothing to fear while
    I hold my peace and await my help.

My house is in flames along with my land;

The beautiful fawn is taken captive;

I am paraded in chains while the One I love is present;

He and all my friends are distant to me;

He has turned into an enemy

Making my life a burden.

Look upon me, my Refuge, help me heal my pain and let me walk free;

I will go to the Temple mount when my redeemer (*go'el*) comes

to Jerusalem. [7]

4/3/3/3

6/6

אָמְרָה כְּתוּשָׁה בַּעֲלִי:/ בַּעֲלִי סָר מֵאָהֳלִי,

אָהֳלִי חָרֵב בְּמַעֲלִי,/ מַעֲלִי הִפְלִיא מַחֲלִי,

מַחֲלִי דוֹמֵם בְּלִי כְלִי,/ כְּלִי שִׁיר נִשְׁבָּה וְכָל חֲלִי.

חֲלִי אֵין לִי/ וְרַב אֶבְלִי/ בְּרֹב הֶבְלִי,/ עֲדֵי כַבְלִי/ בְּרַגְלַי פַּעֲדִי;

5   עֲדֵי הוֹדִי/ בְּיַד רוֹדִי/ וּבָא שָׁדִּי/ וְשָׁב דּוֹדִי/ לְהָסֵר בַּעֲדִי.

בַּעֲדִי יָלִיץ מַעֲנִי,/ מַעֲנִי כְקוֹל אוֹב מֶעֱנִי,

עֶנִי קָם לְפַזֵּר מַחֲנִי,/ מַחֲנִי נְתוּנָה לְשׁוֹטְנִי,

שׁוֹטְנִי שָׂשׂ כִּי דַל אֲנִי,/ אֲנִי תּוֹךְ מְצוּלוֹת כְּמוֹ אֲנִי--

אֲנִי צָלַל/ וְלֵב דָּלַל/ וְהִתְגּוֹלַל/ בְּדַם חָלָל/ וְאֶל חַי שָׁהֳדִי,

10   שָׁהֳדִי עַל/ אֲשֶׁר פָּעַל/ בְּלִיַּעַל/ וְאֵיךְ יַעַל--/ וְלִי יֹאמַר: רְדִי?

רְדִי לָךְ, יְמִין אֵל, בְּלוֹחֲמִי!/ לוֹחֲמִי יָבֻזּוּ לְנָאֲמִי,

נָאֲמִי רַכּוֹת לְהוֹלְמִי,/ הוֹלְמִי יִנְעַם בְּנָעֲמִי,

נָעֲמִי סָף בַּאֲבֹד שְׁמִי/ שְׁמִי תַּם וּמָטָה פַעֲמִי.

פַּעֲמִי צָד/ יְלִיד צַיָד,/ וְשָׁלַח יָד,/ בְּבַת נִכְבָּד/ וְשִׂסַּע כַּגְדִי;

15   גְּדִי עִם גּוּר/ אֲרִי יָגוּר,/ וְאֵיךְ יָגוּר--/ וּפִי סָגוּר,/ עֲדֵי בוֹא מוֹעֲדִי.

מוֹעֲדִי נִשְׂרַף וְהֻצְבִּי,/ צְבִי מַחֲמַדִּי בְּבֵית שְׁבִי,

שְׁבִי אֲהַלֵךְ לְמוּל חוֹבְבִי,/ חוֹבְבִי רָחַק וְאוֹהֲבִי,

אוֹהֲבִי נֶהְפַּךְ לְאוֹיְבִי,/ אוֹיְבִי בְּפֶרֶךְ יִרְדְּ בִּי.

בִּי צוּרִי,/ הַדְרֵךְ שׁוּרִי,/ וְלִמְזוֹרִי/ שְׁלַח צָרִי,/ וְתַרְחִיב צְעָדִי--

---

7. Levin, *Širey Ha-Qodeš...Ibn Ezra*, 1: 305–07.

20 צַעֲדִי אֵל/ נְוֵה הֵרָאֵל/ וּבָא גוֹאֵל/ לְיִשְׂרָאֵל/ בְּקִרְיַת מוֹעֲדִי!

This *ge'ullah* hymn, chanted before the benediction, "Praised are You, Lord, Redeemer (*ga'al*) of the people Israel" on Sabbath and festival mornings, is a *tour de force* in its construction. Built in the form of a metric *muwashshaḥ*, the hymn is enhanced both by internal rhyme and anadiplosis in each line of the strophes. In displaying his virtuosity, Ibn Ezra seems determined to improve on the anadiplosis of earlier Eres Israel poets who confined their linkage to words at the beginning and end of strophes only. [8]

A dominant image in the poem is the abandoned wife—personifying Israel in exile—lamenting her "home [= the Temple]..in ruins" and her life in shambles. "My singers are silent" is a reference to the music played by the Levites in Temple times. "Now foot-shackles are my cosmetics" heightens the contrast between the once pampered wife, "vain in excess" and the pitiable victim. True to conventional theodicy, Israel takes the blame for her suffering ("I was unfaithful and my pain is severe"), although she protests that the nations are no less guilty (Why do they prosper and I am taken down to sit in the dust?") The complaint echoes Jeremiah's question (12: 1), "Why do all who are treacherous thrive?"

Israel is also troubled by the uncommon anger of her Husband [= God]. God, as the enemy of Israel ("even my Husband returns to bar my freedom") is a conceit adapted from Lam. 2: 5, "The Lord has become like an enemy; He has destroyed Israel." She is prepared to accept God's judgment, even as she hopes that it will be extended to her enemies ("He is a witness to the deeds of the barbarians"). Resigning herself to necessity ("The kid must live with the lion") and despite her Husband's action against her, she has no recourse other than to appeal to His mercy ("Look upon me, my Refuge, help me heal my pain").

47.   THE CAPTIVE

A prisoner of hostile men, she is hated and held captive by the sword;
She lives among strangers regretting her failures.
She is heard crying; how sweet is her voice to her Father:

---

8. See Fleischer, *Širat Ha-Qodeš Ha-'Ivrit*, pp. 89, 120.

"Broaden my deliverance; help my redeemer to blossom that he
    may flourish;
The radiant and ruddy, may he ride victoriously! Pardon my faults
And anoint the cherubs! Why must You flee the holy place?
Where will You be as welcome, and find a place to rest?"

Dejected, His soldiers call upon Him
To appear before them in all His glory as in earlier days;
They are stunned hearing once again His majestic voice:
"Nation of sighs, forget the dirge, forsake the wail;
Come, rejoice and sing, for Esau and Ishmael
    Have been laid low! Pray to your God.
    Rely upon Him, not your weapons."

[O God!] Heal the sick at heart; beat back the foe who keeps renewing
    his strength;
Have a regard for Your people, their words come from anguish;
Facing death, they hope for no other than You;
    Make an end to their killers, butchers, and murderers;
    Set a fire of vengeance upon the oppressors who make my life wretched,
    Stoke a flame among them on the day when You will roar like a lion
    Against the vulgar men who pierced me with arrows.

God, may it be Your will to grant my request:
The foe who applauds my distress may he be put to shame
        when You return;
How can I restrain myself when the uncircumcised are in Your holy place,
    Rested and comfortable? Come back and release the prisoners in chains;
    With hooks in their jaws they were led into exile. Spare them

Make ready their ears and open their eyes

When You send Your light to shine upon them. [9]

‐‐ס‐/‐‐ס‐/‐‐ס‐

ס/‐‐/‐‐ס‐/‐‐ס‐‐

אֲסִירַת צָרִים,/ שְׁבוּיַת חֶרֶב,/ מְשֻׂנָּאָה.

בְּאַרְצוֹת זָרִים/ בִּלְבָבָהּ תֶּרֶב/ לַחֲטָאָה;

וְשָׁם קוֹל תָּרִים‐‐/ וְקוֹלָהּ עָרֵב‐‐/ לְבוֹרְאָהּ:

יִשְׁעִי‐‐פְּרַח,/ צִדְקִי‐‐צְמַח/ וֶהְיֵה כְלָח!

וּרְכַב צֶלַח,/ אָדוֹם וְצַח!/ מְרִיַּי סְלַח 5

וּכְרוּב מָשַׁח!/ אֵיךְ מַדְבִּיר תִּבְרַח?

אָן תֶּאֱרַח,/ מְקוֹמְךָ תַנַּח?

בְּרוּחַ נִכְאָה/ מְצַעֵק חֵילוֹ/ לְפָנָיו,

עֲדֵי יֵרָאֶה/ כְּקֶדֶם גָּדְלוֹ/ לְעֵינָיו;

וְאֵיךְ יִשְׁתָּאֶה‐‐/ וְעוֹד הוֹד קוֹלוֹ/ בְּאָזְנָיו: 10

עַם נֶאֱנַח,/ אֲבָל שָׁכַח/ וּנְהִי זָנַח!

קוּם נָא שְׂמַח,/ רִנָּה פְּצָח‐‐/ כִּי סַף וְשָׁח

עֶבֶד וְאָח!/ יָדְךָ לְאֵל תִּשְׁטַח,

עָלָיו בְּטַח/ תְּמוּרַת תּוֹתָח!

רְפָא לֵב רָפֶה/ וְהַךְ צָר חֵילוֹ/ יִגְבַּר! 15

קְהָלְךָ צוֹפֶה/ וּפִיו בַּצַּר לוֹ/ יְדַבֵּר‐‐

וְלֹא יִסָּפֶה/ לְזוּלָתְךָ לֹא/ יְשַׁבֵּר:

רוֹצְחַי רְצָח,/ זוֹבְחַי זְבָח,/ טוֹבְחַי טְבָח!

נוֹגְחַי נְגַח,/ דּוֹלְחַי דְּלָח!/ אֵשׁ אַף קְדַח,

בָּהֶם נְפָח‐‐/ יוֹם כַּאֲרִי תִצְרָח 20

עַל נֶאֱלָח,/ כְּבֵדִי פְלָת.

מְעוֹנִי, הָפֵק/ רְצוֹנִי לִרְצוֹן/ לְבָבְךָ!

וְצַר כַּף סוֹפֵק/ תְּשַׁבַּע קָלוֹן/ בְּשׁוּבְךָ!

וְאֵיךְ תִּתְאַפֵּק‐‐/ וְעָרֵל בִּמְעוֹן/ כְּרוּבְךָ

שָׁכֵן וְנָח?/ שׁוּב נָא וְקַח/ נִלְכָּד בְּפָח, 25

---

9. Levin, Širey Ha‐Qodeš...Ibn Ezra, 1: 313–15.

לְחָיוֹ בְחָח/ בְּגְבוּל חֲלָח!/ עָלָיו פֶּסַח,
אָזְנָיו פְּתַח,/ עֵינָיו עֲדֵי תִפְקָח--
אוֹרְךָ שְׁלַח/ וְעָלָיו תִּזְרָח!

The hymn is a *me'orah* (light) as indicated in its closing line, "...send Your light to shine upon them." It was chanted on Sabbath and festival mornings before the benediction, "Praised are You, O Lord, Creator of light" (*yoṣer ha-me'orot*). Built as a *muwashshah*, it features an elaborate internal rhyme and a variable rhyme scheme, as follows: *abc/abc/abc//ddd/ddd/dd/dd/.   efg/efg/efg//ddd/ddd/dd/dd/* etc.

In this hymn Israel is personified as the prodigal daughter held captive by strangers and now "regretting her failures." She pleads with her Father [= God] to rescue her and to restore their once happy home. The image of God as "radiant and ruddy" riding to her rescue is adapted from Cant. 5: 10 and the rabbinic comment on this verse in *Canticles Rabbah*. Asking her Father to forgive her, she begs him to return to their rebuilt home. "Anoint the cherubs," refers to the Ark of the Covenant, the seat of God's presence; it is based on the practice of Moses [in Lev. 8: 10] who, when consecrating the Tabernacle, anointed all that was in it.

Later in the hymn Israel is represented as a troop of imprisoned soldiers dejected and leaderless. They are happily surprised to hear the Leader's [= God] voice giving them courage ("Come, rejoice and sing, for Esau [= Christians] and Ishmael [= Muslims]/ Have been laid low"). The Leader informs them that their hope is to be found in prayer and not by force of arms. Following the advice of the Leader, the troops pray for an end to the exile, vengeance upon the enemy and reconciliation in their national home.

48.   THE SONG OF A BIRD FRIGHTENS HER

O God, eternal in the heavens, bring back the banished dove;
She was once wounded by a mighty eagle
And now she lives in fear of a wild-boar;
The dove has found no place to rest her foot.

You will find her among the sheepfolds trampled under dust;
Her face is changed and marred, distasteful to the eye.

Seeking shelter she nests by the mouth of a gorge
And falls to her death, to the delight of her neighbors.
The song of a bird frightens her; when they caught her she cried
 Like a violated woman, helpless.

The evil decreed by the stars has overcome her;
But the dove, far from her home, does not protest, though her mate
        has left her;
Her enemies hiss and agitate, "Now we will have her!"
Night and day they strangle her babes as she watches;
She wails and they laugh. When she screams,
 No one says, "Let her be, she is in pain."

Her flaws have brought her to ruin;
Her voice is too weak to grieve, but her foes continue their rage.
Now she remembers her days in the palace
Sheathed in silver, her estate extending to mount Hermon.
By God's command, kings were routed before her advance like
        Zalmon's snow.
 Who will give her wings that she may return to her native nest?

Her neighbors took turns in plucking her wings on purpose;
They spat in her face—and God was watching!
My Refuge, why not pity her when she seeks Your shelter?
Why do You let them tread upon her until she dies in exile?
If she be Your servant, redeem her; if your daughter, let her live!
Remember Isaiah's words (49: 15): "Can a woman forget her nursing child?"
 Bring her home and build a fire-wall to guard her. [10]

6/6

אֱלֹהֵי קֶדֶם מְעוֹנָה/ יְשׁוֹבֵב יוֹנָה הַגְלָה,
אֲשֶׁר פַּעַם רִאשׁוֹנָה/ נֶשֶׁר גָּדוֹל הֶחֱלָה

10. Levin, Širey Ha-Qodeš...Ibn Ezra, 2: 76-78; Schirmann, Ha-Širah Ha-'Ivrit, 1:
618-19.

וְגַם פַּעַם אַחֲרוֹנָה/ חֲזִיר יַעַר הַבְהִילָהּ--
וְלֹא מָצְאָה הַיּוֹנָה/ מָנוֹחַ לְכַף רַגְלָהּ.

5   בֵּין שְׂפַתַּיִם תַּחַת הָאֵפֶר נִרְמְסָה,
בְּשׁוּב מַרְאֶיהָ מָשְׁחַת--/ לְכָל עַיִן נִמְאָסָה,
וּבְעֶבְרֵי פִי פַחַת/ לְהִמָּלֵט קֵן עוֹשָׂה.
הִיא יָרְדָה לַשַּׁחַת--/ וְכָל עוֹף רֹאשׁוֹ נָשָׂא,
וּמִקּוֹל צִפּוֹר תֵּחַת;/ וְצָעֲקָה, יוֹם נִתְפְּשָׂה,

10   כְּמוֹ נַעֲרָה מְאֹרָשָׂה/ אֲשֶׁר אֵין מוֹשִׁיעַ לָהּ.

רָעָה גָזְרוּ שְׁחָקִים--/ וְהִנֵּה בָאָה כַלָּה
לְיוֹנַת אֵלֶם רְחוֹקִים,/ וְסָר מִמֶּנָּה בַּעֲלָהּ;
וְצוֹרְרֶיהָ שֵׁן חוֹרְקִים:/ "כִּי יָכֹל נוּכַל לָהּ."
וְיוֹם וָלַיְלָה חוֹנְקִים/ אֶפְרוֹחֶיהָ לְמוּלָהּ.

15   הִיא תְקוֹנֵן--וְהֵם מְשַׂחֲקִים,/ וְאִם תַּגְבִּיהַּ קוֹלָהּ,
וְאֵין אוֹמֵר: הַרְפֵּה לָהּ,/ כִּי נַפְשָׁהּ מָרָה לָהּ!

הֶעָוֹן הוֹשִׁיבָהּ/ שׁוֹמֵמָה כַיְשִׁימוֹן,
וְקוֹלָהּ כְּאוֹב בְּכָאֵבָהּ--/ וְקוֹל רוֹדְפָהּ כְּקוֹל הָמוֹן;
וַתַּעֲלֶה עַל לְבָבָהּ/ יְמֵי שִׁבְתָּהּ בְּאַרְמוֹן,

20   נֶחְפָּה בְּכֶסֶף וְטוּבָהּ/ נָגַע עַד הַר חֶרְמוֹן,
אָז, בְּפָרֵשׂ שַׁדַּי בָּהּ/ מְלָכִים, תַּשְׁלֵג בְּצַלְמוֹן;
וְלָשׁוּב אֶל קֵן קַדְמוֹן/ מִי יִתֵּן אֵבֶר לָהּ?

מָרְטוּ כָּל שְׂכֶנֶיהָ,/ כְּנָפֶיהָ בְצִדֶּיהָ,
גַּם יָרְקוּ בְפָנֶיהָ--/ וַאדֹנָי שָׁם הָיָה!

25   לָמָה לֹא תַחֲנֶיהָ,/ צוּרִי, כִּי בָךְ חָסָיָה?
פּוּרָה אֵיךְ תִּתְּנֶיהָ/ עַד מוֹתָהּ בַּשִּׁבְיָה?
אִם שִׁפְחָה הִיא--קְנֵיהָ,/ וְאִם בַּת הִיא--נְחָיָה!
וּזְכֹר נְבוּאַת יְשַׁעְיָה:/ "הֲתִשְׁכַּח אִשָּׁה עוּלָהּ?"
וְשׁוֹבְבֶיהָ לִגְבוּלָהּ/ וְחוֹמַת אֵשׁ תִּהְיֶה לָּהּ!

This penitential hymn (selihah) in the form of a pseudo-*muwashshah* was probably the most popular of Ibn Ezra writings for the synagogue. Adopted for liturgical use by the Italians, Franco-Germans, Hispanics, North Africans, Romaniotes, Yemenites and Karaites, it was, presumably, chanted during the Day of

Atonement service. It comes by its wide appeal through a set of striking images with which Jewish congregations in exile could easily identify.

The poem's dominant figure is the banished dove [= Israel in exile], a designation adapted from Cant. 2: 14. "Once wounded by a mighty eagle" [= Babylon, Ez. 17: 3] she lives in fear of her new enemy, the wild-boar (Ps. 80: 14), a reference to the Christian powers. [11] Insecure and defenseless, she is condemned to a vagabond life ("The dove has found no place to rest its foot," Gen. 8: 9).

"The evil decreed by the stars [lit. heavens: šeḥaqim] has overcome her" would seem to be inconsistent with Ibn Ezra's commentary on Deut. 4: 19 where he writes that God has removed Israel from the control of the stars and placed her under His direct supervision. [12] Compounding the dove's distress is the absence of her husband [= God, Jer. 3: 14]: "...her mate has left her." The conceit is adapted from Lam. 1: 1, "How like a widow she has become" and the rabbinic comment [in Lam. Rabbah, Proem #24] that God's presence departed the Temple following its destruction. The graphic images of cruelty in the poem are mainly drawn from Lam. 1: 7 and 2: 16.

The dove admits to her faults in their relationship ("Her flaws have brought her to ruin") and supports herself with remembrance of a happier life in her native land. The hymn closes with the poet's plea that God abide by His own laws. "If she be Your servant redeem her," is based on Lev. 25: 47-54 which calls for the redemption of Israelite slaves sold to aliens. In his argument, "If your daughter, let her live," the poet calls upon God to be no less merciful than Pharaoh who ordered that girls be spared from drowning in the Nile (Ex. 1: 22).

49.   CAN MY COURAGE ENDURE

Alas! can my courage endure and I not tremble
When the impure worship in God's Temple, and I am ruled by gentiles?

They mock my wounds and tell me there is no relief for my hurt;

---

11. See Zunz, Die synagogale Poesie des Millelalters, p. 459.
12. See Langermann, "Astrological Themes in Ibn Ezra," p. 59.

Preying upon my flock, they growl and roar like whelps and lions;

They rebel against You and persist in their treachery; they have
   embittered the life

   Of a nation that was once privy to God's will while standing

   At Sinai. The world's foundation was laid on that delightful day.

Pursuing me and breaking down my walls, they intend to abolish me;

They fancy themselves learned in God's ways while abusing Him.

They broke His laws and forsook [God] the source of life,

   and the dead man they divided [into father and son].

   I will not be drawn to a stranger; God almighty alone I trust.

   I vow never to exchange the glory of the living God for a corpse
      on a crucifix.

I am honored to bear the sweet pain for God's sake!

I care not if the enemy prospers with each day and my people fail.

I am certain that the legatees of lies will perish in an instant;

   My heart, are you sad that your beloved is gone?

      He will not forever

   Reject you; though He tarries in distant places never fail to
      wait for His arrival. [13]

--ס--/--ס-//--ס-/-ס--

אֵיכָה לְבָבִי יַעֲמֹד/ רֶגַע וְאֵיךְ לֹא יֶחֱרַד--

וּבְבֵית אֱלֹהַי יַעֲבֹד/ טָמֵא, וְעָרֵל בִּי יִרַד?

בָּזוּ לְצַלְעִי, אָמְרוּ/ כִּי אֵין לְמַכָּתִי צְרִי,

לִטְרֹף עֲדָרַי נָעֲרוּ/ כִּכְפִיר וְשָׁאֲגוּ כָאֲרִי,

מָרוּ בְךָ וִימָרְרוּ/ חַיֵּי בְּעוֹדָם בֵּית מְרִי--   5

לְעַם אֲשֶׁר עָמְדוּ בְסוֹד/ דָּת נִתְּנָה יוֹם מַעֲמַד

סִינַי, אֲשֶׁר הָיְתָה יְסוֹד/ עוֹלָם בְּיוֹם מַה נֶּחֱמַד!

רָצוּ וְרָדְפוּ לַעֲקֹר/ אוֹתִי וְגֶדֶר פָּרְצוּ,

וּכְבוֹד אֱלֹהַי לַחֲקֹר/ דְּמוּ--וְלִשְׁמוֹ נָאֲצוּ,

13. Levin, Širey Ha–Qodeš...Ibn Ezra, 1: 271–72.

10 חֹק חָלְפוּ, עָזְבוּ מְקוֹר/ חַיִּים וְהַמֵּת יָחֲצוּ.
לִבִּי לְזָר לֹא יַחֲמֹד,/ יִבְטַח בְּאֵל שַׁדַּי לְבָד,
נִשְׁבַּע--וְלֹא יָמִיר כְּבוֹד/ אֵל חַי בְּמֵת נָתוּן בְּבָד!

מֶה עָרְבוּ צָרוֹת עָלַי/ שֵׁם גּוֹאֲלִי, מַה נִּכְבָּדוּ!
מַה לִּי, וְאִם צָר יַעֲלֶה/ כָּל יוֹם--וְעַמִּי יֵרְדוּ.

15 מִבְטָח אֲנִי כִּי נוֹחֲלִי/ שֶׁקֶר כְּרֶגַע יֹאבֵדוּ.
מַה תֶּהֱמֶה, לִבִּי, לְדוֹד/ סָר מִמְּךָ? כִּי לֹא לְעַד
יִזְנַח, וְאִם הִרְחִיק נְדוֹד--/ חַכֵּה לְיוֹם קוּמוֹ לְעַד!

The hymn in the form of a *muwashshah* with internal rhyme is a "permission request" (*rešut*) before the recitation of "Praise the Lord, Source of blessing" (*barekhu 'et 'adonay ha-mevorakh*), the first of the benedictions preceding the *šema'* ("Hear O Israel, the Lord our God, the Lord is One"). The *rešut* provides an opportunity for the cantor-poet to introduce himself to the congregation.

A fierce polemical tone emerges throughout the poem. The resentment that "the impure worship in God's Temple"--based on Ez. 44: 9, "No foreigner, uncircumcised in mind and body shall enter my sanctuary in order to serve me,"--reflects the Crusader occupation of Jerusalem which lasted from 1099 to 1187. The ruling "gentiles"--literally, "the uncircumcised" (*'arel*)--is a reference to Christians who are charged with "embitter[ing] the life" of Israel that stood at the foot of Sinai to receive God's commands. "The world's foundation was laid on that delightful day" is adapted from the rabbinic comment (quoted by RaŠI on Gen. 1: 1) that the world was created for the sake of the Torah.

Ibn Ezra's vow that he will never "exchange the glory of the living God for a corpse on a crucifix" was undoubtedly echoed by his congregation. They, presumably, were the focus of the new Christian proselytizing efforts among Jews in the twelfth century. "They fancy themselves learned in God's ways" hints at a more advanced effort by Christian missionaries to convert their Jewish subjects. Reflective of such an effort was the Christian monk, Peter the Venerable, who quoted from the Talmud in his proselytizing argumentation. [14] The poet closes with an admonition to maintain the hope that God has not rejected His people. Such encouragement was needed in light of the Christian missionaries' argument that the suffering of the Jews and the success of Christianity are proof of the latter's superiority, since God rewards those who are true to Him and punishes the sinners. [15]

50.   MY REDEEMER LIVES

> I know that my Redeemer is alive,
>   Though the day of my deliverance is delayed; I await
>   Him and hope to serve Him;
>   When He hastens to bring help I will rejoice.
>
> In my prison He tested my courage
> That I may bear my burden without weakening!
> I trust my Beloved to rescue me,
> And do not ask for signs and miracles;
> I moan with pain when my assailant
> Turns my holy places into a wilderness.
>   With each passing day he is emboldened
>   Against me; his arrogance increases;
>   Who will peer into the future and tell me
>   If there is an end and purpose to my suffering?
>
> For my trust in You, my oppressor causes me grief;
> I treasure the sorrow, O Father of mercies;
> Though my help is late in coming,
> I have nothing to fear;
> I have memories of days gone by
> When You showed me signs of Your faithfulness;
>   I know that with Your unlimited power
>   You are able to save the nation chosen as Your heritage;
>   They are calling to You from the depths

---

14. See R. Chazan, *Daggers of Faith*, pp. 21–24.
15. Ibid., p. 53.

Show them pity; they writhe in unsparing pain for Your sake.

Why do my enemies rejoice at my plight
When my Beloved leaves me for distant places?
It matters not if He is near or distant,
I will never be attracted to a stranger!
I am happy with my Husband though He punishes me;
I am confident that His promise will be kept
  His presence will once again inhabit His holy
  Mountain in Zion and Jerusalem;
  Then will I throng to His place;
  Then will the slave be free. [16]

(9) 8/6
6/6

אִם יוֹם פְּדוּתִי אֲחַר--/ יָדַעְתִּי, גּוֹאֲלִי חַי, אוֹחִילָה
אֵלָיו וַעֲבֹדוֹת אֶבְחַר/ לִשְׁמוֹ, כִּי חִישׁ בִּיֹשְׁעוֹ אָגִילָה.

בְּחֹן לְבָבִי בַּשֶּׁבִי/ לָשֵׂאת חֲלִי מֵאֵין לְאוֹת!
אֶבְטַח בְּיֵשַׁע אוֹהֲבִי,/ לֹא אֶשְׁאֲלָה מוֹפֵת וְאוֹת,
5   אַךְ אֶהֱמֶה עַל אוֹיְבִי/ יָשִׂים נְוֵה קֹדֶשׁ נְאוֹת
מִדְבָּר, וְיוֹם יוֹם יִגְבַּר/ עָלַי וְרֹאשׁוֹ יָרוּם וְעָלָה.
מִי יַגִּיד פֵּשֶׁר דָּבָר/ אִם לַעֲמָלִי יֵשׁ קֵץ וְתִכְלָה?

רָעוֹת מְעַנַּי יָקְרוּ/ לִי עַל שְׁמָךְ, אָב רַחֲמָן,
לֹא אֶחֱרַד אִם אֵחֲרוּ/ עִתּוֹת פְּדוּתִי רֹב זְמָן.
10   אֶזְכֹּר לְיָמִים עָבְרוּ,/ כִּי לִי בָם אוֹת נֶאֱמָן
כִּי יָדְךָ לֹא תִקְצַר/ לִגְאֹל לָעָם בְּחַרְתּוֹ לְנַחֲלָה,
קוֹרֵא לְךָ מִמֵּצַר/ לַחֲמֹל וָלָךְ יְסַלֵּד בְּחִילָה.

מַה יַּעֲלֹז בִּי גוֹעֲלִי/ אִם אוֹהֲבִי הִרְחִיק נְדֹד;
יִקְרַב, יִרְחַק גּוֹאֲלִי--/ לָעַד לְזָר לֹא אֶחֱמֹד!
15   אֶרְצֶה בְמוּסַר בּוֹעֲלִי,/ בִּבְרִיתוֹ חָזָק אֶעֱמֹד--
עַד שׁוּב כְּבוֹדוֹ אֶל הַר/ קָדְשׁוֹ, לְצִיּוֹן וּלְעִיר תְּהִלָּה,

16. Levin, Širey Ha-Qodeš...Ibn Ezra, 1: 298-300.

וְאָז לְטוּבוֹ אֲנַהֵר/ וְלַנִּמְכָּר תִּהְיֶה לוֹ גְאֻלָּה!

This *ge'ullah* hymn in the form of a *muwashshah* with internal rhyme was chanted on Sabbath and festival mornings before the benediction, "Praised are You, Redeemer (*ga'al*) of Israel." Its designation as a *ge'ullah* is indicated in the closing line, "Then will the slave be free" (*we-la-nimkar tihyeh lo ge'ullah*).

Israel is here personified as the imprisoned slave waiting to be freed by her divine master ("I trust my Beloved [= God] to rescue me"). His help is delayed in order that "He may test my courage,"—a conceit adapted from Jer. 9: 6, "Thus says the Lord of hosts: "I will now refine and test them, for what else can I do with my sinful people?" Israel's travail in exile is related to its prophetic mission as God's people who, like the prophets, would bring His message to the nations. Given the hazards faced by the prophet—who typically dies a martyr—the exile experience is needed in order to help Israel "bear [her] burden without weakening."

The exile tests not only Israel's endurance, but her trust in God's promise as well. Her enemies make the most of her isolation and seek to dampen her loyalty. But she is not persuaded ("It matters not if He is near or distant, / I will never be attracted to a stranger"). The resolute tone of the response is reflective of the proselytizing efforts by Christian monks in Ibn Ezra's day. In the polemical tract, *Milhemet Miswah* (written between 1230–1240) by Rabbi Meir ben Simon of Narbonne, the author gave an account of his disputations with the monks. In Part I the rabbi records the following exchange:

> The priest said that, from the fact that we live in exile and degradation under their [Christian] domination and have remained so for such a long time, we must conclude that their faith is more correct and better than our faith. [17]

---

17. See W. Herskovitz, *Judaeo-Christian Dialogue in Provence*, 19; Chazan, *Daggers of Faith*, p. 53.

51.   GRACE AND CHARM ARE YOUR WEAPONS

[God:]

> O awesome beauty, still desolate, prepare yourself for God's mercy;
>   How fair and pleasant you are!

> O daughter who played on my lap, your face breathes life and
>   your kisses are sweet;
> Charm and grace are your weapons, from the earrings in your ears
>   To your painted eyes.

> O my bride, at night, free yourself from your maidens
> And come dance with me, your breasts like clusters of the vine;
>   If you sin, say you have been enchanted!

> O fairest one, you are wasted among the women,
> You who shines through like the dawn; when they put you to scorn
>   And you fall, I will lift you up!

> My daughter, why complain? Take courage and come with me!
> I will bring you into my sumptuous home; I will betroth you and
>   you will be my wife;
>   I will adorn you and you will be consoled. [18]

6/7

אֵימָתִי, עֶדֶן שָׁמַמְתְּ;/ קוּמִי עֲלִי כִּי רֻחָמְתְּ
מַה יָּפִית וּמַה נָּעַמְתְּ!

בַּת חֵיקִי, בְּפָנַיִךְ/ חַיִּים וְצוּף בְּשִׁנַּיִךְ,
יֹפִי וְחֵן אָזְנֵיךְ,/ עֲגִילַיִךְ בְּאָזְנַיִךְ,
וְעֵינַיִךְ/ בַּפּוּךְ שָׂמְתְּ.   5

---

18. Levin, Širey Ha-Qodeš...Ibn Ezra, 1: 200–01; Scheindlin, The Gazelle, pp. 127–29.

רַעְיָתִי בֵּין יְעֵלוֹת--/ קוּמִי עֲלִי בַּלֵּילוֹת,
וְהֵן תֵּצְאִי בִמְחוֹלוֹת/ וְשָׁדַיִךְ כְּאַשְׁכֹּלוֹת;
אִם אָשַׁמְתְּ--/ בְּאוֹב קָסָמְתְּ.

הֵיךְ הָיִית לְקָצָפָה/ בַּנָּשִׁים הַיָּפָה,
10 כַּשַּׁחַר נִשְׁקָפָה;/ וְכִי שָׁמוֹךְ לִגְדוּפָה
אִם נָפַלְתְּ--/ הוּקַמְתְּ קָמְתְּ!

מַה תִּתְאוֹנְנִי, בִּתִּי?/ קוּמִי לָךְ צְאִי אִתִּי!
אֲבִיאֵךְ לְבֵית תִּפְאַרְתִּי,/ אֲנִי אִישֵׁךְ וְאַתְּ אִשְׁתִּי,
עֲדִי עֶדְיֵךְ/ וְהִתְנֶחָמְתְּ!

In this hymn, formed as a pseudo-*muwashshah*, the poet imagines God speaking in endearing tones to His beloved Israel. She is praised in figures adapted from the Bible and Arabic love poetry. The accolades, "O awesome beauty," "How fair and pleasant you are," and "…your breasts like clusters of the vine" are adapted from Cant. 6: 4, 10; 7: 7; 7: 9. The bold conceit, "O daughter who played on my lap" is based on the account of Wisdom as God's "child" in Prov. 8: 30, "I was daily His delight, rejoicing before Him always."

Israel is designated both as daughter and as bride, from Cant. 7: 2 and 1: 9 respectively. The bride is told to abandon the company of her maidens and dance with her lover in the cool of the evening. She is advised, "If you sin, say you have been enchanted!" In this conceit the poet combines images from Jewish and Arab sources. In Cant. 5: 2ff the maiden relates a dream in which she is asleep at night and her mate knocks on her door, "My beloved thrust his hand into the opening; and my inmost being yearned for him."

"If you sin, say you have been enchanted," is an attempt to justify the lovers' nocturnal tryst and their infatuation. The need to explain this behavior assumes the presence of pious moralists. These "reproachers" are stock characters in Andalusian–Hebrew love poetry. [19]

Concealed in the instruction to the bride to "free yourself from your maidens" is God's admonition to Israel to stay aloof from the nations and remain true to the oracle [in Num. 23: 9], "Here is a people living alone, and not reckoning itself among the nations!" There is no clear indication as to the purpose of this hymn. Presumably, it was an *'ahavah*.

52. I NAMED YOU MY FIRST BORN

[God:]

I named you "my first born" when I took you from Egypt;
I sustained you in the wilderness and carried you on eagles' wings;
I am the Lord your God, who brought you out.

Consider this, you foolish people who pursue the useless,
Can you compare the Most High to another when He is exalted above all?
I, the Lord, am first, and will be with the last.

Observe that I am the One who carries out my wishes;
My creatures are witness to the wonders I do;
Mine are the hands that stretched out the heavens and ordered their host.

My presence fills all space; My light kindles the stars;
My thoughts are deep beyond knowing even by the wisest;

---

19. See Pagis, *Širat Ha-Hol We-Torat Ha-Šir*, p. 269; see also Ibn Nagrela in Weinberger, *Jewish Prince in Moslem Spain*, p. 119: "If you could see with your own eyes the object of my desire, / (You would become his alone) and none of your friends would find you. / When he said, 'Bring me down honey from your swarm of bees,' / I replied, 'Kiss me with your sweet tongue.' / Whereupon he became angry and with ill-temper spoke, 'Shall we sin / Before the living God!' I replied, 'Your sin be upon me, my lord'."

I am the Lord and there is no other; besides me there is no god. [20]

.verse 6/6

אָז מֵאֶרֶץ מִצְרַיִם בְּכוֹרִי כִּנִּיתִיךָ,
עֲלֵי נֶשֶׁר נְשָׂאתִיךָ וּבַמִּדְבָּר מְצָאתִיךָ--
אָנֹכִי יְיָ אֱלֹהֶיךָ אֲשֶׁר הוֹצֵתִיךָ.

בִּינוּ בֹּעֲרִים בָּעָם, רוֹדְפִים אַחֲרֵי תֹּהוּ:
5   אֶל מִי תְּדַמְיוּן עֶלְיוֹן, עֶלְיוֹן--אֵין כָּמוֹהוּ?
אֲנִי יְיָ רִאשׁוֹן וְאֶת אַחֲרוֹנִים אֲנִי הוּא.

רְאוּ עַתָּה כִּי אֲנִי הוּא, אֶעֱשֶׂה כֹּל אוּיִתִי,
וּמִפְעֲלוֹתַי לְאוֹתוֹת עַל מִפְעֲלוֹתַי שׁוִּיתִי--
אֲנִי יָדַי נָטוּ שָׁמַיִם וְכָל צְבָאָם צִוִּיתִי.

10 מָלֵא כְבוֹדִי הַכֹּל, בְּאוֹרִי אוֹרִים נְגוֹהִים,
אַךְ מַחְשְׁבוֹתַי עָמְקוּ וְגָבְהוּ עַל כָּל גְּבוֹהִים--
אֲנִי יְיָ וְאֵין עוֹד, זוּלָתִי אֵין אֱלֹהִים.

This *zulat* hymn was chanted during the morning service following the prayer, "There is no God but You" (*'eyn 'elohim zulatekha*). The intent of the hymn is given in its closing line, "...besides me there is no god" (*zulati 'eyn 'elohim*). Like most authors of the *zulat*, Ibn Ezra favors a strophic form with closing scriptural verses.

The figures in the hymn are largely based on scriptural sources. In the first strophe, "I named you my 'first born,'" and "I sustained you in the wilderness and carried you on eagles' wings," are adapted from Ex. 4: 22, 19: 4, and Deut. 32: 10–11. Later in the hymn, the poet, speaking in God's name, condemns the fools who "pursue the useless (*tohu*)," a reference to idol-worship,—based on I Sam. 12: 21—and

---

20. Levin *Širey Ha-Qodeš...Ibn Ezra*, 2: 403–04; Schirmann, *Ha-Širah Ha-'Ivrit*, 1: 623.

presumably an anti-Christian polemic. It is likely that Ibn Ezra is reacting to the proselytizing efforts of Christian monks in his day. [21]

The closing strophe begins with a conventional biblical figure, "My presence fills all space," based on Is. 6: 3 and Ps. 113: 4. To this the poet adds a conceit from contemporary philosophy, "My light kindles the stars." The reference is to God's supernal light, a source of speculation for Jewish Neoplatonists like Ibn Gabirol (*Keter Malkhut*, 25) and Abraham ben Ḥiyyah (*Megillat Ha-Megalleh*, p. 22).

53.   REJOICE, VIRGIN DAUGHTER

[God:]

> Rejoice, virgin daughter; today I shall make you my bride;
> I have loved you from the first and always.

> I will bring you up from the den of lions to the Temple mount
> When the vision of seers comes true and your sons, heavily armed,
>   will command their troops;
> Then will the daughter of princes be remembered and the foe will
>   be silenced;
>   Mercifully, I will open the prison door for you whom I remember;
>   Only the enemy will be in mourning when I embrace you.

> When Moses went up on Sinai's mountain, it was wrapped in smoke
>   and quaking,
> My people were there with their families, isolated [from the summit],
> They were seen standing at a safe distance when God emerging descended;
>   In His hand He held the complete Torah; with its fine oils I
>   anointed you
>   The bride-price I paid for you is more precious than gold dust and
>   weightier than gold coin.

---

21. See Chazan, *Daggers of Faith*, pp. 21–24.

Distance yourself from error; keep your heart pure from all manner
of evil;

Protect your soul from blemish and your Beloved will encamp
around you;

He will take you to the home you love; I will exact satisfaction
from your accusers

Forever and you will stand tall above them; you are not forgotten;

Even as God, awesome in deeds, had earlier spoken: "I have
made you a sovereign nation."

Beloved daughter, the tent-pegs of your camp will be securely
attached to My own;

You will bring gifts with sweet savor in the land now desolate;

Your help is near; I will remember my promise;

Why are you sick at heart? I have not rejected you;

On my Temple mount I will adorn you with finery like a bride,
and I will bring you home. [22]

--ס-/--ס-//--ס-/--ס-

רַנִּי, בַּת הַבְּתוּלָה,/ כִּי אֲנִי הַיּוֹם בְּעַלְתִּיךְ,
וַהֲלֹא קֶדֶם תְּחִלָּה/ אַהֲבַת עוֹלָם אֲהַבְתִּיךְ.

אַעֲלֵךְ מִבֵּין לְבָאִים/ אֶל נְוֵה קֹדֶשׁ קָדָשִׁים,
יַעֲלוּ יוֹצְאִים וּבָאִים,/ עֵת חֲזוֹת, בָּנִים חֲמוּשִׁים,
5 נִפְקְדָה בַּת הַנְּשִׂיאִים/ אָז, וְצָרִים מַחֲרִישִׁים.
אֶפְתְּחָה דֶלֶת נְעוּלָה/ לָךְ בְּרַחֲמִים, כִּי זְכַרְתִּיךְ,
רַק וְאוֹיֵבַת אֲבֵלָה/ תִּהְיֶה, עֵת כִּי מְשַׁכְתִּיךְ.

בַּעֲלוֹת מֹשֶׁה לְסִינַי/ נֶעֱשַׁן הָהָר וְחָרָד,
עָמְדוּ עַמִּי וּבָנַי,/ כָּל אֱנוֹשׁ מֵהֶם מִפֹרָד,
10 נִצְּבוּ רָחוֹק לְעֵינַי; אַחֲרֵי בֹא צוּר וְיָרַד,
שָׁם בְּיָדוֹ דָּת פְּלוּלָה;/ בָּהּ בְּשֶׁמֶן טוֹב מְשַׁכְתִּיךְ,
נֶחְמְדָה מִפָּז, שְׁקוּלָה/ מִזָּהָבִים, בָּהּ לְקַחְתִּיךְ.

22. Levin, Širey Ha-Qodeš...Ibn Ezra, 2: 224-26.

רַחֲקִי מֵחֵטְא וְלִבֵּךְ/ טַהֲרִי מֵאוָן וְאַשְׁמָה,
בִּהְיוֹת דּוֹדֵךְ סְבִיבֵךְ/ יַשְׁרִי נֶפֶשׁ תְּמִימָה.

15 אֶל מָחוֹז חֶפְצֵךְ יְשִׁיבֵךְ,/ גַּם בְּשׁוֹטְנַיִךְ נָקָמָה
אֶעֱשֶׂה לָעַד, וּמַעְלָה/ תִּהְיִי, כִּי לֹא שְׁכַחְתִּיךְ,
כִּנְאֻם נוֹרָא עֲלִילָה/ אָז בְּרִאשׁוֹנָה: נְסַכְתִּיךְ!

מַחֲנֵךְ, בַּת הָאֲהוּבָה,/ תִּהְיֶה נֶגְדִּי תְקוּעָה,
תַּעֲלֶה מִנְחָה עֲרֵבָה/ לָךְ, בְּאֶרֶץ לֹא זְרוּעָה;

20 כִּי יְשׁוּעָתֵךְ קְרוֹבָה/ הֵן, וְאֶזְכֹּר הַשְּׁבוּעָה.
מַה לְּבָחֵךְ אֲמוּלָה--/ וַאֲנִי עוֹד לֹא מְאַסְתִּיךְ!
אֶעֱדֵךְ עֲדִי כְּכַלָּה/ תּוֹךְ נְוֵה קָדְשִׁי, וְשַׁבְתִּיךְ.

The 'ahavah hymn in muwashshah form with internal rhyme was chanted during the Pentecost morning service. Israel the "virgin daughter" (Jer. 14: 17) became God's bride the day she received His Torah and Pentecost ("today") is the anniversary of that event. The Torah's stipulations and list of reciprocal responsibilities comprise the marriage covenant between the pair. The Torah as a treasure-trove of wisdom, also served as the bride-price by which the marriage was sanctified. [23]

God assures His bride that He will honor His obligation by ending her exile ("I will bring you up from the den of lions...I will open the prison door for you"), punishing her enemies ("Only the enemy will be in mourning...I will exact satisfaction from your accusers"), and restoring her national home ("I have made you a sovereign nation"). For her part, Israel, the bride, is expected to remain faithful to her Beloved ("Distance yourself from error...Protect your soul from blemish"). The intimacy of their relationship is reflected in the image from a rustic setting, "Beloved daughter, the tent-pegs of your camp will be securely fastened to mine."

As befits the occasion, Ibn Ezra reviews the epochal, Giving of the Torah (matan torah) at Sinai based on biblical and rabbinic sources. Upon receiving the Torah, Israel is anointed with its "fine oils," a reference to the account in Ez. 16: 8–14 where the maiden, Israel, is adopted (by marriage) into God's covenant and becomes

---

23. See Targum Pseudo-Jonathan to Ez. 16: 11.

queen ("I...anointed you with oil"). Echoing this conceit is the divine proclamation, "I have made you a sovereign nation."

54. THE VISIONS OF ANCIENT SEERS

Where are the ancient seers and their visions
For my people scattered among the nations?
Exiled and poor they wait wondering,
They had been there a long time.

When we were scorned by the Muslims,
We fled to Christian lands—and perished;
They, never saying, "What have we done?
We have offended against our brother!"

Israel was fearful of his own failings;
It was they who made him an exile;
Not even the Father's power could save him;
A wild animal devoured him.

How could He sell the nobleman's daughter to a stranger?
I remember His instruction in the Torah (Ex. 21: 8),
"When a man sells his daughter as a slave and she displeases [her master],
He shall have no right to sell her to a stranger!"

Sold for a pittance to many masters,
He pleads his case before the living God;
Perhaps He will be merciful
And his redeemer, standing by Him, will come. [24]

8/8

אַיֵּה נְבוּאוֹת נְבִיאִים קָדוּמִים/ לְעַם הוּא מְפֻזָּר בֵּין הָעַמִּים?
בְּגָלוּת וְדַלּוּת יוֹשֵׁב מַשְׁמִים,/ כִּי אָרְכוּ לוֹ שָׁם הַיָּמִים.

---

24. Levin, Širey Ha-Qodeš...Ibn Ezra, 2: 397; Schirmann, Ha-Širah Ha-'Ivrit, 1: 615-16.

בְּיַד יִשְׁמָעֵאל לְבוּז הָיִינוּ,/ נַסְנוּ אֶל אֱדוֹם--לֹא חָיִינוּ,
וְלֹא אָמְרוּ, "מַה זֹּאת עָשִׂינוּ?/ אֲשֵׁמִים אֲנַחְנוּ עַל אָחִינוּ!"

5   רָעַת בֵּן בְּכוֹר הִבְהִילַתְהוּ,/ אִם חַטָּאתוֹ אָז הִגְלַתְהוּ,
גְּבוּרַת אָב לֹא הִצִּילַתְהוּ--/ חַיָּה רָעָה אֲכָלַתְהוּ.

הֵיךְ בַּת נָדִיב בְּיַד זָר מְכָרָהּ?/ כִּי זוֹכֵר אֲנִי בְּתוֹרָה הוֹרָה:
"אִם יִמְכֹּר אִישׁ בִּתּוֹ וְעָבְדָה--/ לְעַם נָכְרִי לֹא יִמְשֹׁל לְמָכְרָהּ!"

מָכוּר בְּלֹא הוֹן--רַבּוּ מוֹשְׁלָיו,/ לִפְנֵי אֵל חַי יַרְבֶּה מְשָׁלָיו,
10   אוּלַי נִכְמְרוּ רַחֲמָיו עָלָיו/ וּבָא גֹאֲלוֹ הַקָּרֹב אֵלָיו.

The hymn is a *ge'ullah* that was chanted during the morning service preceding the benediction, "Praised are You, Lord, Redeemer (*ga'al*) of the people Israel." The closing line in the hymn, "And his redeemer (*go'alo*)...will come" reveals that it was intended as a *ge'ullah*. Unlike his other *muwashshah*-style hymns in this genre, Ibn Ezra now favors an earlier east-Mediterranean strophic form with rhyming quatrains and closing scriptural verse.

The dominant tone of the *ge'ullah* is the poet's complaint about the inordinate length of Israel's exile. "When we were scorned by the Muslims,/ We fled to Christian lands," is presumably a reference to the Almohade invasion of the Maghreb and Andalusia in 1146/47 and the flight of Jewish families to northern Spain, then under Christian rule. [25] Now living among Christians, "we perished"--literally, "we could not live" (*lo' hayyinu*). Presumably, this is a reference to Christian violence during the First and Second Crusades.

Israel's suffering in exile is caused by her own failings. Not even God can intervene once the process of judgment is set in motion ("Not even the Father's power could save him"). However, since Israel has been in exile for "a long time," the poet reasons that the penalty has been paid and justice satisfied. Therefore, he asks how can God permit the nobleman's daughter to remain in slavery. The nobleman is a reference to Abraham, after *Cant. Rabbah* 7. 2. He follows this

25. See Y. Baer, *A History of the Jews in Christian Spain*, 1: 76–77.

argument with a rhetorical flourish by reminding God, as it were, of His own law
[in Ex. 21: 8] with regard to Israelite women that were sold into slavery, "He shall
have no right to sell her to a stranger" [i. e. Christians and Muslims]. [26]

55.   IN THE FAIREST OF LANDS

O dove, I yearn for the days when in the fairest of lands
The presence of your redeemer will abide in your tent;
When your armies will ascend your holy mountain
And He will be drawn to your beauty and crave your service;
When you will prevail over your foes and
Subdue them and bring disgrace upon Edom;
Alas, in your exile there is no relief for your hurt,
Only bitterness and punishment for your sin;
Lift your hearts to God, always,
That He may raise you up from the grimy pit. [27]

--ס-/ס-ס-/-ס--//-ס--/ס-ס-/-ס-.

אֶכְסֹף לְיָמִים הֱיוֹת כְּבוֹד גּוֹאֲלֵךְ,/ יוֹנָה, בְּאֶרֶץ צְבִי בְּתוֹךְ אָהֱלֵךְ,
בַּעֲלוֹת צְבָאֵךְ לְהַר קָדוֹשֵׁךְ,/ וְהוּא/ יִתְאַו לְיָפְיֵךְ וְיַחֲשֹׁק פָּעֱלֵךְ.
רָמָה יְמִינֵךְ עֲלֵי מְשַׂנְאֵךְ וּבוֹ/ תִּרְדִּי, וְתַשְׁלִיךְ עֲלֵי אֱדוֹם נַעֲלֵךְ.

הִנֵּה בְּשִׁבְיֵךְ לְמַחֲלָתֵךְ צֲרִי/ אֵין, רַק מְרוֹרוֹת עֲלֵי מְרִי מַעֲלֵךְ.
5   מִדֵּי הֱיוֹתֵךְ שְׂאִי לְבָבֵךְ לְאֵל--/ מִבּוֹר שְׁאוֹן הַשְּׁבִי יְהִי מַעֲלֵךְ.

This "permission request" (rešut) chanted during the Passover service echoes
the redemption theme associated with Israel's freedom from Egyptian slavery. Its
wistful tone is hopeful that the exiled in Edom's [= Christian] lands will be returned
to their native home [= the "fairest of lands," i. e. Israel, Dan. 11: 16]. The exiles are
compared to the "dove,"—a conventional metaphor for Israel (Cant. 2: 14 and Cant.

---

26. See Ibn Ezra's comment on Ex. 21: 8.
27. Levin, Širey Ha-Qodeš...Ibn Ezra, 1: 47; Schirmann, Ha-Širah Ha-'Ivrit, 1: 616.
The latter's reading בַּעֲלוֹת conforms to the meter, unlike Levin's בַּעֲלוֹת.

Rabbah, ad loc.) who awaits the day of her estranged Beloved's [= God] return. With His help she will prevail over her enemies and bring disgrace upon them. The literal translation of the latter conceit (line 3 in Heb. text), based on Ps. 60: 10, is, "hurl your shoe [i. e. your refuse] upon Edom."

Combined with hopefulness is an admonition drawn in a figure of regret, "Alas in your exile there is no relief for your hurt, Only bitterness and punishment for your sin." Particularly striking is the alliteration in the Hebrew: *raq merorot 'aley meri ma'alekh.* The effect of the repeated use of the letters *mem* and *reš* which when combined spell the word *mar*, "bitterness" was not lost on Ibn Ezra's community.

In closing, the poet's admonition is direct and given in the form of a command, "Lift your hearts to God." Underlying the poet's urging is the assumption that God judges measure for measure, "Lift your hearts…that He may raise you up." In stressing this equation Ibn Ezra employs the homonym set, "*ma'alekh…ma'alekh.*" The first from the noun *ma'al* refers to sin (Lev. 5: 15), the second, "raise you up" is the causative (*hif'il*) form of the verb *'alah* (Ex. 17: 3).

56.   WHEN MY ENEMIES SLANDER ME

> When my enemies slander me
> And I fear that I may fall,
> The God of Abraham gives me strength;
> The Fear of Isaac is my help!

> I immersed myself in the books of prophets;
> The words Isaiah wrote
> Were read before me: "Restoration is near at hand!"
> Generations come and go,
> But the pain of God's people endures;
> For a thousand years their decline was
> A source of amazement; in their agony,
>> They cried, "If You intend to redeem us, do it, and
>> If You will not, tell us!"

"You, Ezekiel, who have seen the future,
And have spoken in parables about us,
Have you sought to learn my fate?
Have you asked the angels:
How long until the end of these awful things,
For there is no relief in sight?"
He answered me as befits a prophet:
"What can even the wisest of men do?
  God has concealed it
  From me and I am not informed."

If only I could meet with
Daniel, the greatly beloved;
He is privy to all secrets
And is at home with allegories and riddles!
In my despair, I would plead with him
Asking that he tell me about
The end time, if it has already come,
Or if his prophecies are for the future.
  But men with good sense tell me:
  "Why do you ask? It is a mystery."

Scholars and sages are dumbfounded;
Not one among them knows;
And my eyes grow dim from much weeping,
For the time of my deliverance remains hidden.
When I searched more closely in God's Torah
I found there what I had sought:
God will restore the captive people,
Even those scattered to the ends of earth!

This gave me comfort.

Of this I must speak and find relief! [28]

7/7

אִם אוֹיְבַי יֹאמְרוּ רַע לִי
וְאָמַרְתִּי: מָטָה רַגְלִי--
אֱלֹהֵי אַבְרָהָם אֵלִי
וּפַחַד יִצְחָק הָיָה לִי!

5   בִּינוֹתִי בְּסִפְרֵי נְבִיאִים,
וְדִבְרֵי יְשַׁעְיָה בְּמִכְתָּבוֹ
הָיוּ לְפָנַי נִקְרָאִים:
כִּי קְרוֹבָה יְשׁוּעָה לָבוֹא.
הֵן דּוֹרוֹת עוֹבְרִים וּבָאִים--

10   וְעַם אֵל עוֹמֵד בְּמַכְאוֹבוֹ,
כִּי אֶלֶף שָׁנִים פְּלָאִים
יָרַד, וּבִמְרִירוּת לְבָבוֹ
יֹאמַר: "אִם תִּגְאַל--גְּאַל, וְאִם
לֹא יִגְאַל--הַגִּידָה לִּי!"

15   רָאִיתָ, יְחֶזְקֵאל, מַרְאוֹת
וְעָלַי נָשָׂאתָ מְשָׁלִים;
הֲבִקַּשְׁתָּ דְּבָרַי לִרְאוֹת?
וְשָׁאַלְתָּ לִבְנֵי אֵלִים:
"עַד מָתַי קֵץ הַפְּלָאוֹת,

20   כִּי לֹא בָאָה שְׁנַת גְּאוּלִים?"
הֱשִׁיבַנִי עַל פִּי נְבוּאוֹת:
"וּמַה יֵּשׁ בְּיַד הַמַּשְׂכִּילִים
לַעֲשׂוֹת? וַאדֹנָי הֶעְלִים
מִמֶּנִּי וְלֹא הִגִּיד לִי."

25   מִי יִתֵּן לִי וְאֶתְחַבָּר
עִם דָּנִיֵּאל אִישׁ חֲמוּדוֹת,

---

28. Levin, *Širey Ha-Qodeš...Ibn Ezra*, 2: 25-26; Schirmann, *Ha-Širah Ha-'Ivrit*, 1: 617-18.

אֲשֶׁר יָדַע פֵּשֶׁר דָּבָר
וְהֵבִין בְּכָל מָשָׁל וְחִידוֹת!
אֶתְחַנֵּן לוֹ בְּלֵב נִשְׁבָּר
30   וְאֶשְׁאָלֶנּוּ עַל אוֹדוֹת
הַקֵּץ, לִרְאוֹת אִם עָבָר
וְאִם עוֹד נְבוּאוֹתָיו עֲתִידוֹת.
אַנְשֵׁי לֵבָב יֹאמְרוּ לִי,
"מַה זֶּה תִּשְׁאַל? וְהוּא פֶּלִיא!"

35   נִבְעֲרוּ חֲכָמַי וּנְבוֹנַי
וְאִישׁ מֵהֶם לֹא יָדַע מָה;
וּמֵרֹב בְּכִי חָשְׁכוּ עֵינַי,
כִּי עֵת פְּדוּתִי נֶעֱלָמָה.
וָאֲחַפֵּשׂ בְּתוֹרַת אֲדֹנָי--
40   וָאֶמְצָא חֶפְצִי שָׁמָּה:
כִּי אֵל יָשִׁיב שְׁבוּת הֲמוֹנַי,
וְלוּ נִדְּחוּ בְּקַצְוֵי אֲדָמָה!
זֹאת הָיְתָה לִּי נֶחָמָה,
עַל כֵּן אֲדַבְּרָה וְיִרְוַח לִי!

The hymn is a *ge'ullah* chanted, probably during the New Year morning service, prior to the benediction, "Praised are You, Lord, Redeemer (*ga'al*) of the people Israel." The *ge'ullah* which Ibn Ezra presumably wrote for Hispanic congregations was later adopted by Franco–German, Yemenite and Allepan Jewries. Although the poet—speaking for Israel—is confident that relief from the oppressive exile is forthcoming ("The Fear of Isaac {Gen. 31: 42} is my help"), he is impatient.

The need to know the exact time of national restoration elicits a tone of urgency that borders on confrontation with Israel's God. "If you intend to redeem us, do it, and If You will not, tell us," is based on language used in Ruth 4: 4. The intent of Boaz's argument before Ruth's unnamed next-of-kin is, "If you are prepared to do your duty as next-of-kin (and marry Ruth, in order to preserve the name of her deceased husband), then do so; but if you will not (and someone must do it), tell me that I may know." Ibn Ezra's use of Boaz' argument almost suggests a threat, "If You (God) will not redeem Israel, someone else will." But who?

The poet recalls Isaiah's assurence [in 56: 1] that, "Soon My salvation will come, and My deliverance be revealed," but he is not persuaded ("Generations come and go, But the pain of God's people endures"). He appeals to Ezekiel who was known to have access to the mysteries of God's "Chariot Throne," and to Daniel who made calculations concerning the "end time." No one can help him. He wonders if "the end time...has already come," or if Daniel's predictions are for the distant future.

The implication of Ibn Ezra's wonderment is startling. If the prophecies concerning the coming of the Messiah have already been fulfilled, as Christian polemicists would argue, [29] what hope is there for the national restoration of the Jewish people? Perhaps the poet's question to Daniel was designed to be provocative, even as was the earlier confrontational challenge, "If You intend to redeem us, do it, and If not tell us!" In framing his question in this way Ibn Ezra may be pressing God to prove that the Christian monks are in error, and the forthcoming appearance of Israel's redeemer would do it.

57.   THEY WATCH MY AGONY AND LAUGH

> Brother and servant threw me into the fire;
> My ashes they swept into the sea.
>
> The time appointed for my release is delayed
> And I suffer stumbling with each step;
>   My assailants hate me; they have put a hook
>   in my nose and do me violence.
>
> They jeer as they pierce my daughters with their swords;
> They watch my agony and laugh;
>   Every day they hunt me; how can they not catch me,
>   my feet are already chained?
>
> My enemies take turns bruising my face;
> They have surrounded me and I am weary of my life;

---

29. See Herskovitz, *Judaeo-Christian Dialogue*, pp. 108-09; Chazan, *Daggers of Faith*, pp. 50-51.

Some urge me: "Sacrifice to our god!"
Others make a sacrifice of me!

What can I say to appease them? They wish only to do me harm!
My foes are obsessed in their rage against me;
They have put me to shame and taunt me: "Give up your hope!".
They trample upon me for no reason. [30]

--ס-/--/-ס--/--ס-/--
-ס--/--ס/-(-) ס-

עַל אָח בְּעֵרוּנִי/ עֶבֶד וְאָח/ בַּיָּם נְעֵרוּנִי.

אֵחֲרוּ זְמַנַּי/ קֵץ מוֹעֲדִי,
וַאֲנִי מְעֻנֶּה,/ צַר צֵעֲדִי.
צָרַי יִשְׁטְמוּנִי,/ נָתְנוּ בְחָח/ אַפִּי, יַחְמְסוּנִי.

בִּתְּקוּ בְנוֹתַי/ וַיִּשְׁרְקוּ,   5
יֵרְאוּ עַצְבוֹתַי--/ אָז יִשְׂחֲקוּ,
יוֹם יוֹם צוֹדְדוּנִי,/ רַגְלִי בְּפָח--/ אֵיךְ לֹא יִלְכְּדוּנִי?

רֹעֲעוּ לְחַיַּי/ בֵּין אוֹיְבִים
עַד קַצְתִּי בְחַיַּי/ מְסוֹבְבִים,
אֵלֶּה יִמְשְׁכוּנִי/ לֵאמֹר, "זְבָח!"/ אֵלֶּה יִזְבְּחוּנִי.   10

מָה אֹמַר?/ וְאוֹיְבַי/ בִּי נִלְחֲמוּ
נוֹעֲצוּ מְרִיבַי,/ לִי זָעֲמוּ,
לִשְׂחוֹק יִתְּנוּנִי/ יֹאמְרוּ, "זְנַח!"/ חִנָּם יִרְמְסוּנִי.

The place of this *muwashshah*-style hymn in the liturgy is not indicated.
Presumably it served as a *ge'ullah* preceding the benediction, "Praised are You, Lord,
Redeemer (*ga'al*) of the people Israel." Its tone of complaint begins in the opening
"belt" which charges that Christians and Muslims [= brother and servant, Gen. 25: 26

30. Levin, *Širey Ha-Qodeš...Ibn Ezra*, 1: 199–200; Schirmann, *Ha-Širah Ha-'Ivrit*, 1:
621.

and 21: 10] have been cruel to exiled Israel. The graphic depictions of physical and mental violence are drawn from allusions to Is. (37: 29), Ez. (16: 40) and Lam. (1: 7), and are based on ancient Near Eastern practices toward a conquered nation.

Israel's helplessness is conveyed in the sarcasm of the rhetorical question, "Every day they hunt me; how can they not catch me, my feet are already chained?" The figure, "Some urge me: Sacrifice to our god! Others make a sacrifice of me!" is a play on the Hebrew, *zevah* and *yizbehuni*. It is likely that the poet had in mind the proselytizing efforts of twelfth-century Christian monks and the uncompromising Muslim revival of the Almohades who brought destruction to Jewish settlements in the Maghreb and Andalusia in 1146/47. [31]

The catalogue of offenses against Israel is capped in the derisive taunt, "Give up your hope!" This indignity can be understood in the context of the "tradition" invoked by Abd 'Al Mu'min, successor to the Almohade, Muhammad Ibn Tumart, that if the Jewish Messiah did not arrive five hundred years after Muhammad's flight (*hegira*) in 622, they should become Muslims. Jews living in Christian lands were subjected to the argument that the promised Messiah has already appeared in the person of Jesus of Nazareth and were urged to leave their wretched condition in exile and become a part of the Christian success story. [32]

---

31. See Chazan, *Daggers of Faith*, pp. 21-22; Baron, *A Social and Religious History of the Jews*, 3: 124-25.
32. See Baron, ibid.; Chazan, *Daggers of Faith*, pp. 53-54.

DIALOGUE AND CHORUS

58. ZION AND ITS FOES

Zion:

"How is it possible that my children have forgotten me?
When they abandoned the Torah entrusted to them on Sinai, God's anger
    flared against them."

The foe:

"It is I who set fire to your home!
Men of Zion, where is your God? Let him come and help you!"

Zion:

"My sons were hunted like birds,
From the fairest of homes they were driven to the lands of strangers;
Feeling secure, they relied upon their strength,
And in their distress did not seek the God exalted;
How could they have forgotten the Lord, a Tower of Strength?"

The foe:

"God's children are without hope;
Their vision is dim because I have snuffed their candle;
By my power I overcame their God.
Here is the proof: His people stand condemned before His eyes!
I keep shouting to them: Call upon your God!"

Zion:

"I cherish the taunts
For God's sake, they give me pleasure.
His rebuke is sweeter than honey.
Exile's end the deliverance of my children is near;
When they repent, God will turn away his anger."

The foe:

"I have seen my wish

Come true; My creed is just and my power unlimited;
How do you, Zion's sons, expect to oppose me?
Your Torah is flawed, why obey it!
Was not God's hand against you and your fathers?"

Zion:
"Enemies of God, have you not heard
The words of His prophets? Why do you defame His Torah
And praise your creed which you stole from Him?
Now He will raise up His right arm and destroy you
Because you have put to death God's people."

The foe:
"The prophecies have already been fulfilled:
If the early seers were indeed faithful and true
Then their comforting words were realized in the Second Temple.
A thousand years have passed, what more can you hope for?
Why do you persist in saying: He will come and save you?"

Zion:
"Be still, my foe who roars like a lion;
The prophets spoke of the future. Tell me
Have the nations broken their swords into plowshares?
The exiles will be gathered in, they are the tribes named in Scripture;
To them will be proclaimed: You are God's priests." [1]

5/5
6/10

אָמְרָה צִיּוֹן:

"אֵיךְ שְׁכֵחוּנִי בָנַי?
בְּצֵאתָם מֵאֵשׁ דָּת הַנְּתוּנָה בְּסִינַי,
בְּעֵרָה בָם אֵשׁ אֲדֹנָי."

---

1. Levin, *Širey Ha-Qodeš...Ibn Ezra*, 2: 256–59.

אָמַר אוֹיֵב: 5

"אִשִּׁי אָכְלָה אֶתְכֶם!
אַנְשֵׁי צִיּוֹן, אַיֵּה נָא אֱלֹהֵיכֶם?
יָקוּמוּ וְיַעְזְרֻכֶם!"

אָמְרָה צִיּוֹן:

"בָּנַי כִּצְפּוֹר נִלְקָחוּ, 10
בְּאַרְצוֹת זָרִים מֵאֶרֶץ צְבִי נִדְּחוּ,
בִּגְבוּרָתָם בִּימֵי שַׁלְוָתָם בָּטְחוּ--
בַּצָּר לָהֶם לְשֵׁם נִשְׂגָּב לֹא בָרָחוּ;
אֵיכָה שָׁכְחוּ מִגְדַּל עֹז אֲדֹנָי?"

אָמַר אוֹיֵב: 15

"בְּנֵי אֵל--אָבַד שִׂבְרָם,
חָשְׁכָה עֵינָם, כִּי כִבִּיתִי נֵרָם.
בְּכֹחַ יָדִי גָּבַרְתִּי עַל צוּרָם,
וְזֶה הָאוֹת: כִּי עַמּוֹ לְעֵינָיו יָחֳרָם,
וָאֹמַר בְּקוֹל רָם, קִרְאוּ בְשֵׁם אֱלֹהֵיכֶם!" 20

אָמְרָה צִיּוֹן:

"רָעוֹתַי לִי טוֹבוּ,
עַל שֵׁם קְדוֹשַׁי תַּעֲנוּגִים נֶחְשָׁבוּ,
כִּי תוֹכְחוֹתָיו לִי מִדְּבַשׁ עָרָבוּ,
וְקִצֵּי יְשׁוּעוֹת בָּנַי עוֹד יִקְרָבוּ, 25
כִּי יָשׁוּבוּ--וְיָשֹׁב חֲרוֹן אַף אֲדֹנָי."

אָמַר אוֹיֵב:

"רָאִיתִי אֲשֶׁר עֵינַי
שָׁאֵלוּ, וְדָתִי יְשָׁרָה וְאֵין קֵץ לְשָׁנַי.
וְאֵיךְ, בְּנֵי צִיּוֹן, תּוּכְלוּ לַעֲמֹד לְפָנַי? 30

וּבַמֶּה תְּשׁוּבוּן--וְהִתְעַוְּתָה דָת סִינַי,
וְהָיְתָה יַד אֲדֹנָי בָּכֶם וּבַאֲבֹתֵיכֶם?"

אָמְרָה צִיּוֹן:

"מְשַׂנְאַי אֵל, הֲלֹא שְׁמַעְתֶּם
35   דִּבְרֵי נְבִיאָיו? וְאֵיךְ דָּתוֹ חֵרַפְתֶּם--
וְתִתְהַלְלוּ בַּחֹק מִמֶּנָּה גְּנַבְתֶּם?
עַתָּה יָעִיר יָמִין עֹזּוֹ וַאֲבַדְתֶּם,
יַעַן אַתֶּם הֲמִתֶּם אֶת עַם אֲדֹנָי."

אָמַר אוֹיֵב:

40   "מִכֶּם נְבִיאִים גָּמְרוּ,
וְהַקַּדְמוֹנִים, אִם אֱמֶת וְתָמִים דִּבְּרוּ--
בְּבֵית שֵׁנִי הַנֶּחָמוֹת עָבְרוּ.
וְעָבְרוּ אֶלֶף שָׁנִים--וְעוֹד מַה תְּשַׂבְּרוּ?
וְאֵיכָה תֹאמְרוּ: הוּא יָבוֹא וְיוֹשִׁיעֲכֶם?"

45   אָמְרָה צִיּוֹן:

"דֹּם אוֹיֵב, אֲרִי נוֹהֵם,
וּנְבוּאוֹת עֲתִידוֹת, אֱמֹר עַתָּה, אַיֵּה הֵם--
וְכֻתְּבוּ גוֹיִם לְאִתִּים חַרְבוֹתֵיהֶם?
וְנִקְבְּצוּ נְפוּצַי, וְאֵלֶּה שְׁמוֹת שְׁבָטֵיהֶם,
50   וְקוֹרָא לָהֶם: אַתֶּם כֹּהֲנֵי אֲדֹנָי!"

This elegy (*qinah*) for the ninth day of Av is in the form of a dialogue between personified Zion and her enemies. The dialogue was an established rhetorical feature in biblical and rabbinic literature. Abraham questions God repeatedly regarding the judgment of Sodom and Gemorrah [in Gen. 18: 22–33] and Moses pleads with God in a lengthy exchange asking that his life be spared, in *Deut. Rabbah*, 11. 10. Writing for the synagogue liturgy, Eleazar Qillir's (7th century) lament for the ninth day of Av paraphrases the rabbinic account [in *Lam. Rabbah*, Proem

24] in which Jeremiah appeals to the Patriarchs to intercede in Israel's behalf. [2] With the emergence of Hispanic-Hebrew poetry the dialogue gained a new structure. Each speaker was assigned a strophe, or a set of strophes, and was formally introduced, as seen in Ibn Ezra's hymn. [3]

Ibn Ezra's elegy lamenting the destruction of the Temple opens with Zion's rhetorical question, "How is it possible that my children have forgotten me?" Not waiting for an answer, Zion regrets that her children have "abandoned the Torah entrusted to them" thereby eliciting divine judgment. Zion's foe disputes this claim and argues that God had no part in her ruin, "It is I who set fire to your home [= Temple]. The taunt, "Where is your God?" is adapted from Ps. 42: 4, 11. Later in the hymn, Zion and her foe debate the relative merits of their religious beliefs, a common practice in the High Middle Ages.

The foe justifies its creed [4] by pointing to its wordly success, a familiar argument used by Christian monks in their mission to the Jews. [5] The polemic, "Your Torah is flawed" echoes the views of Christians, "ministers of a new covenant" which renders "the first one obsolete." [6] The proof that Zion has been rejected is that "God's hand [was] against you and your fathers,"—a paraphrase of I Sam. 12: 15.

Zion reminds her foe of God's promise, through His prophets, to restore Israel to national sovereignty. For good measure, she adds the taunt that "your creed you stole from Him." The foe is not persuaded and argues that the prophecies of Isaiah and Ezekiel for Israel's national restoration were fulfilled with the return of the Judean exiles from Babylon and the building of the Second Temple. [7] Zion

---

2. See *Seder Ha-Qinot*, pp. 98–100.

3. See Fleischer, *Ha-Yoṣerot Be-Hithawwutan We-Hitpatḥutam*, pp. 499–500.

4. The Hebrew term *dat* designates both the foe's "creed" and the Torah called, *'eš dat*, after Deut. 33: 2.

5. See Chazan, *Daggers of Faith*, p. 53.

6. Cf. II Cor. 3: 6 and Heb. 8: 13.

7. This view was shared by several Hispanic-Hebrew scholars, including Moses Ibn Gikatilla (11th century), Abraham Ibn Daud (1110–1180) and Ḥayyim Galipapa (ca. 1310—ca. 1380) among others. See J. Albo, *Sefer Ha-'Iqqarim*, 4. 42, and see A. Silver, *Messianic Speculation in Israel*, pp. 209, 215–16.

counters by turning the foe's citation from Isaiah to her advantage. Isaiah's spoke of the future and his prophecies have not, as yet, been fulfilled. The proof is that "nations [have not] broken their swords into plowshares," as the prophet predicted [in Is. 2: 4].

59.   THE STRAY SHEEP

[Chorus:]

> "Since you are like sheep astray, how could you turn against your master?
> Where now is the Shepherd of your flock?
>
> You lay for days in green pastures
> When Moses led you; then came the time of trials;
> Your Shepherd turned away and you were lost;
>   A spectacle to behold, even your hills denied you shelter;
>   Your crown is removed, there is no end to your misery.
>
> The lion observed your plight as he lay in ambush.
> Who will save you from his hungry jaws when he draws near?
> Who will provide you with water in the heat of the day?
>   Where will you go? Your fences are shattered,
>   You are fully exhausted, even your speech is garbled."

[God:]

> "I am your Shepherd come armed with vengeance;
> I have seen you wounded for your sins;
> The dirt will be removed from you; your plague will vanish.

I have come back to deliver you from the lions
For I remember the devotion of your youth." [8]

---ס/--/--/--//---ס/--/---ס/--
--ס/--//--/--

"אַתְּ שֶׂה פְזוּרָה, אֵיךְ/ מָרִית בְּמוֹרָיִךְ?
אָנָה הָלַךְ/ רוֹעֶה עֲדָרָיִךְ?

בִּנְאוֹת דֶּשֶׁא/ רָבַצְתְּ יוֹם רָעָה
אוֹתָךְ מֹשֶׁה,/ עַד בּוֹא יְמֵי רָעָה;
5   רוֹעֵךְ יֶחְשֶׂה--/ וַתְּהִי תוֹעָה,
מַרְאֶה לְכָל רוֹאֵךְ,/ יִדְפּוּךְ הֲרָרָיִךְ,
מִזְרַח הִשָּׁלַךְ,/ אֵין קֵץ לְצִיָרָיִךְ.

רָאָה צַלְעֵךְ/ הָאֲרִי וְלָךְ אָרַב,
מִי יוֹשִׁיעֵךְ/ מִפִּיו בְּעֵת יִקְרָב?
10   מִי יַשְׂבִּיעֵךְ/ מַיִם בְּבוֹא שָׁרָב?
אוֹ אָן יְהִי בוֹאֵךְ?/ נִתְּשׁוּ גְדֵרָיִךְ,
כָּלִית כֻּלָּךְ,/ לָעוּ דְבָרָיִךְ."

"מַלְבּוּשׁ קִנְאָה/ אֶלְבַּשׁ, אֲנִי רוֹעֵךְ.
עֵינִי רוֹאָה/ פִּצְעֵךְ בְּרֹב פְּשָׁעֵךְ,
15   תָּתֹם חֶלְאָה/ מִמֵּךְ וְסָר נִגְעֵךְ.
שַׁבְתִּי לְהוֹצִיאֵךְ/ מִבֵּין כְּפִירָיִךְ,
זָכַרְתִּי לָךְ/ חֶסֶד נְעוּרָיִךְ."

The hymn, an 'ahavah, is built in the form of muwashshah and has two parts. In the "belt" and opening two strophes the poet's "chorus" admonishes the stray sheep [= Israel] for their perversity. As in the Greek tragedy, Ibn Ezra's "chorus" is the articulate spokesman for traditional religious values.

Israel is admonished for failing the "trials" in the wilderness where Moses led

---

8. Levin, Širey Ha-Qodeš...Ibn Ezra, 1: 338-39.

them into "green pastures." Presumably the reference is to the reconnaissance of Canaan and the majority report of the scouts that formidable obstacles stood in the way of taking the land. Commenting on Num. 14: 1, "Then all the congregation raised a loud cry, and the people wept that night," the rabbis [in *Num. Rabbah* 16. 20] note, "This refers to the punishment which you received as a heritage for future generations. For Israel had wept [at the report of the scouts] on the night of the ninth day of Av, and the Holy One, blessed be He, had said to them, 'You have wept a causeless weeping before Me. I shall therefore fix for you a permanent weeping for future generations.' At that hour it was decreed that the Temple should be destroyed and that Israel should be exiled among the nations." Ibn Ezra alludes to the rabbinic comment in his, "Your Shepherd turned away and you were lost."

In the closing strophe, God the Shepherd of Israel appears--and none too soon. They have been attacked by a mighty nation [= "lion"], lead a wretched life [= "in the heat of the day"] and have no home to give them shelter. Now Israel has paid the penalty for her rebellion [= "I have seen you wounded for your sins"] [9] and she will be restored in her national home. At last, the Shepherd recalls the love that began in the early shared days of their nuptials. He closes with, "I remember the devotion of your youth, [your love as a bride] (*'ahavat kelulotayikh*)." This citation from Jer. 2: 2 designated the hymn as an *'ahavah*.

60.   PERFUMED WITH MYRRH

[Chorus:]

> When the myrrh-scented maiden came up from the wilderness,
> Like a graceful doe with good sense she nestled against her beloved.

> In younger days, the stag gently took her hand and she hastened
> To his side like those who thirst for a river's stream; he aroused her--
> Her heart raged overcome by desire as she spoke:
>> "Would my beloved tell me his pleasure and I will do his bidding;
>> His calming word, a healing balm, is sweeter than honeycomb."

---

9. Is. 40: 2, "She (Jerusalem) has received from the Lord's hand double for all her sins."

She was preferred above all the maidens with surpassing affection;

He protected the delicate girl until he departed

Loathing her; now she scoured the highways asking, "When will he return?"

　At night she stands watch with Orion and Pleiades inquiring

　About him; although he is late in arriving, she waits in silence and hopes.

[God:]

　"Beloved wife, your heart is trembling with fear!

Know that I am promised to rebuild the Sanctuary, now

　　in hostile hands; I will again summon

A redeemer to help you; your land I will return to you and the enemy

　Who defamed us will perish when accounts are closed, and

　　he will admit:

This is the true God and blessed is the nation that He chose for his portion. [10]

-ס-/ס--//--/--ס/ס-ס--

אָז בַּעֲלוֹת מְקֻטֶּרֶת מֹר/ רֵיחָהּ לְמַעְלָה,
הִתְרַפְּקָה בְּמֵיטַב טַעַם/ עַל דּוֹד כִּיַעֲלָה.

בַּלָאט צְבִי מְשָׁכָהּ בִּימֵי/ נֹעַר, וְנֶהְרָה
אֵלָיו כְּרוּץ צְמֵאִים אֶל מֵי/ נָהָר, וְעוֹרְרָהּ;
5　לִבָּהּ יְסָעֲרוּ הֲרֵי מֵי/ חֶשְׁקָהּ, וְאָמְרָה:
'יוֹאֵל יְדִיד רְצוֹנוֹ לֵאמֹר--/ אִמְרוֹ אֲקַבְּלָה,
מִצּוּף לְפִי בְּשַׁלְוָה יִנְעַם/ וְצָרִי בְמַחֲלָה.'

רֹאשָׁה לְכָל עֲדִינוֹת הָיְתָה/ בִּגְאוֹן מְחוֹבְבָה,
רַכָּה בְצֵל כְּנָפָיו הָיְתָה,/ עַד בּוֹא נְדוֹד, וּבָהּ
10　גָּעַל, וְאֶל דְּרָכִים פָּנְתָה:/ מָתַי יְשׁוֹבְבָה?
לַיְלָה כְּסִיל וְכִימָה תִשְׁמֹר,/ תַּעֲמֹד וְשָׁאֲלָה
בַעֲדוֹ, וְאִם יְאַחֵר פַּעַם--/ תִּדֹּם וְיִחֲלָה.

'מַה תִּפְחֲדִי וְלִבֵּךְ זָחַל,/ רַעְיָה מְאֹהֲבָה,
אַקְדִּישׁ שְׁמִי וּמִקְדָּשׁ נָחַל/ צָרִי, אֲשׁוֹבְבָה

---

10. Levin, Širey Ha-Qodeš…Ibn Ezra, 1: 259–60; Schirmann, Ha-Širah Ha-'Ivrit, 1: 622.

15 גּוֹאֵל לִגְאָלֵךְ, כִּי אֶנְחַל/ אוֹתָךְ; וְאוֹיְבָה
אִם גֻּדְּפָה שְׁנֵינוּ--יִגְמֹר/ הַקֵּץ וּמְלֵלָה:
זֶה אֵל אֱמֶת וְאַשְׁרֵי הָעָם/ בָּחַר לְנַחֲלָה.'

The designation of the hymn is not indicated. Presumably, it was chanted as an *'ahavah.* The poet combines figures from Canticles and Arabic love poetry (*ghazal*) in narrating the romance between the Shepherd [= God] and his maiden [= Israel]. The idyllic landscape and lyrical style celebrate the love of youthful days when Israel, recently freed from Egyptian slavery, followed her God into an unsown wilderness. [11] Israel was favored above the nations and enjoyed the protection of her Beloved,--until he departed, loathing her. There is no reason given for the sudden change of heart--unlike Ibn Ezra's other hymns in this genre where Israel's faithlessness is the cause for her Beloved's departure. Here the poet echoes the conventions of the Arabic *ghazal* in which there is a continuous tension between the lover's fidelity, endless yearning and humble devotion, and his beloved's pitiless heart and quick tendency to boredom. [12]

The lover searching the highways for her Beloved is a figure adapted from Cant. 3: 1-3. However, her "watch" at night "with Orion and Pleiadies inquiring/ About him" is a stock image from Hispano-Hebrew love poetry. [13] In the closing strophe, the Beloved returns and reaffirms His devotion. At the end the poet moves from the earlier pastoral landscape into the contemporary setting where Israel is challenged by Christian monks to renounce her religious faith. [14] She is assured that when "accounts are settled" the monks "will admit: This is the true God."

61.   HIS SECRET LIFE

[Israel:]

I desire him, though I know not where
The handsome lad lives his secret life;

---

11. Jer. 2: 2.

12. See A. Hamori, "Love Poetry (*Ghazal*)," 209.

13. See Moses Ibn Ezra, *Širey Ha-Hol*, 1: 185: 3.

14. Chazan, *Daggers of Faith*, pp. 53-54.

Who will direct me to his home,
And to the marks of his foot-prints.

Between my legs passion's ember
Glows like a furnace flame;
My cheeks are flooded from tears
Cascading like a raging sea;
You who know a love-sick heart and its pain
Brought on by a willful beloved, speak up!
  I ask that you bring him my greetings
  (Though he does not ask for them;)
  They come from a vagrant, traveling far and wide,
  And wearily he bears a heavy yoke.

I hear the reproach of my fault-finder;
How sweet is the sound to me!
If I am wretched in prison
Or the young men laugh at me,
In a little while, for my sake,
My beloved will have no mercy (on the lads);
  He will announce: "Let the vagrant,
  Approach, and serve the God who made him;
  I will set my throne,
  With diamonds, encase its feet in fine leather."

[Chorus:]
  The nation He acquired as a heritage,
  The son He called: First-Born,
  How long must he endure this severe beating;
  When will he have enough of disgrace and anguish?
  Much afflicted, he cries out:
  "My Father, remember to be merciful!
    Keep in mind Abraham, the honest
    Man, pure and upright in his manner;
    Do not forget Edom,
    When his deeds were strange, his behavior alien!

[Israel:]

    I am pleased to bear the African's yoke.

    Even the scorn and heaping abuse of Syria and Iraq,

    My passion does not look for rich rewards;

    My deep and sacred desire only needs

    To serve You. Banish the idolator,

      And may the dream be revealed and made clear

      To the son He sold as a slave; long enough

      Has the time of accounting been hidden and sealed up;

      Let his Redeemer arise and go forth. [15]

-ס--/-ס--//-ס--/-ס--

אֶחְשֹׁק-וְלֹא אֵדַע מְקוֹם/ עֹפֶר וְסֵתֶר אָהֳלוֹ;
מִי לִי וְיוֹרֵנִי הֲדוֹם/ רַגְלָיו וּמִדְרַךְ נַעֲלוֹ?

בֵּינוֹת צְלָעַי גַּחֲלֵי/ חִשְׁקוֹ כְּתַנּוּר יִבְעֲרוּ,
לִשְׁטוֹף לְחָיַי נַחֲלֵי/ עֵינַי כְּיַמִּים יִסְעֲרוּ.
5 יוֹדְעֵי כְאֵב לֵב נֶחֱלֶה,/ עַל לֵב קְשֵׁה לֵב דַּבְּרוּ!
אַחֲלַי שְׂאוּ אֵלָיו שָׁלוֹם/ נִדְרָשׁ לְמִי לֹא שׁוֹאֲלוֹ,
יֵלֵךְ לְנוּדוֹ וַהֲלוֹם,/ יִלְאֶה סְבֹל עֹל סַבְּלוֹ.

רִיבוֹת שְׂפַת מֵרִיב אֲנִי/ אֶשְׁמַע, וְלִי מַה מָּתְקוּ!
אִם בַּשְּׁבִי אֶרְאֶה עֳנִי,/ אוֹ בִי צְעִירִים יִשְׂחֲקוּ--
10 עוֹד קָט מְעַט וּלְמַעֲנִי/ רַחֲמֵי יְדִיד יִתְאַפְּקוּ,
יִקְרָא בְקוֹל: יִקְרַב הֲלֹם/ נָד לַעֲבֹד צוּר פּוֹעֲלוֹ!
אֶבְנֶה בְּאַבְנֵי יַהֲלֹם/ כִּסְאִי, וְתַחַשׁ אֶנְעָלוֹ!

הָעָם קְנִיתוֹ נַחֲלָה,/ הַבֵּן קְרָאתוֹ בֶן בְּכוֹר--
עַד אָן בְּמַכָּה נֶחֱלָה/ יֵשֵׁב בְּחֶרְפָּה מַמְרוֹר?
15 יִצְעַק לְרֹב הַמַּחֲלָה:/ אָבִי, חֲסָדֶיךָ זְכֹר!
זָכְרָה, אֱלֹהִים, לוֹ בְתָם/ לֵב זַךְ וְיֹשֶׁר פָּעֳלוֹ,
וּזְכֹר אֲדֹנָי לֶאֱדוֹם/ יוֹם זָר וּמוּזָר מַעֲלוֹ!

---

15. Levin, Širey Ha–Qodeš...Ibn Ezra, 1: 268–70.

מַה טּוֹב נְשׂוֹא בְּשִׁבְיִ שְׁבָא/ לַעֲג, וּבוּז בּוּז וָאֲרָם,
לֹא עַל גְּמוּל יַד רְחָבָה--/ כִּי אִם לְחֵשֶׁק רַב וְרָם;
20   לַעֲבֹד לְשִׁמְךָ אֶתְאָבָה--/ עוֹבֵד לְאֵל זָר יָחֳרָם!
יָגֵל וְיִפָּתֵר חָלוֹם/ אֶל בֵּן מְכַרְתּוֹ, וַהֲלֹא
דֵּי לוֹ סְתֹם קֵץ וְחַתֹּם--/ יַעֲלֶה וְיָבוֹא גוֹאֲלוֹ!

This *muwashshah*-style *ge'ullah* was chanted on Sabbath and festival mornings before the benediction, "Praised are You, Lord, Redeemer (*ga'al*) of...Israel." In the dialogue between Israel and Chorus, the former is personified as the hopelessly yearning lover searching for the elusive beloved. The imagery is a blend of conceits from Canticles and Arabic love poetry (*ghazal*). The influence of the latter is evident in the stock figure of the fickle and unresponsive beloved ("You who know a love-sick heart and its pain / Brought on by a willful beloved, speak up"). Adding to the predicament is the figure of the fault-finder (Heb. *meriv*) who seeks to bring the lover to her senses. [16] She will have none of his cold wisdom, preferring instead the agony that she endures because of him. In elaborating on the "pain," the poet moves from the landscape of the *ghazal* to Israel's current difficulties in exile ("I am wretched in prison"). Yet, the vagrant [= Israel] is hopeful that her beloved [= God] will rebuild their national home.

The Chorus echoes this hope and reminds God of His promise to Abraham and his need to judge Edom for their "strange [and] alien" behavior. The latter figure is adapted from Ps. 69: 9, "I have become a stranger to my kindred, an alien to my mother's children." Concluding the hymn is Israel reverting to the role of the long-suffering lover humbly devoted to her beloved. She is pleased to bear the injustice of the "African's yoke," and the "heaping abuse of Syria and Iraq." [17] Israel will not vulgarize her relationship with God by looking for a reward and desires only to serve Him. Yet, she urges her Lord to "Banish the idolater" and bring the "Redeemer." In comforting his congregation, Ibn Ezra departs from the conventions

---

16. See A. Hamori, "Love Poetry (*Ghazal*)," p. 209.
17. The Hebrew reads *ševa* and *buz wa-'aram*, a reference to north African tribes (Gen. 10: 7; 25: 3) and Syria and Iraq respectively (Gen. 22: 21).

of the *ghazal* where the lover remains in suspense and the flirtation is an end in itself. [18]

62.   THE SPRING OF MY CRAVING

[Israel:]

I am in mortal danger, but not from an erotic
Love–sickness of a desperate suitor,
My desire is to be with the mighty Monarch who has
No weakness; He is the fountain of my craving;
My anguish is hidden in the recess
Of my heart; my face does not show it,
  Lest they say of me: "His base passion killed him—
  Why does he put on airs?"

Love's token is faithful,
Though few are privy to its secret:
If you love a mortal, he will
Find a pretext to evade honor,
If you love the merciful Father,
His honor will stir him to compassion;
  Such is my Beloved and Friend whom I have chosen;
  He stores up a reward for the upright.

[Chorus:]

Many were amazed that the nation
That served its God all of its life,
And looked forward to its deliverance on the acceptable Day,
Had not yet suffered enough.
I told them, "When they (who exited Egypt) faithfully
Trusted Him and His signs
  They witnessed with amazement the wondrous days of redemption;
  And the storms and cries came to an end."

---

18. Hamori, "Love Poetry (*Ghazal*)," pp. 211–13.

[God:]

You who perish in prison, there is relief for you

In the promise of prophets and seers!

Bind up your wounds with their words

Of vision preserved in my Book;

Say to my son caught between

The whelp and the lion:

  Long lasting deliverance I will show him

  And satisfy him, and I will renew the love of our espousal. [19]

$$--\varsigma/--/-\varsigma--//--/-\varsigma--/--/-\varsigma--$$
$$--\varsigma/--/-\varsigma--//-\varsigma--/-\varsigma--$$

אָמוּת--וְלֹא מֵת מֵחָלְי/ הָאַהֲבָה חוֹשֵׁק לְפָנַי!

חִשְׁקִי לְמֶלֶךְ רַב בְּלִי/ רִפְיוֹן וּבוֹ כָל מַעֲינַי,

בַּחֶדֶר לְבָבִי מַחֲלִי/ צָפוּן--וְלֹא נִכַּר בְּפָנַי,

פֶּן יֹאמְרוּ עָלַי: חֵשֶׁק הֲרָגָהוּ,/ מַה לּוֹ לְבַקֵּשׁ לוֹ גְדוֹלוֹת?

5   בָּאַהֲבָה אוֹת נֶאֱמָן,/ לֹא עָמְדוּ רַבִּים בְּסוֹדוֹ:

אִם תֶּאֱהַב שָׁפָל--יְמַן/ פִּיו תּוֹאֲנוֹת תַּחַת כְּבוֹדוֹ;

אִם תֶּאֱהַב אָב רַחֲמָן--/ לַחְמֹל יְעִירֵהוּ כְבוֹדוֹ,

דּוֹדִי וְרֵעִי זֶה, בּוֹ אֶבְחָרָה, כִּי הוּא/ יִצְפֹּן לְיִשְׁרֵי לֵב גְּמוּלוֹת.

רַבִּים תְּמֵהִים כִּי לְאֹם/ עָבַד אֱלֹהָיו כָּל יְמוֹתָיו,

10   וַיָּקֻו שְׁנַת פִּדְיוֹם וְיוֹם/ רָצוֹן--וְלֹא מָלְאוּ שְׁנוֹתָיו.

וְאַעֲנֵם: אִלּוּ בְתֹם/ לֵב הֶאֱמִינוּ בוֹ וּמוֹפְתָיו--

מוֹפְתֵי יְמֵי יֶשַׁע רָאוּ וְתָמָהוּ/ וַיַּחְדְּלוּ בָרָד וְקוֹלוֹת.

'מֵת בַּשְּׁבִי, הֵא לָךְ צְרִי,/ מַעֲשֵׂה יְדֵי חוֹזֶה וְנָבִיא!

לַחֲבֹשׁ כְּאֵב קַח מִפְּרִי/ פִּיהֶם בְּחֶזְיוֹנֵי כְתָבִי.

15   אִמְרוּ לְבֵן, בֵּין גּוּר אֲרִי/ יָגוּר וּבֵין לַיִשׁ וְלָבִיא:

אֹרֶךְ פְּדוּת אַשְׁבִּיעֵהוּ וְאַרְאֵהוּ/ וּנְחַדְשָׁה אַהֲבַת כְּלוּלוֹת.'

---

19. Levin, *Širey Ha-Qodeš...Ibn Ezra*, 1: 300-01; Schirmann, *Ha-Širah Ha-'Ivrit*, 1: 614-15.

The hymn is an *'ahavah* in the form of a *muwashshaḥ*. The dialogue of three parties opens with a parody of the hopelessly yearning lover in the Arabic *ghazal*. Israel's desire is focused on a Beloved who is dependable, unlike the fickle and pitiless flirt in Arabic love poetry. "My face does not show it" is in contrast to the gaunt figure and sleepless eyes of the hapless lover in the erotic setting.

"Lest they say of me etc." is a reference to the "fault-finders" (*merivim*), a stock figure in the *ghazal*. [20] A balanced relationship characterizes the love of God, not the sexual brinkmanship in its secular counterpart. As opposed to the latter where promises are broken, accusations are frivolous, and contrived to keep the wretched partner in suspense, God's love is "faithful." Israel's confession is followed by an intermezzo in which the Chorus echoes the public's scepticism. "Many were amazed" that Israel, the faithful partner who "served her God all her life" is neglected by her Beloved. They are asking whether there is balance in this relationship. Responding to the sceptics, the Chorus cites the historic experience of Israel's exodus from Egypt when she was rewarded for her devotion to the Beloved. Reaffirming this argument, God appears reassuring Israel of His promise. The closing words of endearment, "I will renew the love of our espousal (*u-neḥaddešah 'ahvat kelulot*, based on Jer. 2: 2)" designates the hymn as an *'ahavah*.

63.   SHE LUSTED FOR HER BELOVED

> The gazelle lusted for her beloved;
> Every day she longed to see him;
> At night she combed the highways
> Hoping to find him whom she loved.

[Chorus:]

> She has no right to complain of her suffering,
> And of the pain she is forced to endure;
> She was banished for her sins
> When her secret vices were revealed;
> Now she appeals to You, God,
> And spends long hours in prayer;

---

20. See A. Hamori, "*Love Poetry (Ghazal)*," pp. 209–11.

Seeing that her light has failed
She reminisces of former days;
She recalls an earlier time when
You drew her with bands of love.

[God:]

My bride, why are you cast down?
Be strong, have courage, and be patient;
Cast off your flaws, be rid of your vices
And step up to honesty with resolve;
Say to your foes: "You too will bow your heads,
When you behold Jerusalem's Temple rebuilt."
Keep your eyes from tears,
Remove sorrow from your heart;
My hand will not weaken in support of you;
My love is as strong as death.

[Israel:]

When the enemy saw that I was sick
At heart and filled with remorse,
He began to sing at my hurt
And continued to taunt me;
Muslims kept on saying:
"Are you still waiting for an answer?
You rely on empty promises,
On the scribbling of false prophets!
Where is your Temple? Where is its interior to be inlaid
With love, and where is your beloved?"

[God:]

Why do you sigh, graceful beauty?
Rejoice in Me for I am content with you;
Stay in hiding for the moment until the anger passes,
Then will I open your eyes
And your exiles I will bring back from captivity,
Your scattered remnant I will gather in.

If the invaders come like a flood-tide,
I promise that I will not be false to you;
Great waves cannot
Extinguish our love. [21]

-ס--/--/--//-ס--/--/--

אַיֶּלֶת עַל דּוֹד עָגְבָה/ יוֹם יוֹם לִרְאוֹתוֹ תָּאֵבָה,
בַּלֵּיל בִּרְחוֹבוֹת סָבְבָה/ עַד תִּמְצָא אֶת שֶׁאָהֲבָה.

בַּת לֹא תָלִין אִם חֶלְתָה/ וּבְמַכָּה נַחְלָה [הֻכְּתָה],
כִּי עַל חַטָּאתָהּ הַגְּלֻתָה/ אַחֲרֵי נִסְתָּרָה גָלְתָה,
5 אַךְ פָּנֶיךָ, אֵל, חִלְּתָה/ וּלְהִתְפַּלֵּל לָךְ הִרְבְּתָה.
וּבְשׁוּרָה שִׁמְשָׁהּ יֶחֱשַׁךְ--/ יָמִים מִקֶּדֶם חָשְׁבָה,
זָכְרָה מִקֶּדֶם עֵת מְשַׁכְ-/תָּהּ בַּעֲבוֹתוֹת הָאַהֲבָה.

'רַעְיָתִי, מַה תִּשְׁתּוֹחֲחִי?/ חִזְקִי, אַמְצִי, אַל תֵּחְפְּזִי!
וּזְרִי מַעֲלֵךְ, אֶת חֶטְאֵךְ דְּחִי/ וּבְמַעֲלוֹת יֹשֶׁר אֱחֱזִי,
10 וּלְאוֹיְבָתֵךְ תֹּאמְרִי: שְׁחִי!/ עֵת קִרְיַת מוֹעֵד תֶּחֱזִי.
מֵעֵינַיִךְ מִנְעִי בְכִי,/ הָסִירִי מִלֵּב דַּאֲבָה,
יָד לֹא אֶרֶף מִמֵּךְ, הֲכִי/ עַזָּה כַמָּוֶת אַהֲבָה!'

הַצַּר בִּרְאוֹתוֹ מַחֲלַת/ לִבִּי, כִּי רָוָה לַעֲנוֹת,
הֵחֵל לָשִׁיר עַל מָחֲלַת/ וַיּוֹסִיף אוֹתִי לַעֲנוֹת.
15 וַתּוֹאִיל לֵאמֹר מַחֲלַת:/ 'עוֹד מַה תּוֹחִילִי לַעֲנוֹת?
עַל מֹהוּ לְבֵךְ תִּסְעֲדִי,/ בִּנְבוּאַת שֶׁקֶר נִכְתָּבָה!
אֵי אַפִּרְיוֹנֵךְ, אֵי יְדִי-/ דֵךְ תּוֹכוֹ רָצוּף אַהֲבָה?'

'מַה תֶּאֶנְחִי, יַעְלַת צְבִי?/ בִּי שְׂמְחִי, כִּי בָךְ אֶשְׂמְחָה.
אַךְ עַד יַעֲבֹר זַעַם חֲבִי,/ אַחַר עֵינַיִךְ אֶפְקְחָה
20 וּשְׁבוּתֵךְ אָשִׁיב מִשֶּׁבִי/ וַאֲקַבֵּץ עֵדָה נִדְּחָה.
נַחֲלֵי זָרִים אִם יַעֲלוּ--/ בִּי נִשְׁבַּעְתִּי: לֹא אֶכְזְבָה!
מַיִם רַבִּים לֹא יוּכְלוּ/ לְכַבּוֹת אֶת הָאַהֲבָה!'

---

21. Levin, *Širey Ha-Qodeš...Ibn Ezra*, 1: 220–21.

This is a *muwashshaḥ*-style *'ahavah*. The opening "belt" sets the tone for the lover's [= Israel] predicament with figures adapted from Cant. 3: 1–2 and the Arabic *ghazal*. The Chorus functions as the "watcher" (Arab. *raqīb*) in the poem, and cools the lover's ardor with cold reason, "She has no right to complain...She was banished for her sins." Yet, even the Chorus is in sympathy with Israel who is left with mere memories of happier days.

God enters the dialogue after the Chorus recalls that once "You drew her [to Yourself] with bands of love." Reassuring Israel that they will be reconciled when she is "rid of [her] vices," God hints at a wider acceptance of His sovereignty ("Say to your foes: 'You too will bow your heads, When you behold Jerusalem's Temple rebuilt'"). Israel now reminds her Beloved of the cruelty she endured at the hands of her Muslim captors. (Ibn Ezra employs the term *maḥalat* [from Gen. 28: 9] in line 15 as a reference for Muslims.) The taunting question, "Are you still waiting for an answer?" probably reflects the historic Jewish–Muslim debate concerning the date of the Messiah's arrival. [22]

Concluding the hymn are God's words of comfort and advice to be patient. "Stay in hiding for the moment until the anger passes" is adapted from Is. 26: 20. [23] While judgment is meted out to Israel's tormentors she is to remain protected indoors. The closing "belt" which designates the intent of the *'ahavah* revisits the imagery of the opener: love's ardor will not be cooled by the "flood–tide" of intruders.

64.   RAVISHED BY A LION

> I am continuously in mourning;
> My camp is like a ship
> On a troubled sea; Even
>   When I call for help, my voice is feeble.

---

22. See above Poem #57 and Baron, *A Social and Religious History of the Jews*, 3: 124–25.

23. Presumably the prophet modelled his conceit after the account in Ex. 12: 22–23, "None of you shall go outside the door of your house until morning. For the Lord will pass through to strike down the Egyptians."

I befouled my tent:
When I rebelled against my Maker
Who nurtured me and brought me to life
   I in my folly drifted off-course.

Ravished by a lion, I am still not healed;
Banished by a raging assailant;
He continues to hate me; this is the reward
   For my mutiny; every morning I recall my failure.

My vices led to the loss of my elegant mansion
And the flight of my beloved, handsome as a gazelle.
Dragged from my home, I am tyrranized
   Even in prison; the lion makes war in anger.

O Mighty One, come now and tend to
Your grove, the portion You chose
Graciously. Yoke in the
   The enemy and burden them with darkness.

Turn the Muslim into a servant and punish the African.
Make him a mockery and stop his mouth;
Be a stranger to the Arab until he reels [from your neglect];
   Be sure to remember the love of your first-born son.

Hasten, once more, and face us
As You did at the Burning Bush and wed yourself to Israel's nation;
Build the city and live there;
   Answer the cry of an anguished heart.

[God:]
"I will bring them close to me and exalt them;
I will call them by name and return them to their homes;

I will settle them in their lands and protect them;
I cherish and love them freely." [24]

ס-ס/-ס-ס//-ס/--
ס-ס/-ס//-ס-ס

אֲנִי אֲנִי/ בְּתוֹךְ אֲנִי
וּמַחֲנִי/ כְּמוֹ אֲנִי
בְּיָם עֲנִי/ וְהִנְנִי,
בְּחַנְנִי/ לְמַעֲנִי,/ כְּאוֹבוֹת;

5   בְּחַבְּלִי/ בְּאָהֳלִי,
בְּמַעֲלִי/ בְּפוֹעֲלִי
מְחוֹלְלִי/ וְגוֹאֲלִי,
בְּסִכְלִי/ בְּעָקְלִי/ נְתִיבוֹת.

רְעוּץ אָרִי/ בְּלִי צָרִי,
10   דְּחוּי חָרִי/ בְּשׁוֹרְרִי
מְצוֹרְרִי--/ וְזֶה פְּרִי
דְּבַר מְרִי,/ בְּבַקְרִי/ מְשׁוּבוֹת.

מְכוֹן צְבִי/ בְּתַעֲבִי--
וְאוֹהֲבִי/ דְּמוּת צְבִי,
15   וְסוֹחֲבִי/ וַיֵּרֶד בִּי
בְּבֵית שְׁבִי/ בְּאַף--לִבִּי/ קְרָבוֹת.

חֲסִין, לְכָה/ וְאֶשְׁלָךְ
וְחַבְּלָךְ/ פְּדֵה לָךְ
בְּגָדְלָךְ; וְעֻלָּךְ
20   וְסִבְלָךְ/ וְאָפְלָךְ--/ לְאוֹיְבוֹת!

חֲדַד מְכוֹר/ וְחֵת עֲכוֹר
וְלוֹ הַכּוֹר/ וּפִיו סָכוּר,
בְּבוּז נָכוֹר/ עֲדֵי שָׁכוּר
וְאַךְ זְכוֹר/ לְבֶן בְּכוֹר/ אֲהָבוֹת;

24. Levin, Širey Ha-Qodeš...Ibn Ezra, 2: 394–96.

וְשׁוּב שָׁנֶה/ וְחִישׁ פְּנֵה 25
כְּיוֹם סְנֶה,/ וְעַם קְנֵה
וְעִיר בְּנֵה/ וְתַחֲנֶה,
וְתַעֲנֶה/ לְנַעֲנֶה/ לְבָבוֹת:

'אָקָרְבֵם,/ אֲשַׂגְּבֵם
וְאָקְבֵם,/ אֲשׁוֹבְבֵם, 30
אֲיַשְּׁבֵם,/ אֲסוֹבְבֵם,
אֲחוֹבְבֵם/ וְאֹהֲבֵם/ נְדָבוֹת.'

This pseudo-*muwashshah* is an *'ahavah*. The paronomasia in the opening
strophe serves as an effective means of emphasizing Israel's travail in exile:

> *'ani 'ani/ be-tokh 'ani*
> *umahani/ kemo 'oni*
> *be-yam 'oni;/ we-hinnani*
> *be-hanneni/ le-ma'ani,/ ke-'ovot.*

The phonetic intensive second strophe with staccato use of the letter
bet conveys the sense of urgency in Israel's predicament:

> *be-ḥabbeli/ be-'oholi*
> *be-ma'ali/ be-fo'ali...*
> *be-sikhli/ be-'aqqeli/ netivot.*

The figures in the following strophes reinforce the tone of complaint
combined with self-reproach. The sea imagery in the first strophe ("My camp is like
a ship/ On a troubled sea") is continued in the second ("I in my folly drifted
off-course"). Conceits from Canticles and *Cant. Rabbah* 2. 17 dominate the fourth
strophe ("My vices led to the flight of my beloved [= God], handsome as a gazelle").

In contrast to the "handsome gazelle" is the insatiable "lion,"--Israel's
enemy--who "continues to hate me." In her closing plea, Israel invokes a pastoral
image urging her Mighty One, "Come now and tend to Your grove." The "grove" and
the "portion" are metaphors for Israel, after Gen. 21: 33 and Deut. 32: 9. Following

the plea is a call for judgment upon Israel's oppressors, Muslims, [North] Africans and Arabs. Since Christians are not listed in this imprecation it is likely that Ibn Ezra composed this hymn before leaving for Christian Europe in 1147.

65.   WHAT IS THERE FOR ME AMONG MORTALS

[The soul:]

> Show me, O angels, how to be grateful to
> My Maker? And if I am your kindred what is there for
> > me among mortals?

[The angels:]

> O soul, think and discover that the world and its content is illusion;
> Its charm and wealth are the snares that lure the gullible.
> If you choose to adhere to God and His angels and renounce the faithless,
> > Then take hold of Wisdom's ladder, lower yourself and ascend;
> > You will find a fountain of invention welling within you; with your
> > > own effort draw from it.

> Although your roots are in the heavens, desire has driven you
> To become involved [with the body]; now let it be your agent
> > for the needed
> Task; take the road that will lead you up
> > To the angels who are without form and serve unaided;
> > But sages know that in that place all have immortal lives.

> Now that you have been perfected, prepare yourself to till and keep
> The Garden of Delight that is given to you; in it you will see
> > the Presence
> Of God. Reject the body destined for the grave, its bones
> > Broken, its flesh turned to worms, it had fed on foolishness.
> > If your mind is without blemish, rejoice and be glad.

[The poet:]

> The God who holds my life in His hand, in Him I hope;
> He probes and knows my thoughts before I speak them.

I will prepare myself with every effort and renew each day my resolve.

When I walk in Wisdom's road it will be well

With me and God my redeemer will be my armor. [25]

--ס/ס---//--ס/ס---

אִמְרוּ, בְּנֵי אֱלֹהִים, בַּמֶּה/ אֶתֵּן לְפוֹעֲלִי

חֶסֶד? וְאִם אֲנִי מִכֶּם--מַה/ לִבְנֵי שְׁאוֹל וְלִי?

בִּינִי, נְוַת אֱמוּנוֹת, כִּי שָׁוְא/ חֶלֶד וְיוֹשְׁבָיו,

וּבְהוֹן וּמַחֲמַדִּים מוֹקְשָׁיו/ יַצִּיב לְאוֹהֲבָיו.

5   אִם תִּדְבְּקִי בָאֵל וּקְדוֹשָׁיו/ לִמְאֹס בְּעוֹזְבָיו--

הֵאָחֲזִי בְסֻלָּם חָכְמָה,/ תֵּרְדִי וְתַעֲלִי;

מִמֶּךְ וּבָךְ בְּאֵר לְמִזְמָה,/ תִּדְלִי בְּלִי דְלִי.

רֵאשִׁית הֱיוֹת יְסוֹדֵךְ צוּרֵךְ,/ וַתִּכָּסְפִי אֱלֵי

פֹעַל, וְלַעֲשׂוֹת כָּל צָרֶךְ/ לָךְ נִתְכְּנוּ כְּלֵי

10 גּוּרֵךְ; וְהֵן קְחִי לָךְ דֶּרֶךְ,/ בָּהּ תַּעֲלִי אֱלֵי

צוּרוֹת אֱמֶת, בְּלִי גֵו הֵמָּה,/ עוֹשׂוֹת בְּאֵין כְּלִי--

אוּלָם יְחַשְׁבוּ כִּי שָׁמָה/ כָּל יֵשׁ בְּלִי כְלִי

הִתְאַזְּרִי, כְּלוּלָה, כְּלָךְ/ לִשְׁמֹר וְלַעֲבֹד

גַּן תַּעֲנוּג אֲשֶׁר נִתָּן לָךְ;/ בּוֹ תֶחֱזִי כְּבוֹד

15 הָאֵל; וּמְאַסִי גֵו יִשְׁלָךְ/ בַּבּוֹר, וּבַאֲבֹד

עַצְמוֹ וְשָׁב בְּשָׂרוֹ רִמָּה--/ הֶבֶל תְּכַלְכְּלִי!

אִם אֵין בְּיַד סְעִיפֵךְ אַשְׁמָה--/ רָנִּי וְצַהֲלִי!

מָעוֹן, אֲשֶׁר בְּיָדוֹ רוּחִי--/ אֵלָיו אֲשַׁבְּרָה.

הוּא יַחֲקֹר וְיֵדַע שִׂיחִי/ אִם לֹא אֲדַבְּרָה.

20 אֶתְאַזְּרָה כְּפִי כָל כֹּחִי,/ יוֹם יוֹם אֲעוֹרְרָה.

כִּי אֶעֱבֹר נְתִיבֵי עָרְמָה--/ שָׁלוֹם בְּאָהֳלִי

יִהְיֶה, וְלִי יְצַוֶּה עָצְמָה/ צוּרִי וְגוֹאֲלִי.

This *muwashshah*-style *ge'ullah* was chanted before the benediction, "Praised

25. Levin, *Širey Ha-Qodeš...Ibn Ezra*, 1: 245–47

are You, Lord, Redeemer (ga'al) of the people Israel." The first of its three voices, the soul, unsure of herself, seeks the aid of angels to discover her true identity. They enlighten her to the difference between the illusory sublunar world of appearance and the eternal reality of the supernal realm. Gaining access requires "adhesion" (devequt) to God, a form of mystical union that is achieved by taking "hold of Wisdoms' ladder." Ibn Ezra's model is Jacob's ladder [in Gen. 28: 12] which Ibn Gabirol—quoted by Ibn Ezra in his Bible commentary on Genesis, ad loc.—perceived as an "allegory of the Universal Soul," and the angels of God ascending and descending as "thoughts of Wisdom (mahševot ha-ḥokhmah)."

Before being elevated you must first "lower yourself," like the angels "ascending and descending." This is the response to the soul who questions her mission on earth, "If I am your kindred what is there for me among mortals?" She is informed that her fulfillment will come only after she has met the challenge of an earthly existence. Only by overcoming this challenge will she discover within her divine self her own hidden resources.

Her reward will be to "till and keep The Garden of Delights [= Eden]." This was the gift given to a uncorrupted Adam in Gen. 2: 17 and has been handed down to the "perfected" soul in every generation. There, like Adam, you will see the Presence of God. Following the dialogue between "The soul" and "The angels" is the poet's epilogue. He is persuaded by the argument and resolves to be guided by Wisdom and thereby receive God's blessings.

GLOSSARY OF ARABIC AND HEBREW TERMS

adab. Belles–lettres; refinement; culture.

'ahavah. A liturgical hymn chanted before the benediction, "Praised are You, who in love has chosen His people Israel."

baqqašah. A petition for forgiveness of sins.

barekhu. A permission request before the call to prayer, "Praise the Lord, Source of blessing."

carpe diem. (Latin). "Sieze the day." A call to enjoy the world's pleasures. Its obverse is *mememto mori*, "remember the day of your death" and judgment.

fakhr. Boasting; self–glorification.

genay. Versified lampoon. Counterpart to the Arabic, *hijā.*

ge'ullah. A liturgical hymn chanted before the benediction, "Praised are You, Lord, redeemer of the people Israel."

ghazal. Love poetry.

halakhah. Biblical–rabbinic law. The term is based on Deuteronomy 28:9, "And walk in His ways" [*we–halakhta bi–derakhaw*].

hijā'. Versified lampoon.

khamriyyāt. Hebrew: *širey yayin.* Wine poetry.

kharjah. The closing strophe in the *muwashshah.* It is written in vernacular Arabic or in a Romance dialect.

maqāmah. A narrative in rhymed–prose.

me'orah. A liturgical hymn chanted before the benediction, "Praised are You, O Lord, creator of lights."

merivim. Meddlesome characters in the *ghazal.*

muḥarrak. A permission request before the chanting of the morning prayer, "The breath of all that lives praises You, Lord God."

muwashshaḥ. "Belt-poem." A strophic genre comprising sets of contrasting variable and constant rhyme.

nasīb. Amatory prelude of the *qaṣīdah.*

'ofan. A hymn in the *yoṣer* cycle. It was chanted before, "As in the prophets vision, soaring celestial creatures roar."

petiḥah. The opening prayers in a series of petitions for forgiveness of sins.

qaddiš. A permission request chanted before the prayer, "Hallowed and enhanced may He be throughout the world of His own creation."

qaṣīdah. A poetic genre tradionally represented as "ode."

qerovah. A multi-part liturgical genre embellishing the benediction of the Standing Devotion [*'amidah*].

qinah. Elegy. Common in both synagogue and secular use.

raqīb. The "watcher" or "spy" in the *ghazal.*

rehuṭa. A liturgical hymn comprising variations on biblical verses.

rešut. The poet-cantor's persmission request in which he introduces himself to the congregation.

sevaḥ. Encomium, ususally in honor of a patron.

selihah. Petition to God for forgiveness of sins. The term is based on the verse [in Psalms 130:4], "But there is forgiveness with You" [*ki 'imkha ha-selihah*].

šema'. The affirmation of God's sovereignty, "Hear O Israel: The Lord our God, the Lord alone" [Deut. 6: 4].

tajnis. Paronomasia.

telunah. A plaintive poem. (1) The complaint of a lover about an unresponsive beloved. (2) A plea for relief from an unhappy situation.

tokhehah. Self-rebuke. A type of *selihah.*

yoser. A multi-part liturgical genre embellishing the benedictions before and after the *šema'.*

zekhut 'avot. The merit of the ancestors. Often a reference to the Binding of Isaac [Gen. 22].

zuhdiyyāt. Ascetic poetry.

zulat. A liturgical hymn in the *yoser* cycle attached to the prayer, "There is no God but You."

BIBLIOGRAPHY

Manuscripts

British Museum, Or. #24896.

Jewish Theological Seminary, New York, Mic. #2626.

Jews' College, Montefiore, #34,2.

Oxford, Bodley, Opp. 707 (Neubauer, 2025)

Printed Editions

Abraham b. Ḥiyyah. *Megillat Ha-Megalleh.* Ed. A. Poznanski. Berlin, 1924.

Abū Nuwās. *Dīwān.* Ed. G. Schoeler. Wiesbaden, 1982.

Albo, Joseph. *Sefer Ha-'Iqqarim.* Ed. I. Husic. 4 vols. Philadelphia: Jewish Publication Society, 1929.

Arberry, A. J. *Arabic Poetry.* Cambridge: Cambridge University Press, 1965.

Ashtiany J. et al. *'Abbasid Belles-Lettres.* Cambridge: Cambridge University Press, 1990.

Avishur, Y. "Sippure 'Am Ḥadašim 'Al R. Avraham Ibn Ezra (U-Vno) Mi-Miṣrayim U-Me-'Iraq." In: *Te'udah: Meḥqarim Bi-Yṣirato Šel 'Avraham Ibn Ezra.* 8 (1992), 163–92.

Baer, Y. *A History of the Jews in Christian Spain.* 2 vols. Philadelphia: Jewish Publication Society, 1961.

Baron, Salo W. *A Social and Religious History of the Jews.* 2nd ed. 18 vols. New York: Columbia University Press, 1952–83.

Benjamin b. Jonah of Tudela. *Sefer Massa'ot Šel R. Binyamin.* Ed. and trans. M. N. Adler. London, 1907.

Berger, David. Ed. and trans. *The Jewish–Christian Debate in the High Middle Ages.* Philadephia: Jewish Publication Society, 1979.

Brann, Ross. *The Cumpunctious Poet.* Baltimore: Johns Hopkins University Press, 1991.

Chazan, Robert. *Daggers of Faith: Thirteenth–Century Christian Missionizing and Jewish Response.* Berkeley: University of California Press, 1989.

Cohen, Mark. *Under Crescent and Cross.* Princeton: Princeton University Press, 1994.

DeVane, W. C. *A Browning Handbook.* New York, 1963.

Diaz Esteban, Fernando. Ed. *Abraham Ibn Ezra and His Age.* Madrid, 1990.

Dinur, B. *Yisra'el Ba–Golah.* 2 vols. Vol. 1: 4 books. Vol 2: 6 books. Jerusalem: Mosad Bialik, 1972.

Duran, Profiat. *Ma'aseh 'Efod.* Vienna, 1865.

Fergusson, Francis. *Dante.* New York: Macmillan, 1966.

Fleischer, Ezra. *Širat Ha–Qodeš Ha–'Ivrit Bi–Ymey Ha–Beynayim.* Jerusalem: Keter, 1975.

– – – –. *Ha–Yoṣerot Be–Hithawwutam We–Hitpathutam.* Jerusalem: Magnes Press, 1984.

– – – –. "Yehudah Halevi––Remarks Concerning His Life and Poetical Ouevre" [Hebrew], *Israel Levin Jubilee Volume.* Tel–Aviv: Tel–Aviv University, 1994.

Gerber, Jane. *The Jews of Spain.* New York: Macmillan, 1992.

Goitein, S. D. *A Mediterranean Society.* 6 vols. Berkeley: University of California Press, 1967–.

Guttmann, J. *Philosophies of Judaism.* Trans. D. W. Silverman. New York: Holt, Rinehart and Winston, 1964.

Habermann, A. M. *Toledot Ha-Piyyuṭ Ve-Ha-Širah.* 2 vols. Ramat Gan: Masadah, 1970–72.

al-Ḥallāj, Manṣūr b. Ḥusayn. *Le Dīwān d'al-Ḥallaj.* Ed. and trans. L. Massignon. Paris, 1955.

Halevi, Judah. *Širey Ha-Qodeš Le-Rabbi Yehudah Ha-Levi.* Ed. D. Yarden. 4 vols. Jerusalem, 1978–1985.

Hamori, A. "Love Poetry (*Ghazal*)." In: *'Abbasid Belles-Lettres.* Eds. J. Ashtiany et al. Cambridge: Cambridge University Press, 1990.

– – – –. "Ascetic Poetry (*Zuhdiyyāt*)." In: *'Abbasid Belles-Lettres.* Eds. J. Ashtiany et al. Cambridge: Cambridge University Press, 1990.

al-Ḥarizi, Judah. *Taḥkemoni.* Ed. A. Kaminka. Warsaw, 1899.

Haskins, C. H. *The Renaissance of the Twelfth Century.* Cambridge: Harvard University Press, 1972.

Herskovitz, William. Ed. "Judaeo-Christian Dialogue in Provence as Reflected in *Milḥemet Miṣvah* of R. Meir ha-Meili." Ph.D. diss., Yeshiva University, 1974.

Ibn Daud, Abraham. *Sefer Ha-Qabbalah.* Ed. G. Cohen. Philadelphia: Jewish Publication Society, 1967.

Ibn Ezra, Abraham. *Commentary on Isaiah.* Ed. and trans. M. Friedlander. London,

1873.

- - - -. *Commentary on the Torah: Miqra'ot Gedolot.* New York: Pardes, 1951.

- - - -. *Re'šit Ḥokhmah.* Ed. and trans. R. Levy and F. Cantera. Baltimore: Johns Hopkins University Press, 1939.

- - - -. *Ibn Ezra 'Al Ha-Torah.* 3 vols. Ed. A. Weiser. Jerusalem: Mosad Ha-Rav Kook, 1976.

- - - -. *Sefer Yesod Mora' Ve-Sod Torah.* In: *Yalqut Avraham Ibn Ezra.* Ed. I. Levin. New York and Tel-Aviv: Israel Matz Hebrew Classics and I. E. Kiev Library Foundation, 1985.

- - - -. *Šeney Perušey R. Avraham Ibn Ezra Li-Trey 'Asar.* Ed. U. Simon. Ramat-Gan: Bar-Ilan University Press, 1989.

- - - -. *Sefer Ha-Moladot.* In: Ms. Oxford, Bodley, Opp. 707.

Ibn Ezra, Isaac. *Yiṣḥaq ben Avraham Ibn Ezra: Širim.* Ed. M. Schmelzer. New York: The Jewish Theological Seminary, 1980.

Ibn Ezra, Moses. *Kitab al-Muḥāḍara wal-Mudhākara.* Ed. A. S. Halkin. Jerusalem: Meqiṣey Nirdamim, 1975.

- - - -. *Širey Ha-Ḥol.* Ed. Ḥ. Brody. Vols. 1 and 2. Berlin: Schocken, 1935. Ed. D. Pagis. Vol. 3. Jerusalem: Schocken, 1977.

Ibn Gabirol, Solomon. "*Keter Malkhut.*" In: *Selected Religious Poems of Solomon Ibn Gabirol.* Ed. I. Davidson. Philadelphia: Jewish Publication Society, 1923.

- - - -. *Meqor Ḥayyim.* Ed. A. Zifroni. Jerusalem, 1971.

Ibn al-Rūmī. *Dīwān.* Ed. Ḥ. Naṣṣār. Cairo, 1973-78.

Israeli, Isaac. *Book of Definitions*. In: *Isaac Israeli, A Neo-Platonic Philosopher of the Early Tenth Century*. Eds. A. Altmann and S. M. Stern. Oxford: Oxford University Press, 1958.

JE= Encyclopaedia Judaica. 16 vols. Jerusalem: Keter, 1962.

Kahane, D. Ed. *Rabbi Abvaham Ibn Ezra*. 2 vols. Warsaw, 1922.

Langermann, Y. Tzvi. "Astrological Themes in the Thought of Abraham Ibn Ezra." In: *Rabbi Abraham Ibn Ezra: Studies in the Writings of a Twelfth Century Jewish Polymath*. Eds. I. Twersky and J. M. Harris. Cambridge: Harvard University Press, 1993.

Levin, I. *Avraham Ibn Ezra, Hayyaw We-Širato*. Tel-Aviv: Ha-Qibbus Ha-Me'uḥad, 1969.

- - - -. Ed. *Yalqut Avraham Ibn Ezra*. New York and Tel-Aviv: Israel Matz Hebrew Classics and I. E. Kiev Library Foundation, 1985.

- - - -. Ed. *Širey Ha-Qodeš Šel Avraham Ibn Ezra*. 2 vols. Jerusalem: Israel Academy of Sciences and Humanities, 1975–80.

- - - -. "'He'ahzi Be-Sullam Ḥokhmah,' Hašpaʿat Torat Ha-Nefeš Ha-Neo'aplatonit ʿAl Širat Avraham Ibn Ezra." In: *Teʿudah: Meḥqarim Bi-Ysirato Šel 'Avraham Ibn Ezra*. 8 (1992), 41–86.

- - - -. "'Zeman' We-ʿTevel' Be-Širat Ha-Ḥol Ha-ʿIvrit Bi-Sfarad Bi-Ymey Ha-Beynayim." In: *'Osar Yehudey Sefarad* 5 (1963): 68–79.

Lings, M. "Mystical Poetry." In: *'Abbasid Belles-Lettres*. Eds. J. Ashtiany et al. Cambridge: Cambridge University Press, 1990.

Maimonides (Rabbi Moses ben Maimon). *Koveṣ Tešuvot Ha-Rambam We-'Iggerotaw*. Ed. A. L. Lichtenberg. Leipzig, 1859.

– – – –. *Tešuvot Ha-Rambam*. Ed. Joshua Blau. 4 vols. Jerusalem: Rubin Mass, 1989.

– – – –. *Mišneh Torah*. Ed. M. D. Rabinovitz. 17 vols. Jerusalem: Mosad Ha-Rav Kook, 1972.

– – – –. *Sefer Moreh Ha-Nevukhim*. Ed. Y. Even Shemuel. Jerusalem: Mosad Ha-Rav Kook, 1946.

– – – –. *Peruš Le-Massekhet 'Avot*. Ed. M. D. Rabinovitz. Jerusalem: Mosad Ha-Rav Kook, 1972.

Midraš Rabbah. Eds. H. Freedman and M. Simon. 10 vols. London: Soncino Press, 1951.

Millás Vallicrosa, J. M. *El Libro de los Tablas Astronómicas de R. Abraham Ibn Ezra*. Madrid, 1947.

Mirsky, A. "Ha-Ziqah Še-Beyn Širat Sefarad Li-Drašot Ha-Za-L." *Sinai*, 64 (1969), 248-53.

Mondschein, A. "Li-Yahaso Šel RAB"E 'El Ha-Šimuš Ha-Paršani Be-Midat Ha-Gematria." In: *Te'udah: Meḥqarim Bi-Yṣirato Šel 'Avraham Ibn Ezra*. 8 (1992), 137-61.

Nahmanides. *Commentary to the Pentateuch*. Ed. B. Chavel. Jerusalem: 1960.

The New Oxford Annotated Bible. Eds. B. M. Metzger and R. E. Murphy. New York: Oxford University Press, 1991.

Nykl, A. R. *Hispano-Arabic Poetry*. Baltimore: Johns Hopkins University Press, 1946.

Pagis, D. *Širat Ha-Hol We-Torat Ha-Šir Le-Moše Ibn Ezra U-Vene Doro*. Jerusalem: Mosad Bialik, 1970.

– – – –. *Hidduš U-Masoret Be-Širat Ha-Hol*. Jerusalem: Keter, 1976.

‐ ‐ ‐ ‐. *Hebrew Poetry of the Middle Ages and the Renaissance*. Berkeley: University of California Press, 1991.

Perlmann, M. "Polemics Between Islam and Judaism." In: *Religion in a Religious Age*. Ed. S. D. Goitein. Cambridge: Association for Jewish Studies, 1974.

Saʿadyah Gaon. *Siddur R. Saʿadyah Gaon*. Eds. I. Davidson; S. Asaf; B. I. Joel. Jerusalem: Meqiṣey Nirdamim, 1941.

Sarna, N. "Abraham Ibn Ezra as an Exegete." In: *Rabbi Abraham Ibn Ezra: Studies in the Writings of a Twelfth-Century Jewish Polymath*. Eds. I. Twersky and J. M. Harris. Cambridge: Harvard University Press, 1993.

Scheindlin, R. P. *The Gazelle: Medieval Hebrew Poetry on God, Israel and the Soul*. Philadelphia: Jewish Publication Society, 1991.

‐ ‐ ‐ ‐. *Wine Women and Death: Medieval Hebrew Poems on the Good Life*. Philadelphia: Jewish Publication Society, 1986.

Schirmann, Ḥ. *Ha-Širah Ha-ʿIvrit Bi-Sfarad U-V-Provans*. 2 vols. Jerusalem: Mosad Bialik, 1959.

‐ ‐ ‐ ‐. *Širim Hadašim Min Ha-Geniza*. Jerusalem: Israel Academy of Sciences and Humanities, 1965.

‐ ‐ ‐ ‐. *Le-Toledot Ha-Širah We-Ha-Drama Ha-ʿIvrit*. 2 vols. Jerusalem: Mosad Bialik, 1979.

Schmelzer, *Isaac ben Abraham Ibn Ezra: Širim*. New York: Jewish Theological Seminary, 1980.

Schoeler, G., "Bashshār b. Burd, Abū ʾl-ʿAtāhiyah and Abū Nuwās." In: *ʿAbbasid Belles-Lettres*. Eds. J. Ashtiany et al. Cambridge: Cambridge University Press, 1990.

Scholem, G. "Kabbalah." In: *JE* 10: 489–653.

Seder Ha-Qinot Le-Tiš'ah Be-'Av. Ed. D. Goldschmidt. Jerusalem: Mosad Ha-Rav Kook, 1968.

Septimus, B. "'Open Rebuke and Cocealed Love,' Naḥmanides and the Andalusian Tradition." In: *Rabbi Moses Naḥmanides (Ramban): Explorations in His Religious and Literary Virtuosity*. Ed. I. Twersky. Cambridge: Harvard University Press, 1983.

Shippers, Arie. *Spanish Hebrew Poetry and the Arabic Literary Tradition*. Leiden: E. J. Brill, 1994.

Sifre to Deuteronomy. Ed. Ḥ. S. Horovits and L. Finkelstein. New York: Jewish Theological Seminary, 1969.

Silver, A. H. *A History of Messianic Speculation in Israel*. Boston: Beacon Press, 1959.

Simon, U. "Lešono Ha-Ḥarifah We-Ha-Šenunah Šel RAB"E - Ginuy 'Amiti 'O Derekh Wikkuaḥ Sefaradit?" In: *Te'udah: Meḥqarim Bi-Yṣirato Šel 'Avraham Ibn Ezra*. 8 (1992), 111–20.

Sirat, C. *A History of Jewish Philosophy in the Middle Ages*. Cambridge: Cambridge University Press, 1985.

Solomon b. Abraham b. Adret (RaŠBA). *Še'elot U-Tšuvot Ha-RaŠBA*. Beney Beraq, 1958.

Spiegel, S. *The Last Trial*. New York: Pantheon Books, 1967.

Stern, S. M. *Hispano-Arabic Strophic Poetry*. Oxford: Oxford University Press, 1974.

– – – –. "The Muwashshaḥs of Abraham Ibn Ezra." In: *Hispanic Studies in Honour of I. Gonzales Llubera*. Ed. F. Pierce. Oxford: Oxford University Press, 1959.

Stroumsa, S. "From Muslim Heresy to Jewish-Muslim Polemics: Ibn al-Rāwandi's *Kitāb al-Dāmigh.*" *Journal of the American Oriental Society*, 107 (1987), pp. 767–72.

Tov-Elem, Joseph b. Eliezer. *Sofnat Paneah.* Ed. D. Herzog. Cracow, 1912.

Trachtenberg, J. *Jewish Magic and Superstition.* New York: Atheneum, 1977.

Wasserstein, D. *The Rise and Fall of the Party-Kings: Politics and Society in Islamic Spain 1002-1086.* Princeton: Princeton University Press, 1985.

Weinberger, L. J. "God as Matchmaker." *Journal of the American Academy of Religion,* 40 (1972), 238-44.

- - - -. *Jewish Prince in Moslem Spain: Selected Poems of Samuel Ibn Nagrela.* Tuscaloosa: University of Alabama Press, 1973.

- - - -. "Midraš ʿal Petirat Moše Še-Ne'evad." *Tarbiz,* 38 (1969), 286-93.

Yizḥaqi, M. "Megamot Didaqṭiyot Be-Širat Ha-Hol Šel Avraham Ibn Ezra." In: *Teʿudah: Mehqarim Bi-Ysirato Šel ʾAvraham Ibn Ezra.* 8 (1992): 1-28.

Zulay, M. *Ha-ʾAskolah Ha-Paytanit Šel R. Saʿadyah Gaon.* Jerusalem: Schocken Institute, 1964.

Zunz, L. *Die synagogale Poesie des Mittelalters.* Frankfurt am Main, 1920.

INDEX